THE AD HOC DIPLOMAT:
A STUDY IN MUNICIPAL AND
INTERNATIONAL LAW

MAURICE WATERS

THE AD HOC DIPLOMAT: A STUDY IN MUNICIPAL AND INTERNATIONAL LAW

WITH A FOREWORD BY

HANS MORGENTHAU

MARTINUS NIJHOFF / THE HAGUE / 1963

ISBN 978-94-015-0346-4 ISBN 978-94-015-0897-1 (eBook)
DOI 10.1007/978-94-015-0897-1

Softcover reprint of the hardcover 1st edition 1963

FOREWORD

The special diplomatic agent has played in the history of American foreign policy an important and, it is safe to say, unique role. The names of Colonel House and Harry Hopkins come, of course, right away to mind. But there have been others: John Quincy Adams, Bernard M. Baruch, Henry Clay, Albert Gallatin, James Monroe, John Randolph, Daniel Webster, Wendell Wilkie, for instance.

At the beginning of American history, the use of the special agent was primarily due to the scarcity of available talent. Later it was due to the low quality of many diplomatic representatives, chosen for political reasons and without regard for their diplomatic qualifications. More recently, the President has availed himself of the special agent in order to make sure that his will prevails in the conduct of American foreign policy. The institution of the special agent is indeed inseparable from the preeminent, contested and uncertain role the President plays in the determination of American foreign policy.

Since the Constitution is silent on that point, the ultimate determination of American foreign policy has been throughout American history a subject ot controversy between the President and Congress. As a matter of fact, the President's preeminence in that matter is not open to doubt. Congress can prevent and delay, but it cannot give a positive direction to foreign policy. With his ascendancy over Congress assured, the President faces the continuous problem of making the Secretary of State and, more particularly, the Department of State, a reliable instrument of his will. Secretaries of State and, more particularly, ambassadors have been known to pursue from time to time their own foreign policies, at variance with those of the President, or at least to be half-hearted in the execution of the President's. Thus Presidents have at times tended to bypass the Secretary of State and the bureaucratic hierarchy of his department by either confiding in a particular official of the foreign service regardless of his position in that hierarchy, as Franklin D. Roosevelt did in Sumner Welles, or relying upon a special agent who acted as the President's *alter ego* in the conduct of a particular phase of foreign policy.

The position of the special agent is naturally anomalous both in municipal and international law. It raises a number of interesting legal questions, the answers to which can illuminate broad areas of Presidential power and of diplomatic status. It is the great merit of this book to provide such illuminating answers.

HANS J. MORGENTHAU

PREFACE

In 1953 I became interested in the career of Harry Hopkins as it touched upon United States foreign policy. In discussing my ideas with Dr. Kenneth Thompson, presently Vice President, Rockefeller Foundation, he suggested I consider the possibility of translating this interest into a major study concerned not only with the public career of Hopkins but with an analysis of the status and use of *ad hoc* agents in foreign affairs. This would mean studying them from the perspectives of constitutional and international law. Within this framework the use and status of specific agents could be compared with regular diplomatic agents, thereby allowing some judgments to be rendered regarding their true legal position under U.S. municipal law and international law.

Several problems soon became apparent. In the first place the use of such agents in the United States has numbered in the thousands. Hence any special case studies would have to be limited to a very few where comparable data would be available. Secondly, the practice, though quite popular in the United States, did not seem to play an important part in the foreign relations of other states. In fact, in discussion with officials of other governments they expressed the opinion that such agents were never used by their states' leaders. Yet, despite their limited usage abroad, I knew that such agents had been employed.

This led to the third difficulty – very little attention had ever been paid to the subject.[1] Perhaps this was due to the difficulty of obtaining access to foreign office files. Furthermore, although the League of Nations and United Nations had considered some aspects of the problem, no thorough examination had ever resulted. In brief, no integrated study of any kind existed. Thus it seemed necessary not only to examine the published materials and the private papers of

[1] The one major work was written in the 1920's and did not attempt any examination of their international status. See Henry M. Wriston, *Executive Agents in American Foreign Relations*, (Baltimore: John Hopkins Press, 1929).

certain Presidents and their agents, but to supplement this with correspondence which would reflect the opinions of scholars and the views of officials of major world powers. To this was added the results of interviews with people who had personal contact with such agents and who, therefore, knew their work intimately. Finally, through funds made available by the Rockefeller Foundation, attendance at the United Nations Conference on Diplomatic Intercourse and Immunities held in Vienna, 1961, allowed for a greater insight into the practical aspects of the problem through observation and discussion with the diplomats present. Hence this study combines the methodology of traditional political science with that of the behavioralist. A note on style: rather than attempt to trace the changes in rank of those with whom I corresponded, the rank held at the time of correspondence has been used throughout the text.

One can readily imagine that in a work such as this discouragement and difficulties often appeared overwhelming. Much credit and gratitude must, therefore, be extended to Professors Hans Morgenthau and Max Mark for their continued encouragement and frequent suggestive and incisive comments. I also am indebted to many prominent international law scholars who have provided me with suggestions and insight, among whom mention should be made of William Bishop, Sir Nevile Bland, David R. Deener, Joseph Kunz and last, but by no means least, Lord McNair who so kindly wrote, "No writings dealing with this subject have so far come to my notice, and I feel sure that the result of your work will possess great interest." If this proves to be so it will be due in no small measure to the help of those mentioned above and to the many others left unmentioned in the high echelons of government at home and abroad, in the many libraries throughout this land, as well as, to a degree which one sentence can never convey to my wife.

Appreciation is also felt for the support rendered by Leo M. Butzel, the Irwin Cohn Foundation, and Walter Field, all of Detroit, and to my friends Mr. and Mrs. H. Vane Silberstein, of Pittsburgh.

TABLE OF CONTENTS

INTRODUCTION

It is interesting and somewhat paradoxical to note that the American people have engaged in many long and heated controversies over the question of whether the United States should or should not be actively involved in international affairs, apparently without most of them ever realizing that it has been so involved throughout much of its history. This participation has necessarily put the President, his advisors and agents into positions of great importance, and has made them a subject of much attention.

This study is an attempt to focus upon one aspect of this development, the use of special executive agents in foreign affairs. Although there are many fascinating approaches one could take in such a study, we are here concerned only with the position of the agent insofar as American constitutional and international law is concerned.

It may be pointed out here that the development of the practice of using special agents was a natural concomitant of the importance that foreign affairs itself has held since 1776. From the very inception of our efforts to achieve and maintain independence the leaders of the revolution had to attempt to win the sympathy and support of the leading citizens and statesmen of such European countries as France, Spain, the Netherlands and Poland. Once independence had been obtained the needs of the new nation, particularly for trade and capital, and the alliance signed with France helped maintain that concern which had been so necessary during the Revolutionary War.

As the population grew, and as a desire for economic improvement and new adventures took a hold upon many people, expansion south and west forced our leaders to treat with the rulers of Spain, France and Britain. Thus, although there were many problems of a purely domestic nature, foreign affairs issues including the purchases of Louisiana and the Floridas, the Canadian-United States border, Spain's renewed interest in her former South American colonies, and the clash with Mexico were all of crucial importance.

At the end of the 19th Century, our internal expansion having been completed, many Americans began to covet foreign territory and to demand what at least momentarily seemed so successful in Europe, a colonial policy. Foreign missionaries, traders and enthusiastic supporters of "inevitable destiny" received support in "higher circles." The result was a sphere of influence in the Caribbean and colonies in the Pacific.

Even after World War I despite the desire of many Americans in and out of the legislative and executive branches to restrict our contacts with European powers, they were still continued on a public and private level. These contacts consisted of disarmament efforts, pacts to preserve China's integrity and to renounce war, and loans to the Weimar Republic.

Ever since World War II our major preoccupation as a nation has literally been with foreign affairs. International and regional organizations such as the United Nations, the Organization of American States and the North Atlantic Treaty Organization have received much of the time and attention of our leaders, and direct bilateral negotiations with regard to such programs as Greek-Turkish Aid and "Point Four" were granted a major importance in our foreign policy.

This brief survey has been undertaken to indicate that throughout our history the American Government has been confronted with the need to make many decisions pertaining to foreign affairs, often of a momentous nature. This need has required the attention of Congress and the President. The latter has generally played the predominant role, in part because the nature of such problems has seemed to demand immediate attention under an individual's direction rather than collective responsibility and protracted debate, and in part because of our constitutional provisions. Hence our Chief Executives have been confronted with the need to take many actions which have produced frequent debate among Congressmen and scholars, and a struggle for authority between the two branches of government.

Inasmuch as the President himself could not investigate many of the problems which arose he, perforce, had to rely upon diplomatic agents. Some of those appointed may be termed "regular" agents, that is agents appointed by the President, approved by the Senate, and paid for out of monies appropriated by the Congress. They have been sent either to duly established diplomatic posts abroad, or have been given special assignments, such as representing the United States at international conferences. Others who served the President abroad may be termed "special" or *ad hoc* agents because no appointment in the traditional sense took place. Hence no Senate confirmation was necessary, and when they were paid it was usually out of money provided for in a contingent fund authorized by Congress to be used at the President's discretion. The differences between these two categories was not clear for many years, and in fact confusion has existed on this point even in recent years. Because of this confusion there have been many bitter attacks made upon the President by members of Congress who thought that he was usurping authority, or who were fearful of his gradually increasing power. It should be clearly understood that the whole question of using *ad hoc* agents has been tied closely to the debates regarding the President's power of appointment and his power in foreign affairs. Thus we will have to give attention to both of these issues. Suffice it here to point out the main outline of our problem so far as it pertains to the development of United States constitutional practice.

Under the Articles of Confederation an executive office did not exist, and it was intended that "in Congress assembled" the powers over foreign affairs would lie. (See especially Articles VI and IX).

There was little discussion in the early days of the Philadelphia convention regarding the President's powers and duties in foreign relations except for Hamilton's speech of June 18, 1787.[1] But as the office of the President grew in stature during the Convention more attention was paid to it. This attention focused mainly on the location and extent of the treaty-making power, and to a lesser extent on the appointing power.[2] In the early discussions it was assumed that both of these powers would come under the jurisdiction of Congress, but when the Committee on Detail, headed by Edmund Randolph, was established they were given to the Senate.[3] In effect, from mid-June until the closing days of the Convention a division of the appointing power between the Senate and the President existed.[4]

On August 31 a committee was established of one person from each state to work out those disagreements that still remained. They recommended that the President be given power, "with the advice

[1] Max Farrand, ed., *The Records of the Federal Convention*, (New Haven: Yale University Press, 1911), I, 291. He suggested the President should have the power to make treaties and appointments, but most of his speech was devoted to other problems of government.

[2] *Ibid.*, II, 389, 394, 419, 540.

[3] *Ibid.*, I, 164–65.

[4] Joseph P. Harris, *The Advice and Consent of the Senate, A Study of the Confirmation of Appointments of the United States Senate*, (Berkeley and Los Angeles: University of California Press, 1953), p. 19.

and consent of the Senate, to make treaties, and to nominate and appoint ambassadors ... but no treaty was to be made without the consent of two-thirds of the members present." [1] Thus in the closing days of the Convention a compromise was finally worked out in which the President would nominate the principal officers but the Senate would have to give its consent.[2]

In his arguments in support of this arrangement, Hamilton, writing under the pseudonym Publius, expressed the view that one man would be inclined to make better selections than a body of men to whom the temptations of bargaining might prove irresistible. He felt that there would "be no difference between nominating and appointing," and that the Senate would not readily reject the President's choices "because they could not assure themselves" that their preference would receive attention from the executive. But he felt that there was a value in requiring Senatorial confirmation because this would act as "an excellent check upon a spirit of favoritism in the President" and thereby force upon him a greater degree of caution in making his nominations.[3]

This, in substance, is all that was written on the subject in this great debate, and it will be seen that Hamilton's judgment here did not measure up to the high quality reached in his other arguments.

Thus, we may conclude that the President's appointing power was given to him after some debate with the issue reflecting the differences between those who wanted a strong executive power and those who did not. That this divided authority to appoint would produce a struggle for power was not seen very clearly by Hamilton, although Jay seems to allude to it in *The Federalist*, No. 64. However, the struggle has been a frequent feature on the American political scene, sometimes simmering, sometimes exploding into great constitutional debates. Although the intensity of the debate on the issue has decreased in the past twenty-five or so years regarding his "appointing power," a consistent attitude never did develop on the part of Congress or the President on this matter. As a result the President's leeway to appoint has sometimes been restricted and at other times been left unfettered.

There have been three main bases from which an increase in the executive's authority has stemmed. One is the decisions of courts and

[1] Farrand, *op. cit.*, I, 164–65.
[2] Harris, *op. cit.*, p. 19.
[3] *The Federalist*, Nos. 76 and 77 (New York: The Modern Library, 1941).

the opinions of the attorneys-general. A second has been the acts of Congress, and a third the precedents established by those who held the office of President.

With regard to the first one cannot help but think immediately of John Marshall, that great expounder of a strong national government. He viewed the President's position under the constitution as one "invested with certain important political powers, in the exercise of which he is to use his own discretion, and is accountable only to his country in his political character and to his own conscience ... and whatever opinion may be obtained of the manner in which executive discretion may be used, still there exists and can exist no power to control that discretion." [1]

Many years later this issue arose again and the court spoke out in the case of *Durand* v. *Hollins*. It said, "As the executive head of the nation, the President is made the only legitimate organ of the General Government, to open and carry on correspondence or negotiations with foreign nations, in matters concerning the interests of the country or of its citizens." [2] And more recently in regard to external affairs it used the same strong language. "The President alone has the power to speak or listen as a representative of the nation. He *makes* treaties with the advice and consent of the Senate; but he also negotiates. Into the field of negotiation the Senate cannot intrude; and Congress itself is powerless to invade it." [3]

For that matter, according to Attorney General Cushing, neither can Congress compel the President to employ or not employ certain persons as officers.

> Congress may refuse to make appropriations to pay a person unless appointed from this or that category; but the President may, in my judgment employ him, if the public interest requires it ... Congress cannot by law constitutionally require the President to make removals or appointments of public ministers on a given day, or to make such appointments of prescribed rank, or to make or not make them at this or that place ... It is a constitutional power to appoint to a constitutional office, not a statute power nor a statute office. Like the power to pardon, it is not limitable by Congress ... [4]

In various ways Congress has enacted legislation which revealed an awareness of the President's special position of responsibility in foreign relations. The Department of State, established as the Department of Foreign Affairs in 1789, was organized so as to give it a different re-

[1] *Marbury* v. *Madison*, 1 Cranch, 137.

[2] Blatch 451, 454 (1860).

[3] *U.S.* v. *Curtis Wright Export Corporation*, 299 U.S. 304.

[4] *Official Opinions of the Attorneys-General of the United States*, VII, 215, 217.

lationship to the executive and legislative branches from that intended for the other departments. For example, the Secretary of State is required to "perform and execute such duties as shall, from time to time, be enjoined on or intrusted to him by the President of the United States, agreeable to the Constitution ... and furthermore, that the said principal officer shall conduct the business of the said Department in such manner as the President of the United States shall, from time to time, order or instruct." [1]

Senator Spooner of Wisconsin pointed out in one of the most famous debates on this subject that the statute does not even "direct" the Secretary to transmit information to Congress, which is not true regarding the heads of the other departments. In fact, he noted,

> We *direct* all the other heads of Departments to transmit to the Senate designated papers or information. We do not address directions to the Secretary of State, nor do we direct requests, even, to the Secretary of State. We direct requests to the real head of that Department, the President of the United States, and, as a matter of courtesy, we add the qualifying words, "if in his judgment not incompatible with the public interest." [2]

Another example of Congress's support of executive authority is the establishment of a contingent fund. Congress's most effective check on the President's actions in foreign affairs lies in its control of public expenditures. Here, too, Congress has recognized the President's special position. It is left to the President's judgment whether he should certify the specific uses to which he has put money appropriated as contingent funds. Thus if he deems it inadvisable, his voucher for all or part of this fund may contain no precise information as to how it was spent.[3]

On the other hand it should also be pointed out that the Senate's role has not at all been what it was undoubtedly expected to be with regard to its "advisory powers." By giving the Senate the right to advise the President it was thought that this would contribute to the balance of powers within the government. But with the President taking the Senate less and less in his confidence regarding the negotiators' names and their instructions, the Senate's function assumed a negative aspect. To some extent this negative aspect was there from

[1] *Statutes at Large*, I, 29.

[2] *Congressional Record*, 59th Cong., 1st Sess., XL, 1420.

[3] *Statutes at Large*, I, 128, 299. The statute provides that "... the President shall account specifically for all such expenditures of the said money as in his judgment may be made public, and also for the amount of such expenditures as he may think it advisable not to specify ...", pp. 128–129.

the first for the Senate could never "compel the President to initiate negotiations." [1]

Thomas Jefferson was perhaps the first President to emphasize the special position of the President in foreign affairs. In his correspondence with Genet, November 22, 1793, he said, "*it is from him alone* that foreign nations or their agents are to learn what is or has been the will of the nation; and whatever he communicates as such, they have a right and are bound to consider as the expression of the nation." [2]

A tradition which likewise tended to increase the executive's authority began in the very early days of the government, although it was not widespread until after Madison's administration. Before Madison's term the names of the negotiators of most, though not all, of the treaties entered into by the United States went to the Senate. Since that time, the Presidents have no longer sent their names nor the drafts of their instructions, thus giving them greater latitude in this area.

The practice of using *ad hoc* agents began with Washington's Administration, and without exception was followed by every President since. Obviously, the type of situation confronting the different presidents varied, and thus one would expect that the reasons for their use also varied. For example, Washington was faced with the dual problem of getting recognition for the newly founded State and for preserving its international rights against the Barbary pirates who were interfering with its vitally needed commerce. The agencies of David Humphreys and Thomas Barclay to resolve these issues are appropriate examples here.

Lincoln's most serious concern was preserving the Union. This necessitated the defeat of the rebellion, and it in turn depended in large measure on obtaining large supplies of cotton. Thus, William S. Thayer was sent on missions to Alexandria and London to investigate the possibilities of obtaining this important material from Egypt and India. Lincoln likewise dispatched Robert C. Winthrop to Europe to help promote the Union cause.

Not all missions have been of such vital importance. At the beginning of this century Samuel Gummere was authorized to sign agreements with Britain and Germany to protect American trade-marks in Morocco. But at the other extreme are the famous missions of Colonel

[1] Henry M. Wriston, *Executive Agents in American Foreign Relations* (Baltimore: Johns Hopkins Press, 1929), pp. 118–19.

[2] *American State Papers*, Documents, Legislative and Executive, of the Congress of the U.S., "Foreign Relations," I, 184.

House and Harry Hopkins during World Wars I and II relative to United States' objectives in these wars. Their assignments represent the most significant use of such agents.

Since the last war Presidents Truman, Eisenhower and Kennedy have all continued in this tradition, A. A. Berle's trip to Brazil in the Spring of 1961 regarding the United States-Cuban estrangement being one of the most recent examples of the practice.

Let us now pursue this examination in detail from the view point of the United States' usage, and then turn to an appraisal of these *ad hoc* agents in international law. At the conclusion of this study, in Appendix D, an attempt is made to fuse our conclusions of the status of such agents by presenting case studies of two of the most important who served Presidents of the United States, Colonel Edward M. House and Harry Hopkins.

CHAPTER I

THE NOMINATING AND APPOINTING POWER

The problem of how to establish the whole procedure of making appointments was raised at the Constitutional Convention of 1787. There was a fear on the part of some that if the executive were given a large degree of authority over the other members of the administrative branch an elective monarchy with its own "royal court" might result. Men such as Roger Sherman, Benjamin Franklin and George Mason were afraid of creating a strong executive and preferred giving the appointing power to the upper house.[1] There were others, of course, who, aware of the weakness of the Confederation, were determined that the chief executive should be a fairly strong one. James Wilson, Gouverneur Morris, Alexander Hamilton, and James Madison, to mention a few, felt that responsible government would be jeopardized if the appointing power lay in the hands of the legislature. They pointed out that in the states where such a procedure was followed the appointees were often not of great merit. They preferred giving the President sole authority in the realm of appointments.[2]

As was true of so much of the work at the Convention, the result was a compromise. However, according to one authority, this did not occur until the fears of delegates from large and small states had been quieted by removing the election of the President from the legislature and by giving the power to the lower house should a tie in the electoral college occur. Under this compromise "responsibility would be assured through nomination by the President and security [provided] through the Senate's concurrence." [3]

This arrangement by no means quieted all fears as the John Adams-Roger Sherman exchange in late 1789 illustrates. Adams was not only afraid corruption would easily result but also that the appointees

[1] Harris, *op. cit.*, pp. 17–18.

[2] *Ibid.*, p. 18.

[3] Report of the Committee on Detail, August 6, 1787, Madison, *Debates*, pp. 342, 459, as cited in George H. Haynes, *The Senate of the United States, Its History and Practice* (Boston: Houghton Mifflin Co., 1938), II, 723.

would develop a stronger loyalty to their "patrons in the Senate" than to their chief executive. Sherman denied this and felt the Senators, with their broader knowledge of persons throughout the land would improve the quality of appointments.[1] Just how this shared power would work out in practice no one, of course, could predict. But it has remained the subject of discussion with some authorities taking the view that since the Senate has the right to advise and consent to appointments to public office this gives it the right to participate in selecting the nominee,[2] while others tend to believe that nominating has "for the most part been vested in the President alone." [3] However since the terminology of Article II, Section 2 of the Constitution reads "and he shall nominate, and by and with the Advice and Consent of the Senate, shall appoint ambassadors," etc. etc. the latter view would seem to be the more accurate. Had the authors intended the Senate to have a part in nominating as well as appointing it would seem that they would have put the phrase "advice and consent of the Senate" before the word "nominate" instead of before the word "appoint."

ESTABLISHMENT OF THE PRACTICE

Early Years

But regardless of what construction one places on this section of the Constitution, from the point of view of practice Presidents have not always had a free hand in nominating. The first clash took place in 1789 when Washington sent in a name for confirmation as "naval officer at the port of Savannah." It was rejected without explanation and Washington submitted a new nomination. The Senator from Georgia had objected and his colleagues supported him. Washington's unwillingness to make an issue of the matter by sending the same name back created a precedent which has remained important in a modified form known as "senatorial courtesy," ever since.[4]

The general power of appointment may, in turn, be examined from the specialized view of the power to appoint to diplomatic office. It is clear that this particular office is different from the others especially mentioned in Article II, Section 2 because its historical development as an office is related to the subject of international law.

[1] Harris, *op. cit.*, pp. 29–30.
[2] Herbert W. Horwill, *The Usages of the American Constitution* (London: Oxford University Press, 1925), pp. 126–27.
[3] Quincy Wright, *The Control of American Foreign Relations* (New York: The Macmillan Co., 1922), p. 314.
[4] Horwill, *op. cit.*, pp. 127–29.

Madison specifically addressed himself to this issue. He asserted that "diplomatic functionaries" are not "officers in the constitutional sense because, ... the position of foreign ministers or consuls ... is not created by the constitution, ... by the law authorized by the constitution, ... [nor] by the President and Senate who are to fill, not create offices. ... The place of a foreign minister or consul is to be viewed as created by the Law of Nations, to which the United States as an independent nation, is a party." [1]

Senator O. Horsey took a similar view in a debate in 1814. He found the source of the office of minister in international law. "It is an office without limitation as to number, or duration of tenure, with regard to which neither the Constitution or [*sic*] laws have prescribed the duties .... In short it is an office not created by the Constitution, nor by any municipal law, but emanates from the law of nations and is common to all civilized governments.[2] Insofar as these views attempt to trace the source of the office, they are supported by opinions of the attorney-general,[3] but when the contention is made that this office is not a constitutional one it flies in the teeth of the section of the Constitution quoted above.

Because this view of the basis of diplomatic office was the popular one for over half a century, Presidents nominated to the office of public minister or consul whenever the need for them arose in our intercourse with other countries. This practice is attested to by numerous authorities.[4] The President not only determined the post but also the grade of the diplomat. "Jefferson advised Washington that the Senate could not 'negative the grade' of a diplomatic appointee." [5] Since Congress took no legislative concern in the matter the executive was permitted to organize the diplomatic service as he comprehended customary international law. This he did until 1855.

First Congressional Restriction

On March 1 of that year Congress passed legislation entitled "An Act To Remodel the Diplomatic and Consular Systems of the United

[1] *Writings of James Madison*, ed. Gaillard Hunt (New York: G. P. Putnam's Sons, 1910), IX, 91, n. 1.

[2] *Annals of Congress*, 13th Cong., 1st Sess., XXVI, 711–12.

[3] *Official Opinions of the Attorneys-General of the United States*, VII, 242; XXII, 186.

[4] John M. Mathews, *The Conduct of American Foreign Relations* (New York: The Century Company, 1922), p. 419; Edward S. Corwin, *The Constitution and What It Means Today* (11th ed.; Princeton: Princeton University Press, 1954), p. 115; Wriston, *op. cit.*, p. 30.

[5] *The Writings of Thomas Jefferson*, ed. H. A. Washington (New York: H. W. Derby, 1861), VII, 465.

States." It provided, in part, that "from and after the 30th day of June next, the President of the United States shall, by and with the advice and consent of the Senate, appoint representatives of the grade of envoys extraordinary and ministers plenipotentiary to the following countries." A list of countries follows. Section 9 of the same act provided, "and be it further enacted that the President shall appoint no other than citizens of the United States." Attorney-General Cushing held that these restrictions on the President could only be viewed as recommendatory and not mandatory. "The limit of the range of selection for the appointment of constitutional officers depends upon the Constitution .... The President has absolute right to select for appointment." [1]

Although this mitigated the strength of the legislative enactment, Congress continued to strengthen its position. In the first session of the 43rd Congress it provided that "'Diplomatic Officers' shall be deemed to include ambassadors, envoys extraordinary, ministers plenipotentiary, ministers resident, commissioners, chargés d'affaires, agents, and secretaries of legation, and none others." [2]

Later Acts

Numerous other acts were passed in some way regulating the consular and diplomatic service.[3] For example, the law of 1893 provided for the rank of ambassador and defined the circumstances for his use. Interestingly, Congress passed this measure without request from the executive department for this rank, and in the form of a *rider* to an appropriation bill. It was passed without comment.[4] The act of March 2, 1909 requires that "no new ambassadorship shall be created unless the same shall be provided for by an Act of Congress." [5]

In 1943 the issue of the President's appointing power was again raised, this time in a bill introduced by Senator Kenneth McKellar, and an effort was made to restrict the President on a broad front. Apparently the distinction McKellar wanted to establish between a "superior" officer and an "inferior" one was based on salary. One cent one way or another would make a man a public officer on the one hand

[1] *Official Opinions of the Attorneys-General of the United States*, XXVII, 215, 267.

[2] *Revised Statutes of the United States*, Sec. 1674.

[3] August 18, 1866, *Statutes at Large*, XI, 139; March 3, 1893, *Statutes at Large*, XXVII, 497; April 5, 1907, *Statutes at Large*, XXXIV, 99; March 2, 1909, *Statutes at Large*, XXXV, 672; August 13, 1946, *Statutes at Large*, LX, 1007.

[4] John W. Foster, *The Practice of Diplomacy as Illustrated in the Foreign Relations of the United States* (New York: Houghton Mifflin Co., 1906), pp. 20–26.

[5] *Statutes at Large*, XXXV, 672.

or an inferior one on the other. The bitter feeling which had developed among some of the southern "gentlemen" of the Senate was very clearly reflected in Senator McKellar's attempt to restrict the Executive's appointing power. McKellar introduced a bill in the first session of the seventy-eighth Congress (S 575) which provided that "any person holding an office or *position* in or under the executive branch of the government of the United States ... and receiving compensation at a rate in excess of $4,500 a year for his services in such office or position shall be deemed an officer of the United States to be appointed by the President, by and with the advice and consent of the Senate, and shall not be deemed to be an inferior officer who may be appointed by the President alone or by the head of a department." [1] The bill passed the Senate, but not the House.[2]

Present Requirements

The Statute which is presently operative is the Foreign Service Act of August 13, 1946 which reverts back to the earlier period by merely rephrasing the Constitutional provision. It reads that "the President shall, by and with the advice and consent of the Senate, appoint ambassadors and ministers, including career ministers." [3]

[1] *Congressional Record*, 78th Cong., 1st Sess., LXXXIX, 3341.

[2] *Ibid.*, p. 5826.

[3] *Statutes at Large*, LX, 1007. This matter is the subject of some discussion by both Corwin and Stuart, and it would seem to this writer that the latter's and not the former's position is the correct one. Corwin states that "Today new posts of ministerial rank are dependent on Congressional authorizations, and no new ambassadorships may be created for existing posts 'unless the same shall be provided for by Act of Congress.'" Title 22, Sec. 1-23, 31-40, as cited in Edward S. Corwin, *The President: Office and Powers 1787-1957* (4th rev. ed.; New York: New York University Press, 1957), pp. 205-206. However, as indicated above the statute that is now in force is that of 1946. Corwin's reference in the United States Code is outdated since this refers to the Act of March 2, 1909, which was repealed by the 1946 Act. Although he has acknowledged the error in correspondence with the writer, he does not seem aware of the fact that the prerogative allowed the President by these two acts is vastly different, the earlier being much more restrictive than the latter. It is not, as he indicates, merely an error in citation. Furthermore, Corwin states that the 1909 law was violated by various Presidents, which, although undoubtedly a correct opinion, does not appear to be substantiated by some of the evidence he introduces, but is, however, supported by that introduced by Stuart. The evidence that Corwin introduces are the missions by Elihu Root in 1917 – "Congress was not consulted or informed" – that of Senator's Henry Lodge and Oscar Underwood, who were United States delegates to the Washington Arms Conference of 1922, having been given the rank of Ambassador by President Harding, and the missions of Brigadier General John H. Russel as Ambassador to Haiti, also appointed by Harding, and that of Myron Taylor who was sent by Franklin Roosevelt to the Vatican in 1940. *Ibid.*, pp. 440-41. But none of these would appear to be a violation of the 1909 Statute inasmuch as that probably referred to permanent diplomatic posts, and the missions to which Corwin refers were clearly of a temporary nature, those who went went as personal representatives of the President, and they did not receive an appointment to an ambassadorship in the constitutional sense of the term.

On the other hand Stuart's examples of missions established by the President without

The Foreign Service Act of 1946 reveals, however, that the President is still restricted in other ways. It provides that:

> The President shall appoint Foreign Service officers by and with the advice and consent of the Senate. All appointments of Foreign Service officers shall be by appointment to a class and not to a particular post.
>
> No person shall be eligible for appointment as a Foreign Service officer unless he is a citizen of the United States and has been such for at least ten years.[1]

THE CHANGE IN THE PRESIDENT'S AUTHORITY

Thus we find that Congress has in large measure moved into an area which for 65 years had been left to the discretion of the President. If one examines the debate which preceded the passing of the law of 1855 one would not get any inkling that the members of Congress were aware of the great change they were proposing. There is much discussion on the need for a change from a system that was taken over primarily from the British and that appeared to have grown like Topsy, from a system that permitted consuls to gain an income from an unregulated fee and fine system, and from a system that was based upon "executive, ministerial and consular direction." [2] There is only a slight hint that a motivating factor was the belief that the system then in vogue provided a larger degree of executive discretion and influence than was consistent with the American theory of government.[3] Most of the discussion was devoted to the need to correct inequities in the consular system and to the difficulty in determining the proper compensation for diplomatic work.

After Attorney-General Cushing's opinion was made, a joint resolution was passed in Congress (1856) which again did not reveal the

having been provided for by Act of Congress do seem accurate, as is his interpretation of the President's authority regarding diplomatic grades. He writes, "The question as to the President's control of grades of diplomatic officers has never been definitely settled." Despite the Act of March 2, 1909 which required that new diplomatic posts be authorized by Congress, President Wilson appointed an ambassador to Peru in 1919 without any authorization other than that provided in the appropriation bill for the Department of State. (*Statutes at Large*, XL, 1325.) Confirmation was to be had by the novel route of a joint resolution but was never passed by the House. (*Congressional Record*, 65th Cong., 3rd Sess., LVII, 4537). Coolidge followed Wilson's policy and appointed ministers to Canada and the Irish Free State in 1927 and the appropriation bill covered this. The bill also implied that the President could "reduce the rank of the representative to Turkey from ambassador to minister with a corresponding reduction in salary." Again, in 1935, the diplomatic post in Peiping was raised to an Embassy without prior authorization and Nelson T. Johnson was sent as ambassador. Graham H. Stuart, *American Diplomatic and Consular Practice* (2d ed.; New York: Appleton-Century Crofts, Inc., 1952), pp. 137–38.

[1] August 13, 1946, Sec. 511, *Statutes at Large*, LX, 1007.

[2] Appendix to the *Congressional Globe*, 33rd Cong., 2nd Sess., XXIV, 162–64.

[3] *Ibid.*, p. 356.

reasons for the new legislation. In harmony with the Attorney-General's opinion the resolution permitted the President to decide whether to change the grade of all or any of the existing missions.[1]

Differences exist as to the authority of Congress to pass legislation establishing the rank and posts of diplomatic officers. As has already been noted, the Attorney-General inclined to the belief that the 1855 statute was only recommendatory. Wriston upholds the Congress and says that such statutes "grow out of the power of Congress to originate and control appropriations, for the grade usually determines the salary." [2] Mathews holds that the issue is not settled. However, he writes that since the power of the President and Senate to appoint to these offices is a constitutional one, this ought to "enable them to act even though Congress has not passed a law creating such offices." [3] Wright points to the practical aspect, the fact that Congress has organized the diplomatic service, "and through its control of appropriations it seems able to compel acceptance of its organization." [4] One thing is clear, Congress no longer has any doubts as to its authority on this subject as the list of statutes mentioned above indicates.

The 1946 Act does give the President a greater measure of freedom than he formerly had, although this is primarily true in a general sense only inasmuch as most of the legislation passed since then is restrictive of the President with regard to specific posts, as we will see. However, the President has continued to show his independence in other ways. For example, the reliance upon the use of special agents has grown considerably. And the President sometimes keeps his instructions to missions secret. Congress has frequently asked to see this information but not all Presidents have complied. When Polk was so asked he flatly refused.[5] This same stand has often been taken ever since.

SUMMARY

Although, perhaps, some of the strongest controversies and fears in the debates regarding the establishment of the new State revolved around the subjects of representation in the legislature and the basis of sovereign authority, the question of Executive authority likewise

[1] *Ibid.*, 34th Cong., 1st Sess., XXV, 787.
[2] Wriston, *op. cit.*, p. 133.
[3] Mathews, *op. cit.*, p. 419.
[4] Wright, *op. cit.*, p. 325.
[5] Richardson, *Messages and Papers of the Presidents*, IV 602; cited in Tracy H. Lay, *The Foreign Service of the United States* (New York: Prentice Hall, 1925), p. 115.

came in for much discussion. Some were afraid that too much power in the hands of the Executive would mean that an elected monarch would have replaced an hereditary one. Others were afraid that reducing his independence by requiring that appointment to office be provided for by Congress would only result in weak candidates being selected.

As the practice developed over the next sixty-odd years the President was allowed a fairly free hand regarding the establishment and rank of diplomatic posts. The way in which restrictions did develop regarding the general power of appointment was through the creation of the custom of "Senatorial courtesy."

Thus we find that the President may have been restricted with regard to the "who" of appointments (senatorial courtesy), but not with regard to the "where" (the post) or the grade. From 1855 on, however, Congress passed restrictive legislation which was designed to give it the right to determine where diplomatic posts would be established, and what the grade would be of the person assigned to the post. Although Attorney-General Cushing's opinion was that the 1855 law was "recommendatory and not mandatory" the legislature continued to attempt to restrict the President in this regard. In 1893 it created the grade of ambassador. From 1909 until 1946 Congress insisted that only it could authorize the establishment of ambassadorships. Nevertheless, some Presidents continued to show a sympathy with Cushing's view and appointed men to the grade of ambassador at regularly established posts where such a grade was not provided for by Congress. In 1946 Congress removed its earlier restriction upon the President. The situation would now seem to be that he can establish both the grade and the post. Of course all appointees must receive Senatorial approval. However, appointment to the Foreign Service is restricted as is appointment to many of the international organizations to which this country belongs.

CHAPTER II

HISTORICAL ARGUMENTS FOR AND AGAINST THE USE OF THE SPECIAL AGENT

In making an examination of the constitutional arguments raised and the tradition established concerning the special agent, numerous questions must be answered. How does one define a "special agent"? How does he differ from the regular diplomatic agent, in the way he is appointed, the title or rank, if any, he may have, and the degree of authority he may exercise? In what kinds of situations have the Presidents used such agents? Concomitantly has their use been a rare or common occurrence?

First it should be made clear that the President uses many kinds of special agents. In domestic affairs presidents frequently send agents throughout the nation to gather information for themselves regarding economic and political affairs. Quite often these men are used because they have special contacts in their fields thus making it possible to gather and evaluate information much more readily than if some public official were used. For example, Franklin Roosevelt had many such people doing this for him including his wife.[1] Other agents, the ones this study is concerned with, are sent abroad to represent the President at public occasions, to represent him at conferences and on international commissions, to gather facts and evaluate specific situations, and to attend special sessions of international organizations. These men, as this chapter will reveal, do not hold public office and are on assignments for limited periods. The use of special agents has produced much controversy between supporters and opponents of the practice.

ARGUMENTS AGAINST THE USE OF SPECIAL AGENTS

To answer the above questions it may prove beneficial to look first at the arguments of those who may be identified as critics of the practice. Much of their opposition is based on the grounds that they

[1] Eleanor Roosevelt, interview, July 27, 1955.

believe the practice to be unconstitutional. This, in turn, is often the result of a misconception of the term "office" as used in the constitutional sense. However, it is a subject that is not a simple one to comprehend. No mention of the President's right to use special agents can be found in the Constitution, nor is it possible to ascertain the thinking of the founding fathers on this subject from the debates during and subsequent to the Philadelphia Convention. Therefore, there is much room for debate on the matter.

Opposing Arguments Outside of Congress

An analysis of the debate *pro* and *contra* would have to reveal a differentiation between those who supported or opposed the practice on grounds of expediency or danger to our system of checks and balances, i.e., on practical and moral grounds, and those who supported or opposed it on what they conceived to be constitutional bases. For example, Mathews believes it is an "anomalous practice ... justified in certain cases, especially when the international situation admittedly requires prompt and secret action. But if used to excess [?] it may properly be objected to as a virtual evasion of the Constitution and as tending toward personal and autocratic government." [1] One cannot help but wonder why promptness would not be enhanced by the use of the regular diplomat already on the scene.

Corwin's protest is more constitutional in nature although it also reveals a concern that the executive is enhancing his position at the expense of Congress. He writes, "The established view is clearly that the term ambassadors and other public ministers, which occurs three times in the Constitution, comprehends all officers having diplomatic functions, whatever their title or designation." [2] In another work he comments critically that it is "manifest ... that the practice, considering the dimensions which it has attained, is to be reconciled with the Constitution only by invoking the Hamiltonian conception of residual executive power." [3] It is interesting to note that not only has he cast a jaundiced eye at the practice, but he has also been quite critical of the names given to these agents.

> Though such agents are sometimes termed "secret," yet neither their existence nor their mission is invariably such. While they are sometimes called "private" or "personal" agents of the President, they have at times been appointed under

[1] Mathews, *op. cit.*, pp. 440–41.

[2] Edward S. Corwin, *The President's Control of Foreign Relations* (Princeton: Princeton University Press, 1917), p. 57.

[3] Edward S. Corwin, *The President: Office and Powers, 1787–1948*, *op. cit.*, pp. 252–53.

the great seal. They have been justified as organs of negotiation and so spring from the executive's power in negotiating treaties; yet this, is also a normal function of our regular representatives.[1]

One of the most heated arguments arose as the result of President Cleveland's dispatching James H. Blount to Hawaii with "paramount" authority to the Minister who was already there, John L. Stevens. The Blount affair raised much controversy throughout the country. It was discussed in one of the leading law journals of the day. One of the authors, Francis N. Thorpe, presented the view that Blount was not an officer according to the Supreme Court's definition of "office" in *United States* v. *Hartwell* [2] and *United States* v. *Germaine*.[3] In both of these the Court stressed that a person whose duties are temporary and occasional is not an officer. Thus, because he was "not nominated to the Senate, nor confirmed by them he was not an ambassador, minister or consul." [4] The factor that so confused the issue in the Blount case was the "paramount" authority given to Blount even with regard to Minister Stevens. Thorpe maintained that, "The insertion of the word 'paramount' in his commission, and his subsequent action in obeyance of the intimations implied by that word ... [was] without warrant under the Constitution." [5] As support for his argument and for his view that Blount could be held accountable for his actions he cited the opinion in *Little et al.* v. *Barrieme et al.* In this case, which dealt with a captain in the United States Navy who carried out instructions of the President, Chief Justice Marshall held, "The instructions cannot change the nature of the transaction, or legalize an act which, without these instructions, would have been a plain trespass." [6] It would seem that Thorpe either misconstrued the *Little* decision or used faulty reasoning in attempting to apply it. In that instance the court was referring to a presidential order issued to a naval officer and contrary to international law. This was not the case regarding Blount. The orders dealt entirely with American affairs. In the second place the *Little* case dealt with actions of an officer. Thorpe had already acknowledged that Blount was not an officer.

[1] *Ibid.*

[2] 6 Wallace 393.

[3] 99 U.S. 511.

[4] Francis N. Thorpe, "Is the President of the United States Vested with Authority Under the Constitution To Appoint a Special Diplomatic Agent with Paramount Power Without the Advice and Consent of the Senate," *The American Law Register and Review* (Philadelphia: George W. Pepper, William D. Lewis and William S. Ellis, 1894), 1st Series, XXXIII (New Series, I), 258.

[5] *Ibid.*, p. 263.

[6] 2 Cranch 178.

As to Thorpe's charge that the President did not have power without Senate concurrence, to give Blount "paramount authority" over the regular minister, this could only be determined by the courts, which never were given the opportunity.

Because of the apparent similarity in some of the activities carried out by both the regular and special diplomat many who have discussed the matter have been confused. In fact, confusion has also arisen in the minds of numerous members of Congress.

Opposing Arguments Within Congress

One of the theories put forth when the nation was still fairly young was that of Henry Clay, Speaker of the House, in 1818. He "seemed to regard the contingent fund as designed primarily ... if not exclusively for secret [i.e., private] agencies." [1] Thus, if a man were paid from the contingent fund he was a private agent, if paid from a special Congressional appropriation he was a public officer.[2] This method of distinguishing the private from the public agent is indicative of the fuzzy thinking that was made manifest on numerous occasions when the subject was under discussion. For example when Madison appointed Clay and James Bayard to serve on the commission to establish peace with Britain, both men felt that their membership in the House and Senate respectively required that they resign their seats in order to serve.[3]

Senator Tazewell discussed the practice from a different view when he attacked President Jackson in 1831 for sending a special mission to Turkey. The members, he contended, were officers of the United States whose appointment required the approval of the Senate before the mission could be legal.[4] What were the grounds for his contention? There were two. He claimed they were officers first on the ground that their commission bore the signature of the President and the seal of the United States. "To whomsoever this seal was shown, it proved itself. When recognized by any sovereign, it entitled those who bore the commission it authenticated, to all the rights, privileges and immunities accorded to the ministers of any potentate on earth." [5]

A second reason for asserting that these men were officers was based

1 Wriston, *op. cit.*, p. 222.

2 *Ibid.*

3 George H. Haynes, *The Senate of the United States* (Boston: Houghton Mifflin Co., 1938), II, 596–97.

4 Benton, *Abridgement of the Debates of Congress*, II, 207, as cited in Wright, *op. cit.*, p. 330.

5 *Congressional Debates*, 21st Cong., 2nd Sess., VII, 218.

upon his conception of the relationship diplomatic privilege held to office.

> It is this, at last, that constitutes the true test whereby to ascertain whether the agent appointed to negotiate a treaty is an officer of the United States, in virtue of such an appointment. For as the immunities conceded by the public law are official privileges, he who acquires none such in virtue of his appointment to negotiate a treaty, is not thereby made an officer. But wheresoever the appointment is designed to draw after it pay at home, and immunity abroad, then it creates office.[1]

Tazewell did not understand that any immunities accorded to our diplomatic agents are not the result of our constitutional law.

Senator Tyler supported Tazewell's conclusions but for different reasons. For him it was a question of employment. "If sent on a high embassy, involving the commercial interests of the country, whether his character be publicly known or not is wholly immaterial, he is an officer." [2]

On January 9, 1883 a resolution was introduced into the Senate by William Windom of Minnesota. He objected to the means used to negotiate a commercial treaty with Korea. Commodore Shufeldt was the agent used by President Garfield. He was under instructions from Secretary of State Blaine. The resolution approved the treaty but also contained a restriction on the President's use of the special agent. Despite the fact that the practice had developed since Washington's time the resolution declared that because the Senate approved the treaty this did not mean that it "admitted" or "acquiesced" in "any right or constitutional power in the President to authorize or empower any person to negotiate treaties or carry on diplomatic negotiations with any foreign power unless such person shall have been appointed for such purposes or clothed with such power by and with the advice and consent of the Senate." [3]

Such a position of course left no leeway with the President in his choice of agents used in negotiations. Even the Senate-approved regular diplomat would have to be approved by the same house, before he could be used to negotiate!

Ten years later the same debate blazed up anew. This time the situation was a much more complicated one. The United States had an officer representing it in Hawaii, John L. Stevens. However, because Cleveland suspected that the revolution in Hawaii might have had some

[1] *Ibid.*, pp. 279–80.
[2] *Ibid.*, p. 251.
[3] *Senate Executive Journal*, XXIII, 584–85.

assistance from Americans there he sent a special commissioner, James H. Blount, with "paramount" authority to all other Americans there. Blount's mission was not approved by the Senate. Therefore a number of members of that chamber denounced this action as unconstitutional.[1] Senator Hoar was particularly vehement in his denunciation of Cleveland's action. "If anybody be a public minister within the meaning of the Constitution, it is certainly a person whose authority is paramount in representing the United States over other public functionaries in the kingdom or power to which he is accredited." [2] Hoar acknowledged that the President could use his own agents, but said that such persons never could perform any functions which could be considered "binding" upon the United States.[3] Hoar did not seem to realize that this "binding action" did not occur whether or not the agent was an officer. For either the regular officer or the special agent, actions become binding only when the President, and if a treaty is involved, the Senate, approve. All acts of diplomatic agents must be in line with the President's policies. If they are not they can have no standing. It is on these very grounds that Cleveland could and did disavow Minister Stevens' acts.

Senator Hoar raised one other argument against this use of Blount as a special agent. Blount's actions were binding, he maintained. According to his reasoning he was therefore an officer of the United States and thus unconstitutionally appointed. From a faulty premise he arrived at a fallacious conclusion. As proof of his view he introduced what he described as the "decisive test." "The public minister is not liable to be arrested or held personally responsible for acts done by his superior's orders [whereas] the private citizen has no exemption from full responsibility to all the laws of the country where he happens to be." [4] Since Blount was not arrested by the government of Hawaii at a time which was critical and when it normally would have acted against a private citizen, Blount must have been considered a public officer, the Senator reasoned.

There was one other basis for disapproving of Cleveland's use of Blount, a position which was taken by Senator Cushman Davis during the debate in the upper house, *viz.*, if the President were permitted to give an agent such authority in Hawaii, he, by the same token could

[1] Senate Report 227, 88, Serial 3180, 53rd Cong., 2nd Sess.

[2] *Congressional Record*, 53rd Cong., 2nd Sess., XXVI, 128.

[3] *Congressional Record*, 53rd Cong., 2nd Sess., XXVI, 430–31.

[4] Wriston, *op. cit.*, p. 298. Wriston gives no citation for this analysis by Hoar. It appears in *Congressional Record*, 58th Cong., 2nd Sess., XXVI, 431.

create agencies with paramount authority over duly approved officers everywhere. As Davis pointed out this could be especially disastrous in the armed services.[1] It may be noted that this is a political and not a legal argument and one which no one bothered to answer and which therefore does not merit any attention here.

ARGUMENTS FOR THE USE OF SPECIAL AGENTS

Let us turn now to an examination of the views of those who have been sympathetic with the President's use of special agents and who have contended that the practice does not do violence to the Constitution.

Supporting Arguments Within Congress

One of the first important debates arose as the result of the sending of a mission to Turkey by Andrew Jackson in 1829. Senator Edward Livingston held the creation of such missions was quite proper, especially where secrecy was necessary, and did not require Senate approval. He pointed to the fact that the Senate was not informed regarding David Humphrey's mission to Algiers in 1795. And, he added significantly, since Washington and others around him had attended the Philadelphia Convention, they would have been in a position to know best what the founders had intended. Hence he assumed that appointment of these agents without confirmation was proper.[2]

Livingston presented other reasons for the President's right to use special agents with perhaps even more force. He claimed that under international law there were "two classes of agents by whom diplomatic intercourse may be carried on ... public ministers and private agents." [3] He held that both classes have equal powers but that there are limitations under the Constitution with regard to the President's appointments to the one class but not with regard to the other. Thus "the President has it without restriction." [4]

The Senator also stressed the fact that the Constitution gave the executive the right to negotiate treaties. It would be inconceivable, he held, to suppose that the President could not do the negotiating himself. Why, therefore, could he not have someone else do it for him?

[1] Thorpe, *op. cit.*, pp. 262–63; *Congressional Record*, 58th Cong., 2nd Sess., XXVI, 698.
[2] Wright, *op. cit.*, pp. 330–31.
[3] *Congressional Debates*, 21st Cong., 2nd Sess., VII, 247–48.
[4] *Ibid.*

And if this be not denied him why "must such others be ambassadors or public ministers? Where is the clause that restricts him to such agents? ... What title in the Constitution, what forced construction of any word it contains, can be made to show that he may not make choice of them [secret agents] when he deems it expedient? There is none." [1] In fact, Livingston insisted, "he *must* employ them whenever he thinks publicity would endanger the failure of his object." [2]

Part of the argument that emerged in this debate was based on the use of the presidential seal on the commissions of Jackson's agents to Turkey. Livingston contended that "the use of the seal makes no difference in the nature of the mission. They are private agents for the transaction of the business of the Nation ...." [3] Perhaps one of the most important points raised in Livingston's presentation was the opinion that even the Secretary of State, if sent to negotiate a treaty, was a special agent just as any private citizen would be.[4]

Livingston's arguments showed much merit except where he alluded to international law as providing for the existence of the private agent category. He cited no source for this belief and there is no reason to believe that he could have in his day.

Senator Bedford Brown, who was among Jackson's supporters, added one other point to the discussion which should be reported. He commented that these agents had been "appointed for a special designated purpose [and were] not clothed with the usual powers of public ministers." [5] He further claimed that Senate confirmation of special agents was not necessary because the President's constitutionally derived authority to direct foreign affairs permitted him the power to carry out his duties in this sphere.[6]

It is rather interesting to observe that even one of the members of the upper house who opposed Jackson's appointments agreed to the executive's right to use special agents, but was misled into believing that those sent on the mission to Turkey were not in that category. Senator Littleton Tazewell said, "I do not mean to doubt the power of the President to appoint secret agents when and how he pleases; nor do I mean to advance any claim on the part of the Senate to participate in the exercise of any such power .... And it is only because

[1] *Ibid.*, p. 253.
[2] *Ibid.*
[3] *Ibid.*, p. 251.
[4] *Ibid.*, p. 258.
[5] *Ibid.*, p. 271.
[6] *Ibid.*

secret agents are not officers of the United States, but the mere agents of the President, or of his Secretaries, or of his military and naval commanders, that I disclaim all participation in their appointment." [1] This is probably one of the soundest statements made *apropos* this practice, and yet ironically it came from a man who was confused as to how to differentiate between the public officer and the private agent, believing that any commission carrying the seal of the United States and of the President *ipso facto* made the bearer an officer.[2]

Another debate arose regarding "secret agents" in 1842. The occasion was the debate over an amendment to the general appropriation bill which provided that no part of the appropriation could be used to pay special agents abroad who are appointed without the consent of the Senate or an authorization of Congress.[3] Senator James Buchanan objected to any denial of the President's right to use special agents whenever, in his judgment, it might be necessary to use them. "There was no Government on the face of the earth that had not secret agents abroad unless it were our own." [4] He pointed out that it might soon be necessary to send an agent into the Caribbean region, and to be forced to use the method of appointment required for officers would destroy the secrecy that was a *desideratum.* "This amendment would deprive the executive of this power, so essential to the interests of any country that no Government on the face of the earth was destitute of it .... I admit that such discretion may be abused; that it has been abused. But the question is can we take it away altogether?" [5] Buchanan's appeal carried the day.

The first person to appreciate that the executive not only had the authority to appoint special agents but also to give them high diplomatic rank was Charles Sumner. Interestingly, as with the Tazewell opinion cited above, his views were elaborated as a part of an attack *against* the President. Grant had requested that "by joint resolution the executive be authorized to appoint a commission to negotiate a treaty with the authorities of San Domingo for the acquisition of that Island." [6] Sumner denied that such a resolution was necessary.

The President has all the power this pretends to give. He may, if he sees fit, appoint agents, calling them any name that he pleases, calling them com-

[1] *Ibid.*, p. 233.
[2] *Ibid.*, pp. 217–18.
[3] *Congressional Globe*, 27th Cong., 2nd Sess., XI, Append., 469.
[4] *Ibid.*, p. 473.
[5] *Ibid.*
[6] James D. Richardson, *A Compilation of the Messages and Papers of the Presidents* (New York: Bureau of National Literature, 1908), VII, 100.

missioners; calling them embassadors [*sic*] perhaps, if he will, though this might raise a constitutional question; but he may appoint agents to any extent, of any number, to visit this island and report to him with regard to its condition.[1]

His objections to the mission were based on opposition to the idea of annexation, and not to the use of agents.

Sumner did not really oppose this practice. This is exemplified by his behavior regarding the Nicholas Trist claim. Trist believed that he had not received all he was entitled to as Polk's commissioner to Mexico in 1847 and 1848. His claim was reported favorably by Sumner, who was Chairman of the Foreign Relations committee. It was eventually approved by Congress with little opposition.[2]

One of the most heated debates on the issue of special agents took place in 1886. It was a confused debate, but arose over Cleveland's appointment of three agents to work out the difficulties that had long been smoldering with Britain regarding the Canadian Fisheries Treaty of 1818. A resolution had been passed in the Senate that such a commission should not be provided for by Congress. Cleveland, therefore, went ahead and provided for it himself. The results of the negotiations were sent to the Senate and there attacked, in part on the grounds that the plenipotentiaries had not been approved by that house. A minority report of the Senate Committee on Foreign Relations answered the charge by issuing a report concerning the precedents that existed. This report indicates that of all "diplomatic agents" sent to "negotiate and conclude conventions, agreements, and treaties with foreign powers since 1792," 438 were appointed without Senate or Congressional approval, whereas only 32 had received such. It furthermore indicated that between 1827 and 1880 no President had asked for Senate approval.[3]

One would have thought that such a list of precedents plus the numerous cogent arguments put forth on behalf of the practice would have satisfied any doubting Thomases. Yet another critical debate on this same topic occurred only eight years later. This was the Hawaiian situation referred to above. President Cleveland, it will be remembered, had sent James H. Blount to Hawaii with "paramount authority" to the regular minister stationed there, John L. Stevens. Blount was to investigate the conditions which led to the overthrow of the Hawaiian government, and particularly the part the American troops played in

[1] *Congressional Globe*, 41st Cong., 3rd Sess., XLIII, 227.

[2] *Ibid.*, 42nd Cong., 1st Sess., XLIV, 809.

[3] U.S. Senate, Committee on Foreign Relations, 50th Cong., 1st Sess., Serial 2517, Senate Misc. Doc. 109.

that event. As was mentioned earlier when Congress learned of Blount's mission and authority, there ensued one of the liveliest debates on the subject of diplomatic agents the Senate had seen. Several Senators stood by Cleveland in a report by the Foreign Relations committee. Senator Morgan, who was one of them, wrote,

> The employment of such agencies is a necessary part of the proper exercise of the diplomatic power ... precedents .... show that the Senate of the United States, though in session, need not be consulted as to the appointment of such agents, or as to the instruction the President may give them .... There seems to be no reason why the Government of the United States cannot, in conducting its diplomatic intercourse with other countries, exercise powers as broad and general, or as limited and peculiar, or special, as any other government.[1]

Morgan did not attempt to make a strong constitutional case but was content to point to the frequency of the practice in this and other countries as support for the President's action.

Not so Senator Gray of Delaware. He argued that Senatorial confirmation of appointments was unnecessary where those involved held only employment and not office. He reminded his colleagues that Blount had been assigned a specific task and that with its accomplishment his employment was at an end. Therefore, according to numerous judicial decisions, he had never held an office within the meaning of the Constitution. With regard to his specific task no one had preceded him and no one would succeed him.[2]

During the McKinley administration the discussion arose again but in a different form. The President had been appointing members of Congress to various conferences and Congresses. There began to be some strong feeling that this was improper and in fact contrary to the constitutional provision that a member of Congress may not hold an office under the United States government. The judiciary committee of each house examined the cases of those who had been appointed. The Senate Committee never issued a report; one of its members had a "heart to heart" talk with McKinley instead, during which the President expressed an appreciation of the difficulty a member of the Senate was in when he had to pass upon a treaty which was a part of his own handiwork.[3] Meanwhile the House Committee made a very careful investigation regarding its members. It called in numerous witnesses including several legal experts. Their conclusions gave the

[1] U.S. Senate, Committee on Foreign Relations, 53rd Cong., 2nd Sess., Serial 3180, Senate Report 227, p. 25.

[2] *Congressional Record*, 58th Cong., 2nd Sess., XXXVIII, 2126–27.

[3] Wriston, *op. cit.*, p. 306.

President and their colleagues a "clean bill of health." It was found that all of the positions were "merely transient, occasional or incidental in their nature." [1] The practice continued at an increasing rate.

Five years later, in 1903, Senator Augustus Bacon joined those whose views were that the President was empowered to use special agents, but he was not satisfied that this included Senators. Once again we see an example of confused thinking in Congress. He thought that if the President had the power to use special agents in treaty negotiations it rested "not upon his power to appoint officers, but upon his power to negotiate treaties. The President merely employs agents to perform certain specific duties under his direction ... and the constitutional requirement as to the confirmation by the Senate of Presidental appointments is not applicable." [2] Bacon understood well the views of his predecessors concerning this practice but was unwilling to accept them regarding Senators. This unwillingness was shown again in his 1906 debate with Senator John Spooner of Wisconsin. The appointment by Theodore Roosevelt of Henry White as ambassador to the Algeciras Conference had aroused the opposition. Wisconsin's Senator stood by the President. "He may employ such agencies as he chooses to negotiate the proposed treaty [including] the ambassador ... minister ... chargé d'affaires, or ... a person in private life whom he thinks by his skill or knowledge of the language or people of the country with which he is about to deal is best fitted to negotiate the treaty." [3] Bacon was not completely willing to accept this at the time, but eight years later supported Wilson's use of John Lind in his work in Mexico and "accurately defined his status." [4]

Even one of Wilson's bitterest critics, Senator Lodge, supported his right to use a personal agent to work out peace terms after World War I, based, however, upon his prerogatives in negotiating treaties.[5] It may be noted that the names of those chosen to attend the treaty conferences did not go to the Senate although it was in session. There were even "evidences of dissatisfaction that no Senator was appointed." [6]

[1] U.S. Congress, *Appointment of Members of Congress to Military and Other Offices*, 55th Cong., 3rd Sess., Serial 3841, House Report 2205.

[2] *Congressional Record*, 57th Cong., 2d Sess., XXXVI, 2907.

[3] *Ibid.*, 59th Cong., 1st Sess., XL, 1418.

[4] Wriston, *op. cit.*, p. 309.

[5] Wright, *op. cit.*, pp. 332–33.

[6] Wriston, *op. cit.*, pp. 311–12.

Supporting Arguments Outside of Congress

Several authorities who have addressed themselves to this question have pointed out that the power to appoint is an executive power. Although they accept the consequences of this power, they are not always in agreement as to its source. For example, Attorney General Nelson held in 1843 that "the power of appointment results from the obligation that the laws be faithfully executed.[1]

Mathews, on the other hand, states:

> The President ... is recognized as having control over the negotiation of treaties, and may appoint for their negotiation special agents who act solely under his direction.
>
> ... The President exercises not only legal control but predominating practical influence, both through his power to negotiate treaties and through his power to appoint and remove diplomatic officers and agents.[2]

Another writer discussing this subject believes that the Constitution does not specifically take this matter up because it cannot fully define all the modes by which the power may be carried out. Nevertheless, he believes, it may be assumed that when a branch of the government is charged with a duty it has, inherently, powers necessary and proper to perform it.[3] However, the writer seems to have forgotten that in certain specific situations the Senate shares with the President duties regarding foreign affairs.

Quincy Wright puts forth an interesting argument in support of the President's right to use such agents. He points to the decision of the Supreme Court, *In Re Neagle* as an authoritative source for their use. This was the case in which a federal marshal, Neagle, was assigned by the Attorney-General to protect Justice Field of the Supreme Court while he rode his circuit in California. The Justice, who had been threatened, was assaulted, and the marshal shot and killed one Terry, the assailant. Because the latter and his wife had been popular in the state, the sheriff proceeded to arrest Neagle and Justice Field. The Governor of the state used his influence to have the charges dropped against the Justice but the marshal was still under arrest. The issue which the Supreme Court had to decide, once the lower courts' dismissal of the case was appealed, was since there was no statute author-

1 *Official Opinions of the Attorneys-General of the United States*, IV, 248, as cited in Wriston, *op. cit.*, pp. 123–24.

2 Mathews, *op. cit.*, pp. 91–92.

3 Henry Flanders, "Power of the President To Appoint Special Diplomatic Agents Without the Advice and Consent of the Senate." *The American Law Register and Review* (Philadelphia: George W. Pepper, William D. Lewis and William S. Ellis, 1894) 1st Series, XXXIII (New Series, I), 177.

izing such a use of the marshal, on what grounds could it be assumed that such employment was proper. The Court decided that "any obligation fairly and properly inferrable from [the Constitution] ... is a 'law,'" and it is the President, who, under the Constitution "shall take care that the laws be faithfully executed." [1] To Wright this indicates that executive authority can be delegated even when Congress has not created an office, but he cautions that one can go no further than to recognize that the President can create subordinate agencies but not necessarily offices.[2]

Wright states, "The President's authorization of personal 'agents' for conducting diplomatic negotiations and representing the United States in international conferences is justified under the same inherent power." [3] But this is, perhaps, an extension of the court's view that may not be entirely justified. What the Court struck down was the argument that Neagle's action was unauthorized because "there exists no statute authorizing any such protection as that which Neagle was instructed to give Judge Field in the present case ...." [4] The Court was really addressing itself to the contention that the use of an established office for matters which are not specified is *ultra vires*, there being no statutory authority for it. But in the use of special agents there is no office that has been created nor is one always used. One would have to argue that using an officer in a situation where the authority to use him was only implicit is creating an agency, and that that is tantamount to creating a special agent to fulfill an obligation whenever the authority to fulfill it is implicit in the office of the President. Such a position could be taken but that it could be based on the court's decision in the Neagle case is questionable in those instances where a private citizen is employed as a special agent.

Another writer states his views with much force:

> Congress has no power whatever to limit the President in his choice of negotiators. In contemplation of law, the President is the negotiator of all treaties. The actual discussion is usually committed by the President to an agent, but there are *no limitations upon his choice of a representative*. He may select a diplomat or other official, a private citizen, or even a foreigner .... Whether his agents, be they called commissioners or delegates or by some other title, shall receive compensation is the only question which must be decided by Congress, and then only in the absence of money available from the contingent or some other funds.[5]

[1] 135 U.S. 1.
[2] Wright, *op. cit.*, p. 313.
[3] *Ibid.*
[4] 135 U.S. 1.
[5] Wriston, *op. cit.*, pp. 139–40. My emphasis.

These views are probably an accurate reflection of the authority the President has exercised in appointing agents to represent him in negotiating with other powers. Nevertheless, as we will note, Congress has seen fit to reduce seriously this power and no strong protest has been made.

It should be noted that not only Congress but also Presidents have shown some confusion in their thoughts on the subject. Both Jackson and Grant thought that a person who signed a treaty on the part of the United States necessarily became an officer.[1] And Madison referred to his commissioners to the Treaty of Ghent as holders of "office." [2]

SUMMARY

The Presidential use of special agents has produced heated controversy throughout much of our history. Most of the arguments raised regarding the practice have been based on either a moral or constitutional position. Many have shown very little insight into the true nature of the practice and the arguments have as often been partisan as not. This chapter has been divided into the arguments presented for and against the practice; by members of Congress and scholars.

The moral argument revolves around the propriety of the President's using such agents often. Apparently the fear has been that frequent use of an agent who is not responsible to Congress but only to the President gives him a power advantage over Congress. Such an advantage makes possible a breakdown in the checks and balance principle, at least with regard to the area of foreign relations, an area where the Executive already has certain definite advantages.

One of the popular arguments has dealt with the contingent fund, a fund the significance of which will be examined in the next chapter. Some have felt that any agent who was paid from a special appropriation had to be a public officer. The only way a person could be sent on a mission without being an officer was to give him his pay from the contingent fund. The existence of the contingent fund in the minds of some was just for that purpose. It is interesting to point out that in order to distinguish him from a public officer the special agent was often referred to as a "private" agent, a title which generally would not be correct anymore than would the title "special" agent be proper merely because the person was paid from the contingent fund.

[1] *Ibid.*, p. 164.
[2] *Ibid.*, p. 187.

Another view that was commonly expressed until World War I was that a member of Congress could not hold his seat and also serve as a Presidential agent. This, of course, reflected confused thinking because it assumed that such an agent was an officer. In the past four decades, however, many members of Congress have accepted such assignments, some with a title, others without.

Some critics of the President argued that any commission which bore both the seal of the United States and the President's signature would indicate that the bearer was an officer. It is rather difficult to comprehend the line of reasoning for such a position and it seems to imply that there is an analogy here with signing a public law or order. The use of a signature merely identifies the authorizing source, and to assume that everything that the President signs makes it a public document would be fatuous. Likewise, affixing the Seal merely indicates that the signature is authentic. This will be discussed in detail in the next chapter.

One argument that was extremely weak was that since private citizens would not ordinarily have any diplomatic immunities one who has such would not be a private citizen. Ergo he must be a public official. But this too makes little sense. The view would come closer to providing a sound analysis if the question raised was, Why has a State extended diplomatic immunities in any particular case? There may be different reasons for the extension to an individual of what are known as diplomatic privileges and immunities. The mere existence of them, therefore, would not necessarily reveal the status of the individual. This is a subject that is examined in great detail later on. Suffice it to say here that immunity is established by international law or treaty, that if a Government decides to grant diplomatic rank to a group of persons who would not normally get such consideration, that is its privilege. But this does not mean that such consideration can be demanded of a State. Thus it cannot be assumed that if a State grants such diplomatic status to foreigners, that the home State of the foreigners must consider them officers.

Congress continued to show an increasing concern over the President's use of such agents. Its ire was probably more highly aroused over Cleveland's use of special agents than over any President's. In each of his two separated terms Cleveland used a special agent in a situf ation that seemed to deny the basic right of one or both Houses o- Congress. In 1886 when Congress was aroused over the fishing controversy in Canadian waters it passed a resolution refusing to send commissioners to work out the controversy as the President requested. Upon being informed of their decision Cleveland went ahead and appointed the men on his own. To support the President the minority party drew up a list of 438 names of agents who had been sent abroad by the President without Senate approval. They hoped to ward off obstructive tactics by relying on custom if not constitution. But success for the mission did not result because of the effectiveness of the arguments in support of the President (the list had a number of errors in it), but because of the tact and flexibility of the British delegates when the commission met two years later. The Bayard-Chamberlain agreement seemed to provide enough advantages to the United States so that the attack upon the President was diminished.

However, in Cleveland's second administration he was subjected to, if anything, an even more bitter attack. This was the "Blount episode." It was perhaps understandable that Congress should have been more perplexed than ever. The President's critics could not understand how anyone other than an officer could have an authority paramount to an officer. If he had the authority he must have been an officer, if he were not an officer he could not have had the authority. The courts never were given a chance to test the merits of this argument but it is certainly clear that the President could dismiss his diplomatic representative. Furthermore he could rescind his orders and recall him. And all of this could certainly have been done through the Secretary of State at the President's direction. Using someone else instead for such a temporary mission would not have changed the President's authority to do so. At no time did Blount take on the status of an officer. Hence Senate approval was not necessary. Of course, one would have to view this episode as well as the 1886–87 Canadian fishing dispute in true perspective. Congress and much of the country being aroused at the President's mildness in the face of the British arrests of United States fishermen for alleged violations of the 1818 treaty, and being more than aroused because of Cleveland's opposition to the growing imperialist policies, these missions presented ideal clubs with which to beat the President. In all of these arguments only one Senator saw full well the legal issues at stake and accurately distinguished between office and the employment of a special agent.

CHAPTER III

THE QUESTION OF OFFICE

So far we have examined the thoughts of members of Congress and of scholars on the subject of the use of special agents. These arguments in some cases were based upon the wisdom of the use of such agents, and in other cases the question of whether their use, wise or unwise, was sanctioned by the Constitution. But most crucial to a proper analysis of the legality of the practice is an understanding of the term "office."

MARSHALL'S OPINION

It should be noted that few who argued on constitutional grounds were aware of this, and yet fairly early in our history John Marshall provided the "understanding" which was necessary. It is the question of whether the President's agents are officers, by virtue of their commissions and tasks, which has aroused the most controversy. If they are officers (of other than an "inferior" status), then their appointment requires Senate approval. In one of the early federal court cases that involved this question, Marshall spoke for the Circuit Court of Virginia. He said:

> The Constitution ... is understood to declare that all offices of the United States, except in cases where the Constitution itself may otherwise provide, shall be established by law ... An office is defined to be "a public charge or employment" and he who performs the duties of the office is an officer. If employed on the part of the United States, he is an officer of the United States. Although an office is an employment it does not follow that every employment is an office. A man may certainly be employed under a contract, express or implied, to do an act, or perform a service, without becoming an officer. But if a duty be a continuing one, which is defined by rules prescribed by the government, and not by contract, which an individual is appointed by the government to perform, who enters on the duties appertaining to his station, without any contract defining them, if those duties continue, though the person be changed, it seems very difficult to distinguish such a charge or employment from an office, or the person who performs the duties from an officer.[1]

[1] *United States* v. *Maurice*, Federal Case No. 15,747.

It will be noted that Marshall emphasized three ideas, (1) though an office required employment, the reverse was not necessarily so, (2) the duties of an office are continuing duties, (3) the duties continue on regardless of whether the same person remains to fill them. There is nothing here that refers to the nature or character of the duties. Whether they be of serious moment or trivial apparently does not enter into it. In the *Matter of Hathaway* the court took the same position. It pointed out that "the term 'public office' as used in the Constitution has respect to a permanent public trust or employment." In this particular case a man acting as surrogate for the regular officer had the powers, duties and authority that the latter would have had. Yet the court held that the person acting for the officer was not himself an officer.[1] It very carefully defined office as "an employment ... not merely transient, occasional, or incidental." [2]

LATER DEFINITIONS OF OFFICE

In a very similar vein Mr. Justice Miller spoke for the Supreme Court in 1878. The Court held that the defendant was not an officer as defined by the Constitution because his "duties are *not* continuing and permanent." It added several other criteria that establish office and determined that he did not meet any of them. He kept "no place of business for the public use," he gave "no bond" and took "no oath," no "regular appropriation [was] made to pay his compensation," and there was "no penalty for his absence from duty or refusal to perform." [3]

This is clearly a description that could be used in determining the position of the special diplomatic agent. Its emphasis is on the continuity and *regularity* of the performance of duties by the officer, which is not a characteristic that applies to the temporary agent. In *United States* v. *Hartwell* the Court stressed these same characteristics. Office "embraces the ideas of tenure, duration, emolument and duties." [4]

THE PROBLEM OF RANK

Much of the confusion that has surrounded the practice of employing special agents has stemmed from the fact that some agents have been

[1] 71 New York 238.

[2] *Ibid.*

[3] *United States* v. *Germaine*, 99 U.S. 512.

[4] 73 U.S. 385. See also 15 Court of Claims, 151; 40 Court of Claims, 110; 43 Court of Claims 69; 107 U.S. 414; and *Official Opinions of the Attorneys-General*, XVI, 414, XXII, 483.

given no title or rank, e.g., Washington's use of Gouverneur Morris on a mission to England in 1789, and others have held the highest rank in the diplomatic service, e.g., Wilson's dispatch of Elihu Root with the rank of ambassador and as head of a mission to Russia in 1917. In both of these instances the men were special agents, not officers. There are many examples of persons sent on special missions by Presidents who fit into one or the other of these categories. While there is little quarrel with the opinion that men like Morris were special agents of the President, it has not been so clear to all that men who go on missions carrying diplomatic rank may also be.

It was with this kind of problem that the Court was concerned in the Wood case. Judge Richardson, speaking for the Court, held that rank and office are not necessarily identical. "Rank is often used to express something different from office." It may only be a term of honor used to confer distinction and position.[1]

The same conclusion, although for very different reasons, was held in the case of *United States* v. *Smith*. In this opinion the Court took a position which cut the ground from the argument that Presidential use of special agents was in some cases a usurpation of the appointing power. Justice Field spoke for the court. "An officer of the United States can only be appointed by the President, by and with the advice and consent of the Senate, or by a court of law, or the head of a department. *A person in the service of the government who does not derive his position from one of these sources is not an officer of the United States in the sense of the Constitution.*" [2]

This was not the last time that this question arose. Much confused thinking also was revealed in the Senate and House debates on appointments of delegates to the United Nations. The bill which dealt with this matter was S 1580. It provided that appointments to the Security Council be approved by the Senate, but the appointments to the Economic and Social Council and the Trusteeship Council would be subject to Senate ratification only if the appointees were not members of Congress or officers already so approved. Senator Donnell argued that (1) if the appointees who were not members of Congress or officers of the federal government had to be passed upon by the Senate it meant that they were being considered with regard to public office under the Constitution, (2) that, therefore, appointments of *all*

[1] *Wood* v. *United States*, 15 Court of Claims 151.

[2] 124 U.S. 532. My emphasis. This is perhaps a little too strong, inasmuch as men who are given so-called recess appointments are officers though not approved by the Senate.

to such posts would necessarily require Senatorial approval.[1] He seemed unaware that they would not be officers merely because of Senate approval, but that if the intent was to create an office then the members of Congress who were appointed would lose their seats. This matter was raised by others, however, and will be discussed later.

Senator Connolly in reply made some attempt to refute the notion that all of these offices were constitutional offices, but placed more emphasis upon the aspect of the traditional right of the President to appoint to conferences without Senate approval. He said that the Security Council was different from the other organs inasmuch as it was conceived to be an organ continually in session whereas the others would meet for only short periods of time during the year. Hence appointment to it was to a permanent office, whereas appointment to the others was appointment to temporary assignments. But his main argument was that all Presidents including President Truman appointed members to international conferences without having to get the approval of the Senate. He mentioned as examples Senator Thomas (of Utah) who had been a delegate to the recent conference of the International Labor Organization, the missions of Senator Vandenberg and himself to the San Francisco Conference, and those of Senator Austin and himself to the recent Food and Agricultural Organization Conference in Mexico.[2] The delegates to these conferences, he insisted, were not officers but personal representatives of the President.

Senator Donnell vehemently protested this interpretation and claimed that they were not representatives of the President alone but of the entire United States and as such had to be constitutional officers. He furthermore attacked Senator Connolly on his own ground and maintained that these specific posts were not temporary. As proof of this he pointed to Article 61 of the United Nations Charter which provided that the members of the Economic and Social Council would be elected for three years. It was not clear, he said, how long the members of the Trusteeship Council would serve, but he did not feel that their term would be brief either. As for the tenure of members of the General Assembly he was not sure but his close collaborator, Senator Millikin argued that there was nothing in the Charter which would indicate that the representatives would serve temporarily, either.[3]

[1] *Congressional Record*, 79th Cong., 1st Sess., XCI, 11241.

[2] *Ibid.*, p. 11243.

[3] *Ibid.*, p. 11244.

None of these Senators, including Senators Taft and Vandenberg who occasionally spoke, gave much evidence that they understood the true nature of these appointments. And Senators Donnell's and Millikin's arguments that these were permanent positions because the United Nations' Charter provided for three-year terms for the members showed a gross miscomprehension of the meaning of the term "member" in an international treaty. Instead of interpreting "member' to mean State they thought it meant delegate. Thus they were unaware that a treaty can only define the terms of memberships for States, who are the principal characters of an international agreement, and not the terms of appointment of delegates. The latter is a matter of concern to the municipal law of each member State.

The President's right to appoint such agents is attested to by numerous scholars. Willoughby has written, "The President, as well as other executive officials may, for their assistance in executing their official duties, employ persons to perform certain specific duties. Those persons have, however, legally speaking, no official powers ..." [1] Still others have maintained that "A public office is the right, authority, and duty created and conferred by law ... for a given period, either fixed by law or enduring at the pleasure of the creating power ..." [2] or that "Persons appointed for a special and temporary purpose in connection with foreign affairs, and whose employment ceases when the purpose is accomplished are mere *pro tempore* aids to the President in the performance of his executive functions." [3]

When the question of appointing Senators or Representatives as delegates to the United Nations was considered under S. 1580 in the United States Congress, the members of the House Foreign Affairs Committee asked whether, due to the Constitutional provision prohibiting a member of Congress from holding office, acceptance of such an appointment would result automatically in that member's losing his seat. A memorandum on this subject by Senator Connally which contained a ruling by Attorney-General Harry A. Daugherty, was introduced. Daugherty's ruling was *apropos* the appointment of Representative Burton and Senator Smoot to the Debt Funding Commission following the first World War. Confirmation of appointment

[1] Westel W. Willoughby, *The Constitutional Law of the United States* (2nd ed.; New York: Baker Vorhis and Co., 1929), p. 1178.

[2] Floyd R. Mechem, *A Treatise on the Law of Public Offices and Officers* (Chicago: Callaghan and Co., 1890), pp. 1–2.

[3] Flanders, *op. cit.*, p. 179.

was required by the Joint Resolution which created the Commission. The memorandum with the Attorney-General's ruling read,

"I have failed to find any judicial interpretation of the section of the Constitution now under consideration, and in the absence of such finally authoritative interpretation, great weight must be attached to the practical construction put upon the Constitution from the beginning of the Government. In such practical construction a distinction has always been made between special employment on the one hand and offices on the other, and between offices – using that term in a general sense – which serve only a temporary purpose, and those which have duration and permanency. From the very beginning of the Government Members of the Senate and the House have, from time to time, been asked to render services and it has never been decided that such temporary employment for a special purpose and to serve an immediate exigency constituted a civil office within the meaning of the constitutional provision above referred to ....

"Where, therefore, a position does not have continuancy and permanency and its function is restricted to a single matter, the position seems to be that of an executive agent and not an 'office' within the meaning of the Constitution ..."

The Senate Judiciary Committee, to whom the question was referred, recommended against the confirmation of the nominees on the basis of the alleged constitutional ineligibility. A minority report, however, agreed with the views of the Attorney-General. After a full debate of the matter on the floor of the Senate, Messrs. Smoot and Burton were confirmed by a vote of 47 to 25. There are numerous other cases in which Members of Congress have been appointed on commissions to settle international disputes such as boundary commissions or other arbitration commissions.[1]

The fact that some agents carry commissions with the United States seal affixed and others do not, and that some commissions carry high diplomatic rank and others do not, has no bearing on whether a man is an officer or not. Wriston has put it well when he says,

While it is unquestioned that credentials vary in character in accordance with the nature of the task, there is no place where a line may be drawn; it cannot be said, "Those with a commission under the President's hand are officers, those otherwise commissioned are not."

This would be operating on the false premise,

that official character depends upon the duties to be performed. *The commission does, indeed, fix the status of the agent as a diplomatic functionary, but it has no necessary relation to his being an officer of the United States in the constitutional sense.*[2]

It is this last point that has not been comprehended by many critics of the practice. When Attorney-General Cushing said, "the expression 'ambassadors and other public ministers' in the Constitution must be understood as comprehending all officers having diplomatic

[1] *Congressional Record*, 79th Cong., 1st Sess., XCI, 12322.

[2] Wriston, *op. cit.*, pp. 169–79. My emphasis.

functions whatever their title or designation," [1] he was misinterpreted. As Wriston points out he did not mean that all agents or persons "having diplomatic functions are officers." [2] Even a prominent authority on American constitutional law was confused about this.[3]

One could fall into the same error regarding the U.S. Statutes which state that "'Diplomatic Officers' shall be deemed to include ambassadors, envoys extraordinary, ministers plenipotentiary, ministers resident, commissioners, chargés d'affaires, agents, and secretaries of legations, and none others." [4] But this likewise cannot be interpreted to mean that anyone who holds one of the ranks enumerated is an officer.

Perhaps the best summation of the fact that office and employment are not the same, and that the President has the constitutional right to employ agents came in the great debate on Cleveland's use of Blount. Senator James George argued,

> "The President may appoint persons called envoys, ministers, ambassadors, commissioners, or chargés d'affaires, or whatever you may be pleased to call them, for the specific purpose of making a treaty. It has been conceded that he may make the appointment during the session of the Senate and without submitting to the Senate the name of the person so appointed." In the same way the President may appoint agents for other duties. Whatever the duties or the title, they are immaterial. "The true rule is, that in the sense of that clause of the Constitution which requires appointments to office to be made by and with the advice and consent of the Senate, an appointment or employment to do a particular thing, or specific things, is without constitutional tenure and is not an office. This idea is plain in the Constitution." The idea is plain because "in every instance in which an office is established the tenure or term of the estate of the Officer in the office is invariably fixed, either by express words or by an implication clear and indisputable. The Constitution ... refers alone to appointments of officers whose terms or tenure of office are determined by afflux of time ..." [5]

In every case, regardless of the title or rank bestowed, the decisive factors are whether or not the agents' assignment is temporary, and whether the duties are transient.

It has sometimes been thought that because rank confers certain privileges upon the agent in carrying out his diplomatic work, that this, perforce, makes him an officer. But such privileges as may be given to these agents are not, as was mentioned previously, the result of United States statutory or constitutional law. The choice of the

[1] *Official Opinions of the Attorneys-General of the United States*, LXX, 186.

[2] Wriston, *op. cit.*, pp. 161–62.

[3] See the discussion in Corwin, *The President's Control of Foreign Relations*, *op. cit.*, p. 108.

[4] Revised Statutes, Sec. 1674.

[5] *Congressional Record*, 58th Cong., 2nd Sess., XXVI, 3133–34, quoted in Wriston, *op. cit.*, pp. 301–302.

rank on the other hand, is a matter of municipal law since only the duly-constituted national authorities can assign rank to their agents whether they render service in domestic or international affairs.[1]

Perhaps one other illustration of the fact that special agents are not officers should be pointed out. According to Article I, Section 6, paragraph 2 of the Constitution, no member of Congress may hold any office "under the authority of the United States," and "no person holding any office under the United States" shall be a member of Congress. This is an airtight provision prohibiting anyone from holding both an office and a seat in Congress concurrently. Yet since 1921 when two Senators were appointed as United States delegates to the Washington Arms Conference there have been numerous occasions when members of Congress have received appointments to represent the United States at international gatherings. Were these delegates at the conferences United States officers, the incompatibility with the constitutional requirement would be patently clear. This is the nature of the situation that Clay and Bayard thought they were in when Madison appointed them as United States delegates to the peace conference with Britain in 1814, hence their resignation from their Congressional seats.

THE PRESIDENTIAL SIGNATURE AND THE UNITED STATES' SEAL

It will be recalled that Senator Tazewell argued that a commission which contained the President's signature and the Great Seal of the United States explicitly defined the bearer as an officer. But there are really no grounds for such a conclusion. The President's signature merely indicates that the holder of such a commission has been duly

[1] David Jayne Hill, "The Classification of Diplomatic Agents," *American Journal of International Law*, XXI, 737.

It should not be thought that the problem of differentiating the official from the non-official agent is peculiar to appointees in diplomatic work. Other departments of the executive branch have found difficulty in making the proper distinction. In 1830 Attorney-General Berrien gave as his opinion that although under the Act of March 3, 1809 the Secretary of the Navy could appoint special agents who might be called on frequently to perform duties normally filled by a permanent agent, he still could only be considered as temporary. *Official Opinions of the Attorneys-General of the United States*, XX, 321.

A similar situation arose almost 100 years later in the Census Office. This office had been created in 1902, and Section 5 of the Statute referred to "all employees of the Census Office." A question arose whether the special agents permitted under the Act of March 3, 1899 to help take the census were to be considered as coming under the provision of Section 5. The Attorney-General ruled that special agents could not be considered as regular employees. See *ibid.*, XXIII, 533. The Treasury and War Departments have also adopted this view.

authorized by the President to fulfill a certain assignment. It has the same standing that any signature has, it supports an allegation by the bearer that a certain act has been authorized by the signatory.

The use of the Seal likewise confused Tazewell. The United States Seal, which was authorized in 1782, is affixed to public documents. But the Seal does not indicate that the bearer of the document is a public officer. It merely authenticates the signature of the signer, who is the President of the United States. This was made clear by John Marshall in 1803 when he said, "It attests by an act supposed to be of public notoriety, the verity of the presidential signature." [1] Thus, whenever the President writes a communication to foreign governments, makes official agreements with other states, gives commissions, etc., he signs and affixes the Seal to indicate the authenticity of the signature.

THE CONTINGENT FUND

An important question that needs examination is, does a special agent get paid, and how is the amount determined? It cannot be that there is a certain, fixed amount allocated to him by law for this would then establish one of the characteristics that the Supreme Court has defined as an attribute of office. Of course not all agents have been paid. Colonel Edward M. House, one of the most important agents, made one trip abroad at his own expense.[2] It is up to the President to decide whether and what the agent shall be paid, unless a special appropriation is allocated by Congress. If a special appropriation is not furnished by Congress from whence comes the money to pay such agencies? It comes from what is known as the contingent or secret fund. This fund is one of several at the disposal of the President for a variety of matters of concern to the executive. In foreign affairs it gives the President a degree of freedom which he could not possibly have without it. It makes it possible for him to spend any amount of money within, of course, the limits made available by Congress, and for whatever purposes he wishes except for any which may be specifically denied.

Establishment of the Fund

Such a fund for foreign affairs has existed almost from the very first days of our government. Apparently it was created in large measure

[1] 5 U.S. Reports 158.
[2] His spring, 1914 trip.

as the result of Jefferson's influence based upon his experiences abroad. A Senate committee was considering how to provide for the expenses for foreign affairs. Jefferson, who was Secretary of State, appeared before the committee and "as a result of his illuminating exposition of diplomatic methods in Europe, the committee agreed to strike out the specific sum to be given to any foreign appointments, leaving a lump sum to the President for foreign intercourse.[1]

Restrictions on Use of the Fund

Shortly after this was put into law Congress approved, on July 1, 1790, an act authorizing the President to draw from the Treasury not more than $40,000 annually for the support of such persons as he shall commission to serve the United States in foreign parts, and for the expense incident to the business in which they may be employed.[2] An amendment was approved February 9, 1793 which required the President to make an account of the money expended in foreign affairs "wherein the expenditures thereof may, in his judgment be made public." [3]

In 1818 although "the names of the existing or anticipated diplomatic missions [were] introduced into the appropriation acts, and certain sums of money ... allotted to each," the contingent fund was continued.[4] But the executive's freedom continued to be inhibited. By act of March 26, 1842, Congress prohibited "any payments to agents or commissioners thereafter to be appointed except out of specific appropriations to be made by law." [5] This was a serious restriction on the general use of agents. However the contingent fund was still made available for use in diplomatic work.[6] This may be considered an indication that it was anticipated that the President, in carrying out his duties in foreign relations would need more latitude of action in foreign than in domestic relations.

[1] Maclay's Journal, p. 272, as cited in Mathews, *American Foreign Relations, op. cit.*, p. 423.

[2] I Stat. 128. There is no comparable fund today. The Government's operations having grown so complex, Congress now provides several contingency funds. Those for Mutual Security and Foreign Assistance are each to be approximately 300 million dollars in 1962. That fund which is closest in nature to the original contingent fund is $1,000,000. Public Law 87–125, 75 Stat. 270, 87th Congress, August 3, 1961.

[3] *Statutes at Large*, I, 299.

[4] Mathews, *American Foreign Relations, op. cit.*, p. 421.

[5] *Statutes at Large*, V, 533.

[6] The law stated that the restrictions on the use of agents "shall not extend to the contingent fund connected with the foreign intercourse of the Government, placed at the disposal of the President ..." *Ibid.*

Effect on Presidential Authority

There are differences of opinion as to what authority Congress intended the President to derive from the existence of such a fund. Mathews finds that the fund, and various sections of the Revised Statutes which authorize payments from the fund "on Presidential receipts or certificates without vouchers ..." is a source of authority for the use of special agents.[1] Williams is of a similar mind and finds that the fund not only aids the President in avoiding the need for Congressional allocations for each agent, but also gives tacit approval of the agent and/or the function he is to perform.[2] This would seem to be reading quite a bit into the reasons which Congress had in creating such a fund.

Secretary of State Seward was even more forthright in his belief that the contingent fund was a source of authority for the use of special agents. On January 28, 1838 he wrote to Senator Sumner regarding a bill introduced in the Senate prohibiting the appointment of special agents. He hoped this would not apply to those agents connected with foreign affairs, and said they had "always been indirectly sanctioned" by appropriations for the contingent fund.[3]

Wriston, in what appears to be a much sounder analysis, disputes the contention that the contingent fund confers

> any power upon the President to appoint agents. If that were the case, the power of appointing agents would be limited to use of them in diplomatic business ... But the fact is that the agents used in the conduct of our foreign relations constitute only a very small fraction of the whole number of executive agents. The power of appointment arises not from legislative enactment, but from the general grant of executive power by the Constitution.[4]

[1] Mathews, *American Foreign Relations*, *op. cit.*, pp. 436–37. Mathews raises an interesting argument regarding a possible use of the contingent fund. "If Congress by act constitutes the position of a delegate to an international conference an office under the United States and attaches thereto a definite salary, it can doubtless require the President to submit nominations to the Senate. But it is difficult to see how compliance with the act could be compelled by any means short of impeachment, so long as the delegate is paid from the contingent fund on Presidential certificates or is willing to serve without compensation. Such an act would be indicative of the opinion of Congress and entitled to respect, but it would not necessarily be mandatory upon the President ... Congress might, however, provide that no compensation should be paid out of the public funds to delegates to an international conference unless the Senate has advised and consented to their appointment, and this would probably have controlling effect as to the compensation of such delegates, even though a contingent fund for the general purpose of foreign intercourse should at the same time be provided." See p. 439.

[2] Benjamin H. Williams, *American Diplomacy, Policies and Practices* (1st ed.; New York: McGraw Hill Book Co., 1936), p. 423.

[3] U.S. Report Book, IX, 387, as cited in Wriston, *op. cit.*, p. 265, n. 116.

[4] *Ibid.*, p. 123.

It is interesting to note that members of the legislature have not always exhibited clear thinking with regard to this matter. In the debate over the Turkish Treaty of 1831, for example, Senator Forsyth of Georgia, who championed Jackson's use of special agents to negotiate the treaty, seemed to imply that the fund was there to enable the President to appoint "spies" and agents for special missions.[1]

The availability of the contingent fund has often served to confuse the issue of the President's right to use special agents. However, it is probably accurate to say that the fund, which has been made available to the executive from the very early days of the nation's history, is to be used in foreign affairs at the President's discretion, and one of the major uses Presidents have made of it has been to pay special agents to carry out assignments in foreign affairs.

SUMMARY

From the numerous cases cited it seems patently clear that most of the confusion regarding the use of special agents has stemmed from insufficient attention to the distinction between office and employment. The courts on numerous occasions have stated that office implies continuing duties which go beyond a specific assignment, that the duties are not created with regard to a specific individual in mind and that the general duties are prescribed in law, as is the tenure of the performer of those duties. Employment implies temporary or occasional occupation, specific to the individual without reference to regularity or oath. Many officers of the Government employ through their departments, bureaus, etc., agents for limited needs. In fact, in certain departments such as Commerce and Post Office, special agents are frequently hired. In no instance, however, do such agents get any rights which exist only as a result of holding office.

The use of the contingent fund has at times added to the confusion on the subject. Jefferson's familiarity with the existence and use of such a fund in European Governments helped lead to its establishment here. The President has broad discretion regarding the use of such a fund, which has grown considerably since its inception, except that he may not use it to pay the salaries of those "agents or commissioners" who are appointed presumably upon congressional authorization. The

[1] *Congressional Debates*, 21st Cong., 2nd Sess., VII, 295, as cited in Wriston, *op. cit.*, pp. 241–42.

President has felt entitled to use it to pay secret and public special agents and has continued to do so.

But the existence of such a fund is not solely for payment of special agents and hence its existence cannot be considered as the source of authority for the use of special agents.

CHAPTER IV

THE PRESIDENT'S APPOINTING POWER WITH RESPECT TO SPECIAL AGENTS

We have seen how the President's authority was unrestricted in the early period of our history with regard to creating diplomatic posts and assigning title or rank to those officers who filled them. After 1855 this appointing power was curtailed.

Restrictions upon the President that were passed also applied to the appointment of special agents. It may now be of some value to examine the nature of these restrictions.

EARLY ATTEMPTS AT RESTRICTIONS

Not all of the attempts materialized. For example, Senator Gore's attack in 1814 against Madison's recess appointments of Messrs. Gallatin, Adams and Bayard to work out peace terms with Great Britain was based upon the belief that the President was creating new offices without the necessary statutory authority, but the protest was never put to a vote.[1]

Other criticisms were leveled over a decade later. In 1826 John Quincy Adams had asked Congress for funds to send ministers to the Panama Conference. The "House of Representatives considered a proposition expressing the sense of that body as to what the Ministers ought and ought not to do." Because the legislators provided the funds they thought this enabled them to impose conditions. This effort was defeated.[2]

Another attempt suffered the same fate in 1842. An amendment was added to the general appropriation prohibiting the use of any of the funds for agents who were not approved. This was in response to a report by Secretary of State Webster that there were agents stationed abroad drawing a regular salary from the contingent fund. But it was

[1] Wright, *op. cit.*, pp. 326–27.

[2] Benton, *op. cit.*, IX, 94–95, cited in Mathews, *American Foreign Relations*, *op. cit.*, pp 455–56.

defeated in place of the substitute motion by Senator Buchanan which prohibited paying regular dispatch agents from contingent funds.[1]

RESTRICTIONS SUCCESSFULLY PASSED

The next effort by the Senate to restrict the President succeeded in passing. It was the resolution mentioned previously by Senator Windom in 1883. Although approving of the treaty with Korea, negotiated by Commodore Shufeldt, Windom's resolution did not want approval of the treaty to imply approval of the use of an agent whose name had not been sent to the Senate. He thought the resolution of protest was necessary lest the means employed in the mission be interpreted as creating a precedent. President Arthur ignored it.[2]

The succeeding attempt against the executive's appointing power came in 1886. Cleveland's use of special agents to resolve the fisheries dispute with England was attacked by a number of Senators on many grounds, but only one dealt with his methods of negotiation. Even on this score Senator William E. Chandler was the only one willing to introduce outright a resolution that the appointment was unconstitutional. It read, "The President has no right under his implied power of making preliminary negotiations of treaties to appoint without the concurrence of the Senate, private citizens as plenipotentiaries to make and sign such treaties in behalf of the United States." [3] The resolution died without being voted on.

Cleveland was, of course, subject to attack for the use of Blount in Hawaii. The minority of the Foreign Relations Committee declared that giving Blount paramount authority was an unconstitutional act, and Senator Hoar supported this by a resolution which was based upon the belief that Blount must have been an officer by virtue of his authority over the regular officer. The majority who supported Cleveland carried the day.

Although only one effort to limit the President in his power to use special agents had been successful, that of Senator Windom in 1883, efforts along this line did not cease. Significant success was finally achieved in the year just prior to the outbreak of the Great War.

In 1913 the Senate added an amendment to the House bill authorizing a general deficiency appropriation. The amendment was to the

[1] Serial 398, Sen. Doc. 253, 27th Cong., 2nd Sess., pp. 1841–42, cited in Wriston, *op. cit.*, pp. 260–61.

[2] *Senate Executive Journal*, XXIII, 584–85, cited in Wriston, *op. cit.*, pp. 276, 278.

[3] *Congressional Record*, 50th Cong., 1st Sess., XIX, 6568.

effect that "hereafter the Executive shall not extend or accept any invitation to participate in any international Congress, conference or like event without first having specific authority of law to do so.[1] Without any discussion or comment on such an important matter it was passed. There is, therefore, no way of knowing what the Congress had in mind when it accepted this amendment. It has never been legally construed by the Attorney-General or the courts. The President has ignored this at times.[2]

Still another limitation was imposed on the executive's appointing power. When the Senate gave its consent to the treaties of World War I with Germany, Austria, and Hungary, it included a reservation that "the United States shall not be represented or participate in any body, agency or commission, nor shall any person represent the United States as a member of any body, agency or commission in which the United States is authorized to participate by this Treaty, unless and until an act of the Congress of the United States shall provide for such representation or participation." [3]

RESTRICTIONS WITH RESPECT TO INTERNATIONAL ORGANIZATIONS

Although the United States did not join the League of Nations, had she done so review of appointments by the Senate would probably have been necessary. Reservation No. 7 in the Senate debate on the Versailles Treaty provided that the United States representatives would have to be approved by the Senate. This was later changed to provide that representation in the League or any other agency established by the peace treaty would have to be in accordance with acts of Congress which would not only approve the appointments, but also define the powers and duties of all delegates. Senator Lodge supported this view with the contention that in such matters the delegates represented the entire United States government. "Unofficial" agents, therefore should not be involved.[4]

THE UNITED NATIONS "BATTLE"

When discussion arose in 1945 over the Senate's part in the appointment of delegates to the international conferences and organi-

[1] *Ibid.*, 62nd Cong., 3rd Sess., II, 4411.
[2] Wright, *op. cit.*, p. 328.
[3] *Statutes at Large*, XLII, Part 2, 1945, 1949, 1954, as cited in Wriston, *op. cit.*, p. 152.
[4] *Congressional Record*, 67th Cong., 1st Sess., LXI, 5772.

zations which were planned or which might be created, the view seemed to be taken for granted that appointments were not simply a matter of Presidential prerogative. The Foreign Relations Committee bill required Senatorial confirmation of the representative and deputy representative on the Security Council but not necessarily for the General Assembly, Economic and Social Council and the Trusteeship Council. For the last three an exception was to be made for delegates who were members of Congress or officers already approved.[1]

Senator Millikin objected to the bill put out by the Committee. He proposed an amendment that all appointments should require Senate approval. In this he was joined by Senator O'Mahoney who believed that this would give the desired prestige to all delegates. Some argued that if Senate approval was needed for appointment to the General Assembly or that if the appointment was for a specific period of time, six months or a year, that such delegates would be officers in a constitutional sense and hence members of Congress would be ineligible. The Millikin amendment was defeated.[2]

Senator Connolly gave several reasons for supporting the right of the President to appoint the delegates to the General Assembly without check, including the belief that the President had the right to appoint delegates to international conferences since these conferences were temporary and since, therefore, the delegates would only be executive agents. He pointed out that his and Senator Vandenberg's names were not sent to the Senate when they went to the San Francisco Conference. Senator Millikin replied that the reason was Senatorial confidence in Connolly and Vandenberg, thus implying the Senate had the right to insist on passing on such appointments. Senator Donnell agreed with Millikin. To smooth matters over Senator Connolly then brought in an amendment which met Senator Millikin's objections.[3] In its final form it was decided that approval of "the representatives of the United States in any commission that may be formed by the United Nations ... to which the United States is entitled to a representative" would be necessary.[4]

So far as the procedure for appointing delegates to the United Nations is concerned, the United Nations Participation Act of December 20, 1945, requires that Presidential appointments of representa-

[1] *Ibid.*, 79th Cong., 1st Sess., XCI, 10969–78.

[2] *Ibid.*, pp. 11315–20.

[3] *Ibid.*, p. 11390.

[4] Public Law 264, 79th Cong., 1st Sess. The same provisions were inserted into the Economic Cooperation Administration Act of 1948.

tive and deputy representative of the United States to the United Nations both have the rank and status of envoy extraordinary and ambassador plenipotentiary and require the advice and consent of the Senate. Additional deputy representatives are to be appointed the same way as are the regular representatives and delegates to the General Assembly.[1]

The Act also requires that any United States representative to any United Nations Commission must get Senate approval. It further provides that,

> The President may also appoint from time to time such other persons as he may deem necessary to represent the United States in the organs and agencies of the United Nations but the representatives of the United States in the Economic and Social Council and in the Trusteeship Council of the United Nations shall be appointed only by and with the advice and consent of the Senate, except that the President may, without the advice and consent of the Senate, designate any officer of the United States to act without additional compensation, as a representative of the United States in either such council (A) at any specified session thereof where the position is vacant or in the absence or disability of the regular representative, or (B) in connection with specified subject matter at any specified session of either such Council in lieu of the regular representative.[2]

The Congress's ability to restrict the President by virtue of its power to approve appointments was revealed very sharply with regard to President Truman's first nomination of the United States representative to the Economic and Social Council. Francis Biddle was nominated January 29, 1947. The Senate Foreign Relations Committee opposed Biddle, probably because of his New Deal past. (He was considered by many to belong to the left-wing of the New Dealers). Hence, his nomination was pigeonholed for six months. President Truman finally gave in by withdrawing his name.[3] In its place was submitted the name of Willard Thorpe, whose name was immediately approved by the Committee and the Senate.[4]

[1] United Nations Participation Act of 1945, 22 *U.S. Code*, Sec. 287.

[2] *Ibid.* The Amendment to the United Nations Act, October 10, 1949, Public Law 341, 81st Cong., 2nd Sess., maintains these requirements. Senatorial approval to the United Nations Educational, Scientific and Cultural Organization is also necessary (Public Law 565, 79th Cong., 2nd Sess.). Interestingly, for a change it was the House of Representatives which insisted on Senatorial approval, the Senate reluctantly going along (*Congressional Record*, 79th Cong., 2nd Sess., XCII, 5389).

[3] *New York Times*, March 17, May 13, 14, 24, July 13, 14, 1947.

[4] *Congressional Record*, 80th Cong., 1st Sess., XCIII, 9046–47.

SPECIAL AGENTS AND THE QUESTION OF RANK

One question which may be asked is what title or rank, if any, may the special agent hold. The early practice generally was to send the agent's name to the Senate for approval, if he was to be given rank. When, for example, Washington decided not to give Samuel Bayard, whom he sent on a special mission to London in 1794 a formal appointment, the latter complained. He was told, interestingly, that there was doubt that the executive had the power "to give a formal commission" (without Senate confirmation).[1]

With the exception of Thomas Barclay who was sent to Morocco while the Senate was in recess in 1791, the names of all of Washington's special emissaries who held rank or title were sent to the Senate for confirmation.[2] John Adams followed the same procedure, as did Jefferson and Madison.[3] As Wriston points out none of the executives who were closely connected with the events at the Constitutional Convention felt justified in giving rank or title to agents without sending their names to the Senate.[4] The same tradition was followed by other Presidents including John Quincy Adams, James Polk, Ulysses Grant, and Rutherford Hayes.[5]

Apparently the first time anyone in the government suggested that the executive not only could appoint special agents but also give them rank without the need for Senatorial approbation was in December, 1870. That was the incident referred to above in which Senator Sumner expressed the belief that the President could give any title he wished to his agent, possibly including that of "ambassador." [6]

The doubt in Sumner's thinking probably was based on the belief that anyone having the title of ambassador would possibly fall under the constitutional provision dealing with the appointment of officers. Since the Constitution (Article II, Section 2, paragraph 2) requires that those appointed as ambassadors must be nominated to the Senate, confusion on this subject was bound to result. But, as has already been related, the term "ambassadors" in the Constitution refers to Officers of the United States and not to those who merely hold employment.

1 MS Instructions to United States Ministers, III, 208–11, cited in Wriston, *op. cit.*, pp. 183–84.

2 *Ibid.*, pp. 180, 184.

3 *Ibid.*, pp. 184–86.

4 *Ibid.*, p. 188.

5 *Ibid.*, pp. 188–89.

Congressional Globe, 41st Cong., 3rd Sess., XLIII, 227.

That this was not perceived by many is undoubtedly the reason why even those special diplomatic agents who were given a lower grade than ambassador were nominated to the Senate during the eighteenth and most of the nineteenth centuries. However, once the practice of assigning top diplomatic rank began, it developed with great speed. Wriston suggests, with much logic, that the reason for this change lay in the circumstances of the time. The United States had gotten over its strong distaste for ceremony, and had also resented being forced to take positions of lesser prominence than many smaller nations in ceremonial affairs abroad. Before the United States used the rank of ambassador, protocol required that its diplomats should not have all the privileges carried by higher ranking diplomats of other states.[1] This situation was changed by the Act of March 3, 1893 which "authorized 'the President to appoint' ambassadors in certain cases." [2] Hence the President was not "breaking new ground" in the fullest sense when McKinley sent Whitelaw Reid to Queen Victoria's Diamond Jubilee celebration in 1897 with the rank of Ambassador Extraordinary. But, it was not because of the 1893 Act that McKinley could do so since this Act concerned officers of the United States and Reid went as a special representative of the President. Nevertheless, since the authority to appoint to the rank of ambassador had already been granted, it made it easier for McKinley to use this rank for a special agent. Reid would, of course, stand at the ceremony for the President of the United States. It seemed necessary, therefore, that he have the highest diplomatic rank.[3]

It should be recalled from previous discussion that holding such rank did not make him an officer anymore than the fact that he performed a function that many officers of highest rank often perform. The courts had spoken to this point many times stating that rank is not office nor does appointment to a given rank confer office.[4]

Soon the practice of sending special agents with rank to ceremonial affairs became commonplace. But it was not confined merely to these occasions. Delegates to international conferences were given diplomatic rank, as for example those who went to the Second Hague Conference in 1907 with the rank of "Ambassador Extraordinary," and others with the rank of "Commissioner Plenipotentiary" or "Minister Plenipotentiary." [5]

[1] Wriston, *op. cit.*, pp. 192–94.
[2] Wright, *op. cit.*, p. 325.
[3] Wriston, *op. cit.*, pp. 194–95.
[4] *Supra*, pp. 35–36
[5] *Foreign Relations* (1907), p. 1110, cited in Wriston, *op. cit.*, p. 196.

At the Washington Conference of 1922 the United States delegates held the rank of ambassador despite the fact that two of them were Senators.[1]

Apparently once the Executive began to assign rank and title to an agent he felt free to choose any rank or title he wished. Furthermore, not only did he exhibit such authority, but the practice was extended to cover agents sent on all kinds of missions. Thus it may be assumed that the President is not restricted in assigning any rank or title he deems fitting and proper for the personal agents he sends on special missions or if he wishes, he may assign none at all.

SUMMARY

It is interesting that almost from the beginning of the new nation's history Congress seemed to be more critical of the President when he attempted to use special agents than it was when he created regular diplomatic posts. When the President would appoint individuals to special missions invariably some criticism would be voiced in Congress implying that the President was violating the provision of the Constitution regarding appointment to office. These criticisms generally indicated a misinterpretation of the position of the agents and assumed that they were officers.

These attacks and attempted restrictions did not prove successful until 1883 when a protest in the form of a resolution was passed with regard to the Shufeldt mission to Korea. After that, and perhaps emboldened by this success, Congress succeeded in passing a much more serious restriction in 1913. The President was then forbidden to extend or accept any invitation to an international conference on behalf of the United States without Congressional authorization. After World War I with the serious split that developed between the Executive and Congress it was perhaps natural that this zeal for restricting Executive action should continue. Congress not only required that its approval was necessary in order to join any organization which was es-

[1] *New York Times*, November 1, 1921, cited in Wriston, *op. cit.*, p. 197. The two were Henry C. Lodge and Oscar Underwood. This is the first example of Senators having conferred upon them the rank of Ambassador, and it is interesting that Lodge should have been one of them. Lodge, who so strongly attacked the proposition that the United States should join the League of Nations, partly on the grounds that membership would diminish the Senate's authority in foreign affairs, allowed himself to be put in the position that Senator Hoar attacked years earlier, namely, that Senators could not exercise the independent judgment that the Constitution expected from the principle of separation of powers if they joined the Executive in negotiations which they would later be expected to pass judgment upon as Senators.

tablished as a result of the peace treaty we signed with the Central European powers, but clearly intended to have a veto over any possible appointments the President might make if we joined the League of Nations.

When the Congress prepared to pass legislation which would authorize United States membership in the United Nations it debated with some feeling the question of appointing United States delegates. Although the attitude which permeated the Congress in 1919 and 1920 regarding the danger confronting United States independence if it joined an international organization did not exist in 1945, as in this earlier period, Congress did show concern for the need to restrict the President's use of the appointing power. Senator Connolly tried to keep the President's hands unfettered by permitting him to appoint those he chose without Senate control. He even went so far as to say that the President had the right to do this. But under Senators Millikin's and Donnell's attacks he gave way, and when the Senate and House finished with this matter the Presidential appointees no longer could hold the status of special agent but had to be public officers. What better example could there be of the Senate's tactical success than that represented by the Biddle nomination? Had Senator Connolly had his way President Truman could have appointed Francis Biddle. By Senator Millikin's victory he could not.

How many times this story may be repeated no one can say, but clearly with the United Nations becoming so involved in international affairs, in scope if not yet in influence, and the United States being so interested in having the United Nations take on so many different problems, the victory that Congress won in 1945 may take on significant proportions at some future date.

In the early period of our history it was customary for the President to send the agent's name to the Senate for approval if he held a diplomatic rank. The status of such an agent was apparently not very well understood by either the President or his advisors, and they assumed that the mere holding of a diplomatic rank put the agent in the category which fell under the constitutional provisions dealing with officers. But once Congress authorized the use of the rank of ambassador Presidents began to give this rank to their agents without first seeking Senatorial approval. Thus, strangely, the right to use the highest diplomatic rank seemed to convey the idea that the President no longer had his hands tied and the special agents who held this rank rarely had their names submitted to the Senate from then on.

From the Appendix it can be seen that the Presidents have used personal diplomatic agents on a great variety of missions. They have been asked to represent the President personally at public ceremonial functions and personally at private conferences *tête à tête* with high-ranking officials including chiefs of state. They have been authorized to gather statistical information, to act as unofficial observers at international meetings, to prepare for the coming of official diplomatic missions and to act in their stead whenever official missions were thought to be inappropriate.

At times such agents have been given rank and title and at other times not at all. Some have gone on secret missions which were not supposed to be known by anyone but the President, and the few to whom they might have had to confide such information. Still others have gone on similar missions in which even the officials of the countries to which they were dispatched were not informed.

On the other hand many missions were not kept secret at all and in fact the intention was to give as much publicity to them as possible. The use to which such agencies have been put would seem, therefore, to deny strict definition or limitation. And, although it has taken a long time, and although Congress has passed legislation which somewhat restricts the President in his use of these agencies, it is now accepted by almost all authorities within the government and without, that the President may appoint such agents for his purposes, and that Congress has no constitutional grounds upon which to challenge him.

The practice has not grown into any rigid pattern. Not only have the types of missions varied depending upon the needs of the moment, and not only has the diplomatic rank of the agents varied, depending upon the President's wishes, but the credentials have also varied. These credentials have varied according to the nature of the mission and also according to what the President has thought necessary or desirable. One authority's analysis of this matter made in the 1920s can no longer be followed. In fact it was not even true of all agents then, e.g. Colonel House. He wrote,

If the mission be one of inquiry and investigation merely, in which he [the agent] is not required to deal with the national officers of the foreign state, he is likely to have a special passport. If his conversations with foreign officials are informal and unofficial, he may have as informal a letter as that of Gouverneur Morris, already referred to, or that which Thurlow Weed carried when he went to England for Seward. When the agent is to deal with a viceregal government or with the representatives of the minister of foreign affairs of the foreign nations, a certificate of the Department of State suffices. But if the American representative is to approach the foreign sovereign directly, or if he is to negotiate with representatives of that sovereign, for example in signing a treaty, his full powers will be signed by the President and the seal of the United States must be employed.[1]

Certainly neither Col. E. M. House nor Harry Hopkins would fit into this description regarding their several missions abroad. The flexibility of the practice, which is one of its outstanding characteristics, has remained.

[1] Wriston, *op. cit.*, pp. 168–69.

CHAPTER V

STATUS OF THE REGULAR DIPLOMATIC AGENT UNDER INTERNATIONAL LAW

It would be well now to examine the status of the regular diplomatic agent under international law in order to compare it with that of the special agent. Our discussion will have to be arbitrarily limited because an analysis of the regular diplomat's status could become a topic in itself, and also because of the lack of comparability, in many instances, between the special and regular diplomat. In addition, certain aspects will require our attention because of their relevance to our discussion of the establishment of the position of special agents under United States municipal law.

For example Stuart distinguishes between diplomatic rights and privileges and diplomatic immunities. Under the former category he discusses the status of the ambassador en route through third states, the use of the diplomatic passport in third states during a war, exemption from customs, exemption from taxes, the right of chapel, the right to the title "Excellency," and the diplomatic list. Under the latter category he discusses the inviolability of the person of the ambassador, the immunity of his family, of his correspondence and communications, of his residence and archives, his exemption from court testimony and his general reputation.[1]

Although some of these topics will have to be examined for the special agent, clearly a discussion of others would make no sense at all. For example the exemption from personal income taxes would not normally be a matter of concern to the special agent because his stay is generally under a year, although in such cases as Myron Taylor's mission to the Vatican this would not be true. And whether he receives the courtesy of the address of Excellency is hardly worthy of investigation.

The regular diplomat is generally accredited to a specific State, although for the sake of convenience it has been an accepted practice that a diplomat may represent his State in two or more States. When

[1] Stuart, *op. cit.*, chs. 13 and 14, *passim.*

such a practice is followed it is expected that each of the receiving States will give its assent. This does not mean that the *agrément* must be established in the narrow sense, i.e. that the agent must be acceptable, for this is always true. What it does mean is that State A has, in effect, the right to decide whether Mr. X may represent his State in A, if he is at the same time representing his State in B. This practice has been confirmed at the second Vienna Conference on Diplomatic Intercourse and Immunities. It is interesting to note that it was found acceptable despite the concern expressed by the Soviet delegate that the right of each State to object could create serious difficulties.[1] And it should also be noted that with the increasing importance of international organizations, representatives bearing the highest diplomatic rank and title have also been appointed to such organizations.[2] His appointment is, of course, a matter of municipal law and not international law. Custom has established that in the United States such appointments may be made on a patronage basis. The Senate generally approves the President's nomination although involved investigations have taken place.[3]

AGRÉATION

Although international law does not yet require it, it has been a matter of comity to ascertain before the appointment is made whether the appointee will be acceptable to the government to which he has been assigned. This is the *agréation*. If objections are raised the appointing government must honor them whether or not reasons are given, and whether or not, if given, they appear to be satisfactory grounds for rejection.[4] If there is no objection, the *agrément* is then established. The obligation to inquire regarding the acceptability of

[1] United Nations Conference on Diplomatic Intercourse and Immunities, Provisional Summary Record of the Fourth Plenary Meeting, 10 April 1961, A/Conf. 20/SR 4, p. 116. The reader is cautioned that here, and in all subsequent references to the provisional records, changes may occur in the final form of the official records when they are published.

[2] The first permanent functional organization was the Rhine River Commission in 1804 established to control navigation on the Rhine. The first attempt to establish a permanent universal organization was the International Telegraphic Union in 1865, and the first permanent multi-purpose organization was the Inter-American Organization established in 1889. Norman Hill, *International Organization*, (New York: Harper & Bros., 1952), pp. 28–29.

[3] See for example the debate regarding the nomination of Charles E. Bohlen as ambassador to the Soviet Union, *Congressional Record*, 83rd Cong., 1st Sess., 16, 2156, 2187, 2277, 2285, 2373. See also statements by United States Congressmen quoted in the *Detroit Free Press*, July 15, 1957 or the *Detroit News*, July 14, 1957, re Senate approval.

[4] Pasquale Fiore, *International Law Codified and Its Legal Sanctions*, Transl. E. M. Borchard, (New York: Baker Vorhis & Co., 1918), 235. Foster, *Practice of Diplomacy*, *op. cit.*, p. 38.

the agent, and the right to refuse the *agrément* has been accepted in article 4 of the Vienna Convention on Diplomatic Relations, concluded April 18, 1961.[1]

There have been several examples of difficulties in the annals of American diplomatic history. For example, a Mr. Keiley was rejected as Minister to Austria-Hungary by that government in 1885. Presumably the Austrians objected to him on grounds that he was married in a civil ceremony to a non-Christian. Although President Cleveland objected to the protest Keiley was not sent.[2] The Chinese Government likewise objected to an appointment, that of Mr. Henry W. Blair, in 1891. This action was taken due to reports in a newspaper that Blair supported the exclusion of Chinese from the United States.[3] Although the United States objected to the protests it again acquiesced.

The most recent example of a problem of *agréation*, and one with a rather novel twist, is that concerning the intent to appoint Earl E. T. Smith as the United States Ambassador to Switzerland. It was novel because both Smith and the public knew he was being considered before an *agrément* had been reached. It was likewise novel in that the Swiss objections, though never formally stated, were apparently based on the fact that Smith had been the U.S. Ambassador to Cuba and had made obvious his opposition to the Castro Government. When the break in diplomatic relations between Cuba and the U.S. occurred, Switzerland was asked by the U.S. to look after its interests in Cuba. The Swiss apparently felt it would be embarrassing to have such a man as Smith represent the U.S. at Bern, while it was honoring the U.S. request. For this reason Smith's name was withdrawn from consideration upon his own suggestion and the *agrément* was never established.[4]

During much of its early history this country did not make a deliberate effort to establish the *agrément*, but commenced to do so once the grade of ambassador was created, on the grounds "that they stand in closer relation to the sovereign than a minister." [5] However, even as far back as 1792, Jefferson acknowledged the obligation of accepting a refusal to receive an envoy.[6]

[1] United Nations Conference on Diplomatic Intercourse and Immunities, 1961, Vienna, Convention on Diplomatic Relations, 16 April, 1961, A/Conf. 20/13.

[2] Foster, *op. cit.*, p. 37.

[3] *Ibid.*, p. 45.

[4] *New York Times*, 2/7/61, p. 1; 2/23/61, p. 1.

[5] Sen. Ex. Doc., 4, 49th Cong., 1st Sess., 10, quoted in Foster, *op. cit.*, p. 37.

[6] John B. Moore, *A Digest of International Law*, IV, (Washington: Government Printing Office, 1906), p. 473.

LA LETTRE DE CRÉANCE

Before leaving for his post the envoy is given his credentials called a "lettre de créance," in duplicate. The official copy is sealed and the other is an "open" copy. In this country the great seal is affixed, and the President and Secretary of State sign their names.[1] The "open" copy is sent to the foreign office of the receiving state to let it be known that he has officially arrived. The original is submitted personally "by the envoy to the head of the State to whom he is accredited." [2]

In addition to the letter of credence the diplomat will also have a copy of instruction defining his duties.[3] Upon arrival at his post he will get in touch with the foreign minister who, unless his grade is that of *chargé d'affaires*, will arrange for his audience with the chief of state.[4]

If the envoy is entrusted with a special mission in addition to his regular diplomatic work, he will receive special credentials, the *pleins pouvoirs*, "limited or unlimited ... according to the requirements of the case." [5]

His acts will be in accord with his instructions, unless he exceeds them, in which case they are open to the possibility of a disavowal. But this possibility always exists if the Chief of State believes it to be necessary.

THE NATURE OF DIPLOMATIC PRIVILEGES AND IMMUNITIES

There is no doubt that the heart of the subject of the legal aspects of diplomatic relations pertains to the privileges and immunities of a diplomat, his staff and suite, his States' property in the form of the embassy or legation, archives and other items, as well as his personal effects. It is in fact to this subject that our later discussion of the basis of these privileges and immunities will relate. Although there are many other matters that receive attention in such a discussion of diplomacy, without a wide degree of acceptance as to the nature of these immuni-

[1] Foster, *Practice of Diplomacy*, *op. cit.*, p. 51.

[2] L. Oppenheim, *International Law: A Treatise*, (London: Longmans, Green & Co., 1905), I, 426–27.

[3] Foster, *Practice of Diplomacy*, *op. cit.*, p. 52.

[4] *Ibid.*, p. 56; Mathews, *American Foreign Relations*, *op. cit.*, pp. 395–96; Oppenheim, *op. cit.*, pp. 431–32; U.S. Dept of State, *Instructions to Diplomatic Officers of the United States*, (1897), Secs. 7–10.

[5] Oppenheim, *op. cit.*, p. 427. Wright, *op. cit.*, pp. 42–44.

ties, international relations would be chaotic and more frought with peril than it is. For there is no doubt that despite the instabilities in international affairs that result from the search for power, from the desire to maximize the degree of security for one's country, from the need for markets to buy and sell the products required by the economy of the nation, agreement through custom and convention of the rights and privileges of diplomatic agents have added a valuable and necessary quality to the conduct of foreign relations.

Because of the significance of the subject one can find hundreds of works, court cases and Foreign Office memoranda devoted to it. Suffice it for our study that only a brief reference shall be made to what these privileges and immunities are generally conceded to be.

The "embassy or legation buildings and grounds" are inviolable. In some quarters it is argued that this stems from the "sacredness" of the Ambassador's position.[1] On the other hand it has been said that this is not the reason, but rather that such inviolability exists "by reason of the fact that the premises are used as the headquarters of the mission." [2]

Whatever the reasons it is accepted that the receiving State will not permit its agents to enter the premises for any reason unless the head of the mission agrees, and that it has a special obligation to protect the mission from any violence or damage. This inviolability is even expected to cover such actions as the serving of a writ.[3]

It is interesting to note that when this subject was discussed at the second Vienna Conference on Diplomatic Relations, all efforts to reduce the scope of this inviolability were beaten down. Concern had been expressed that a very narrow view of obligations was being followed which resulted in restrictions on the receiving State but not on the sending State. Thus, for example, the Indian delegate was anxious for the rights of the lessor whose property might be damaged unless inspection and redress were authorized in the convention.[4]

Others, such as Mr. Bouziri of Tunisia and Mr. McDonald of Canada expressed concern that an emphasis on only the prerogatives of the sending State could mean that when exceptional circumstances arose,

[1] John M. Mathews, *The Conduct of American Foreign Relations*, (New York: The Century Co., 1922), p. 85.

[2] Report of the International Law Commission, Tenth Session, 1958, G.A.O.R.: Thirteenth Session, Supp. no. 9 (A/3859) p. 17.

[3] *Ibid.*

[4] United Nations Conference on Diplomatic Intercourse and Immunities, Committee of the Whole, Provisional Summary Record of the Twenty-Second Meeting, 20 March 1961, A/Conf. 20/C. 1/SR.22, p. 7.

such as a fire, earthquake or epidemic, authorities of the host State would not have the right to enter if it were deemed necessary.[1] Most other delegates, however, opposed such views not because there was no merit to such a position but because they felt that the convention had to emphasize the principle of inviolability and not the occasional exceptions that might arise, exceptions that might be said to involve a moral obligation but not a legal one.[2]

In addition to the obligation to protect the premises of the mission, the archives and other official papers and documents are likewise considered inviolable. They are held to be so by many authorities.[3] The same is true for the diplomat's papers and correspondence. This principle was incorporated into the Final Act of the Vienna Convention on Diplomatic Relations, in Article 24. It was argued by many authorities at the Conference that inviolability of these items does not derive from that extended to the premises. Rather, it was insisted, this inviolability attaches to them regardless of where they are if they are marked so as to indicate their nature. Some delegates argued that if such papers were found in unauthorized hands, the host State was not obligated to honor their inviolability. This view, however, did not prevail.[4]

Probably the most important object of concern in this subject of immunities is that of the diplomatic representative himself. One could undoubtedly trace the belief in the "sacred and inviolable" status of the ambassador back to ancient times.[5] It is perhaps because of this long tradition of immunity from the jurisdiction of the receiving State that so little debate exists regarding the nature of his inviolability, with most discussion generally directed to its basis. In fact it produced very little discussion at the 1961 Vienna Conference. The final agreement that he was immune from "arrest or detention" and that the receiving State was obligated to show him respect and to prevent

[1] *Ibid.*, pp. 4, 6.

[2] *Ibid.*, A/Conf.20/C.1/SR 21–22–23, *passim.*

[3] Mathews, *American Foreign Relations, Conduct and Policies, op. cit.*, 405; *Respublica* v *Longchamps*, 1 Dallas 116; Report of the International Law Commission, Tenth Session, *op. cit.*, Art. 22.

[4] United Nations Conference on Diplomatic Intercourse and Immunities, Committee of the Whole, Provisional Summary Record of the Twenty-Fourth Meeting, 21 March, 1961, A/Conf.20/C1/SR 24, pp. 2–7.

[5] *Respublica* v *Longchamps*, 1 Dallas 111; Sir Travers Twiss, *The Law of Nations Considered as Independent Political Communities*, (2nd ed., Oxford: Clarendon Press, 1884), p. 365; Oppenheim, 8 ed., *op. cit.*, p. 789; Charles C. Hyde, *International Law Chiefly as Interpreted and Applied by the United States*, (2nd ed., Boston: Little Brown and Co., 1922), I, 782; Fiore, *op. cit.*, p. 237; Report of the International Law Commission, Tenth Session, *op. cit.*, Art. 27.

attacks "on his person, freedom or dignity," was identical to the 1958 draft considered by the International Law Commission.[1]

The immunity of the agent is absolute regarding criminal jurisdiction of the receiving State, but qualified with regard to its civil and administrative jurisdiction. A rather protracted discussion on this latter point developed at the Vienna Conference particularly with regard to the means whereby the citizens of the receiving State who are injured by a diplomatic agent can obtain recovery. Most of those who spoke were desirous of finding some means whereby recovery could be obtained as in the case of an automobile accident, through an insurance provision, or by some clause establishing the principle that sending States would provide compensation for damages where warranted. All such efforts at restriction failed, leaving only those pertaining to "real action[s] relating to private immovable property..., [pertaining to] succession in which the diplomatic agent is involved as executor, administrator, [etc.] as a private person ..., [or] ... any professional or commercial activity by the ... agent ... outside his official functions." [2]

In addition to this immunity from jurisdiction, it has been widely held that the diplomat's personal and household effects, as well as his conveyances are exempt from seizure.[3] And his special status entitles him to "the free importation of effects for his ... official use," and to him and "his immediate family" for their personal use.[4]

There are other exemptions which he has. With regard to taxes he is exempt from personal taxes and property taxes, as are the embassy or legation buildings. [5] "But this exemption does not usually extend to water rents and lighting charges." [6] Neither may the envoy be compelled to testify in a court case, to appear as a witness, or for other purposes.[7] The instructions for diplomatic representatives of the United

[1] Vienna Convention of Diplomatic Relations, *op. cit.*, art. 29.

[2] *Ibid.*, art 31.

[3] Moore, *op. cit.*, p. 622; *Official Opinions of the Attorneys-General of the United States*, III), 69; Willian E. Hall, *Treatise in International Law*, (8th ed.; Oxford: Clarendon Press, 1924) p. 224; Hyde, *op. cit.*, p. 740; Oppenheim, 8th ed., *op. cit.*, pp. 438–39; J. L. Kunz, "Privileges and Immunities of International Organizations," *American Journal of International Law*, XLI, (1947) 828; Vienna Convention on Diplomatic Relations, *op. cit.*, art. 30.

[4] Foster, *The Practice of Diplomacy*, *op cit.*, p. 172; Mathews, *American Foreign Relations*, *op. cit.*, p. 404; Fiore, *op. cit.*, p. 237; Vienna Convention on Diplomatic Relations, *op. cit.*, art. 36.

[5] Fiore, *op. cit.*, p. 405; Hall, *op. cit.*, p. 235; Graham H. Stuart, *American Diplomatic and Consular Practice*, (2nd ed.; D. Appleton-Century Co., 1952), p. 229; Foster, *The Practice of Diplomacy*, *op. cit.*, p. 171; Vienna Convention on Diplomatic Relations, *op. cit.*, art. 34.

[6] Foster, *op. cit.*, Vienna Convention on Diplomatic Relations, *op. cit.*, art. 34.

[7] Mathews, *American Foreign Relations*, *op. cit.*, p. 405; Foster, *The Practice of Diplomacy*, *op. cit.*, p. 161; Vienna Convention on Diplomatic Relations, *op. cit.*, art. 29.

States contain the regulation that permission from the President is necessary before any testimony may be given even if the case has nothing to do with the diplomat's mission.[1]

DURATION OF DIPLOMATIC IMMUNITIES

One can raise here the question of the duration of these privileges and immunities. As could be expected there are different views on this, and they turn in part on whether one emphasizes a functional or representational basis to such immunities. In the case of *Salm* v *Frazier* the Court took the view that immunity attaches to functions and does not continue beyond them.[2] According to the Harvard Research Draft Convention such immunities commence as of the time the agent or member of the mission enters the territory of the receiving State, or if he is already there as of the time he becomes a member of the mission.[3] The latter provision is rather vague because obviously the host Government must be notified of such an appointment, yet neither the instrument nor process are mentioned. Nevertheless, obviously the emphasis here seems to be more on representation than function. And also the view that immunities commence only after the official reception is likewise not supported. Briggs, in referring to this point, quotes the comment to the above mentioned article that, "the effect of a formal reception is merely to confirm and acknowledge a pre-existing status." [4]

Gould, on the other hand, supports the contention that these immunities commence as of the day when the diplomat is officially accredited.[5] He further argues that these immunities remain until accreditation ceases.[6]

The matter also came up at the Vienna Diplomatic Convention in 1961. The Conference adopted with little change the provisions of the International Law Commission Draft which practically adopted the Harvard Draft referred to above. There is clarification regarding the agent who is already in the country when he receives his appointment, for it provides that immunity begins "from the moment when his appointment is notified to the Ministry for Foreign Affairs." [7]

[1] Foster, *op. cit.*, p. 162.

[2] *AJIL* (1934), p. 382.

[3] Art. 16, as cited in Briggs, *op. cit.*, p. 780.

[4] *Ibid.*

[5] *Foucault de Mondion* v. *Tcheng-Ki-Tong*, 19 *Clunet* (1882), p. 429, as cited in Gould, *op. cit.*, p. 275.

[6] *Musurus Bey* v *Gadbam* [1894] 2 *Q.B.* 352, *Ibid.*

[7] Vie nna Convention on Diplomatic Relations, *op. cit.*, art. 39, par 1.

Again the question regarding the moment immunities commenced was debated. The French, Italian and United States' delegates were unwilling to support the view that they began as of the time of entry on the soil of the receiving State. M. Vaucelles of France argued that the competent authorities had to be notified.[1] Professor Tunkin of the Soviet Union staunchly supported the ILC Draft, and it was in fact upheld. The United States view, expressed by Mr. Warde Cameron, that at least exemption from customs duties and taxes should be related to the continuation of functions was not even supported, and as to the termination of privileges and immunities, paragraph 2 of Article 39 provides that they shall cease when the agent leaves the country, "or on expiry of a reasonable period in which to do so." This phrase, of course, refers to the possibility of a demand by the receiving State for the recall of the agent.[2]

Communication with his home government free from interference is likewise due the diplomatic agent. During the Franco-Prussian War the German Government acknowledged the protests of the diplomatic corps against restrictions on the traditional right of sending dispatches without interference or inspection.[3]

Along with the debate on who is entitled to diplomatic immunities, the issue of communication between a mission and its home government, or other missions was one of the most controversial at the 1961 diplomatic conference. In fact many of the delegates consider that it produced the most heated of all the discussions. Rather than analyze in depth the nature of the disagreements, it would be better merely to indicate the major reasons for the difficulty.

In large measure the sides which were in opposition were the large, more technologically advanced nations against the newer, or at least smaller, less advanced ones. And this fact was frankly acknowledged by Mr. Matine-Daftary of Iran. Thus the extent of familiarity with radio as a means of communication probably had much to do with a delegation's position on this matter. It is also probable that the larger and older States have more diplomatic missions with which to keep in contact, and thus one can see here too an explanation for the desire to rely, in part, on wireless communication.

[1] United Nations Conference on Diplomatic Intercourse and Immunities, Committee of the Whole, Provisional Summary Record of the Thirty-Fifth Meeting, 29 March 1961, A/Conf. 20/C1/SR. 35, p. 2.

[2] Vienna Convention on Diplomatic Relations, *op. cit.*, Art. 39, par. 2.

[3] Foreign Correspondence, United States Foreign Relations (1870), 127; Washburn's Recollections, 159, 308, cited in *Ibid.*, p. 173. Also Kunz, *op. cit.*, p. 838.

Actually article 25 only alludes indirectly to the use of radio. But the matter was brought up both before the International Law Commission and the Vienna Conference. In the commentary to the Commission's Report it is stated that a mission interested in using such a transmitter must apply to the host State for permission, which request must not be refused. You have further the view that international conventions on telecommunications must be observed, and the condition that regulations established for the use of radio by a mission must apply to all and be honored.

One of the arguments that received much support was that of India, viz. that unless the receiving State's permission were necessary, radio, television and radio-telephonic broadcasts would be undertaken solely on the grounds decided by the sending State and chaos in communications would result. This view was supported by the Swiss and, with some modification, by the Viet Namese and Brazilians. It was opposed by the representatives of the United States, United Kingdom and Soviet Union, the latter arguing that the sovereign right of the receiving State was now being considered to the detriment of the sending State.[1] With so much resentment, it was only natural that in the final version (article 27) permission of the receiving State was required, with no mention of its obligation to grant it.

The inviolability of the person and house of the diplomatic agent is so sacred that any violation of either "is a crime against the state." [2] The Statutes of the United States provide that he is to be "afforded complete protection, and that his goods and chattels are not subject to seizure or attachment," and that anyone who violates this law "is to be imprisoned for not more than three years and fined at the discretion of the court." [3] Violations of his privileges are likewise dealt with severely in Britain.[4] Should he or a member of his suite commit a crime he could not "rightfully be arrested, tried, or punished." [5] It would, of course, be possible for the receiving state in such circumstances to declare the diplomat *persona non grata.*

[1] U.N. Conf. on Diplomatic Intercourse and Immunities, Committee of the Whole, Provisional Summary Record of the Twenty-Fourth Meeting, 21 March 1961, A/Conf.20/C./SR 24, 25, 26, 29, *passim.*

[2] *Respublica* v. *Longchamps*, 1 Dallas 111, cited in Moore, *op. cit.*, p. 627.

[3] *U.S. Code*, Title 18, Sec. 112, and Title 22, Secs. 252 and 253.

[4] Oppenheim, 8th ed., *op. cit.*, p. 561.

[5] Mathews, *American Foreign Relations, op. cit.*, p. 405; Hall, 8th ed., *op. cit.*, p. 223; Oppenheim, 8th ed., *op. cit.*, p. 290.

THEORIES OF THE BASIS OF DIPLOMATIC IMMUNITY

Representation

The existence of these immunities, which date back to the time of the Greeks and Romans, and the observance of which was supported by Cicero, has been explained in various ways. Grotius and many early writers supported the immunity of diplomatic agents on the grounds of their "representative character." They stand in the place of the sovereign and thus represent their states.[1] This idea, Kunz reports, "has undoubtedly exercized a powerful influence [in international relations] hence the pomp and ceremony, the importance of 'diplomatic rank' and of the problem of precedence." [2]

Bishop seems to be supporting the "representation" position when he writes that diplomatic privileges and immunities "result only from being sent as a diplomatic representative and received as such." [3]

Exterritoriality

Kauffmann ties the "representation" theory to that of exterritoriality, the fiction that the minister, his suite and property are legally outside the territory of the receiving State and hence not subject to its laws.[4] For him the two mean that since the Chief of State would be exempt from local jurisdiction on the basis of exterritoriality, and the diplomatic agent is merely his representative, the latter likewise enjoys exemption from local jurisdiction. With regard to the importance of the representative's position he quotes from the report of the Committee of Experts of the League of Nations who noted that one of the most important reasons for giving diplomatic immunities is the necessity "de maintenir la dignité du représentant diplomatique et de l'Etat qu'il représente." [5] Sir Cecil Hurst has likewise stressed the principle of exterritoriality as the basis of diplomatic privileges and immunities. He believes that the purpose of the principle is effective representation.[6]

[1] Hugo Grotius, *The Rights of War and Peace, Including the Law of Nature and of Nations*, Trans. by A. C. Campbell, (London: M. Walter Dunne, 1901), Book II, Ch. XVIII, Sec. IV, p. 5; Hyde *op. cit.*, p. 783; Oppenheim, 8th ed., *op. cit.*, p. 788.

[2] Kunz, *op. cit.*, p. 837.

[3] William W. Bishop Jr., Correspondence, May 19, 1958.

[4] Siegmund Kauffmann, *Die Immunität der Nicht-Diplomaten, ein Beitrag zur Kodifikation des Völkerrechts* ("Frankfurter Abhandlungen Zum Modernen Völkerrecht," Hft. 33, Leipzig: Robert Noske, 1932), p. 32.

[5] League of Nations, S.d.N.C. 196 M. 70, 1927, U.V. 76.

[6] Sir Cecil Hurst, "Diplomatic Immunities – Modern Development," *British Yearbook of International Law* (1929), 4–5.

Francis Deak, writing at about the same time as Sir Cecil, disagrees strongly with this view.

> The inviolability of the *domicile* of the diplomatic agent was a natural consequence of the doctrine of exterritoriality .... But with the decline of the theory of exterritoriality, and with the greater restriction of the conception of immunity, the practice naturally reaches a point where courts expound another principle namely that the fiction of exterritoriality, and with it the inviolability of residence, in modern international law, 'goes no further' than is necessary to insure the personal inviolability of the envoy and his suite.[1]

He notes further that,

> First, we have to reckon with the fact that the doctrine of exterritoriality as a basis of diplomatic privilege is not in accord with modern juristic conceptions. While recognizing the traditional element in law making, we should dispense with so much of the tradition as may give rise to misunderstanding and, hence, tend to create a false conception of the extent of jurisdiction.[2]

Function

A third explanation has become the most acceptable in recent years. This is the so-called "functional theory." It is really not a new explanation and was offered by Grotius and Vattel.[3] In effect the immunities are held to exist because of the necessity of permitting diplomats the fullest freedom so that they may perform their duties effectively.[4]

Today the tendency is greater than ever "to approach the whole question on a functional basis ..." [5] The dictum *officium ne impediatur* is held to be the underlying principle for the diplomat's immunities, and Kauffmann points out that this view was foremost in the opinion of the Committee of Experts of the League of Nations. "... la seule base solide de l'étude de la question [des immunités diplomatiques] est la necessité de permettre l'exercice absolument libre des fonctions diplomatiques." [6]

There is, therefore, fairly widespread agreement concerning the manifestations of these immunities of diplomats and the reasons for them. Their existence does not rest on treaty law but, according to Oppenheim, is based upon "rights given by the Municipal Law of the

[1] Francis Deak, "Classification, Immunities and Privileges of Diplomatic Agents," *S. Calif. Law Rev.*, I (March & May, 1928), 249.

[2] *Ibid.*, p. 342.

[3] Vattel, *Le Droit des Gens*, Book IV, Chs. 7, 92, as cited in Kunz, *op. cit.*, p. 838.

[4] Charles G. Fenwick, *International Law* (3rd ed.; New York: Appleton-Century Crofts, Inc., 1948), p. 468.

[5] David R. Deener, correspondence, June 13, 1958.

[6] League of Nations, S.d.N.C. 196 M 70, 1927, U.V. 76, as cited in Kauffmann, *op. cit.*, p. 64.

receiving states in compliance with an international right of their home States. For international law gives a right to every State to demand for its diplomatic envoys certain privileges from the Municipal Law of a foreign State.[1] Others base these rights on custom [2] or on comity.[3]

Kunz argues that some confusion exists regarding the subject of immunities. He believes that

> the exemption from local jurisdiction ... pertains exclusively to the private acts of diplomatic agents. Their exemption from local jurisdiction for their *official acts*[4] has nothing to do with diplomatic privileges and immunities, their official acts are acts of state and are legally imputed not to them but to the sending state. That this is so can be seen from the fact that the same immunity from local jurisdiction pertains also to the official acts of consuls who enjoy no diplomatic privileges ... But these immunities constitute only an immunity from local jurisdiction, not from local law. That is why diplomatic agents can be held liable after the termination of the diplomatic mission. There is further the possibility of bringing civil action against them in their own countries. A means of conciliating the exemptions from local jurisdiction with the necessities of local life, is the institution of the waiver of diplomatic privileges. But as they are functional, not personal, privileges such waiver must, in the case of subordinate diplomatic officers, be made by the chief of their mission and in the case of a chief of mission by his government.[5]

This is much the same point of view to be found in Harvard Law School's *Research in International Law.* Article 18 reads:

> Although immunity from the jurisdiction of the receiving State for private acts is attached to the person of the member of a mission and therefore does not survive the period of his functions ... the immunity for official acts is permanent. Insofar as the member acts in his official capacity, his immunity confounds itself with that of the sending State and depends, not upon the person of the representative, but upon the intrinsic nature of the act performed. International law imposes upon the courts of the receiving State an incompetence *ratione materiae* in the case of public acts. The incompetence of the court in the case of official acts does not constitute a diplomatic privilege in the sense that it is imposed by international law as an exception to the competence which the courts would normally possess. Immunity for official acts, as the application of a general principle of international law, and attaching to the intrinsic nature of the acts themselves, does not constitute a part of 'exterritoriality' or diplomatic immunity in the strict sense, which imposes upon the court an incompetence

[1] Oppenheim, 3rd ed., *op. cit.*, p. 560.

[2] Fenwick, *op. cit.*, p. 467.

[3] *Tsiang* v *Tsiang*, 194 Misc. 259, N.Y.S. 2nd, 556, (1949).

[4] My emphasis.

[5] Kunz, *op. cit.*, pp. 838–39. Commenting on Kunz's statement Deener writes, "With the trend toward giving diplomatic immunity a functional basis and toward asserting jurisdiction *in rem* rather than *in personam*, the position that 'local jurisdiction "pertains exclusively to the private acts" of diplomatic agents and has "nothing to do" with exemptions in re official acts' may have to be changed." David R. Deener, "Some Problems of the Law of Diplomatic Immunity," *American Journal of International Law*, L (1956) 118–19.

ratione personae. It applies to all public acts by whomsoever performed, and to all State agents whether diplomatic or otherwise.[1]

WHO RECEIVES DIPLOMATIC PRIVILEGES AND IMMUNITY

A pertinent question which may be put forth at this juncture is who is entitled to this inviolability. It has been one of the most controversial aspects of our subject. Stuart's position is a rather sweeping one. "The right of inviolability embraces all classes of public ministers – the chargé d'affaires enjoys this immunity as fully as does the ambassador. It extends to all persons who either officially or unofficially are connected with the diplomatic mission, regardless of their nationality." [2] However, he excepts from this position nationals of a state who are serving with a foreign mission whose position depends upon the "terms" of their own state. [3]

Deak is in complete accord. "... The privileges of a diplomatic agent have no connection whatever with his rank. His legal status and the privileges and immunities attached to his position are defined by international law regardless of his being an ambassador, chargé d'affaires or attaché of an embassy." [4]

One writer who has delved deeply into the development of the principle quotes Sir Cecil Hurst approvingly that to be entitled to diplomatic immunity a person "must be concerned with the work of the head of the mission or the channel of communication with the Government to which he is accredited.'" [5] This very general definition would, of course, cover all those referred to by both Stuart and Deak. But obviously none of these definitions, least of all Hurst's, really comes to grips with the problem.

The International Law Commission, and particularly the delegates at the recent Vienna Conference on Diplomatic Relations, became involved in more controversy on this point than on almost any other. The difficulty has arisen because within the past century the scope of interests of States has greatly widened. With attention now being given to economic, social and cultural matters, in addition to those of a more

[1] Harvard Law School, *Research in International Law* (Cambridge: Harvard Law School, 1932), p. 98. (Hereafter cited as Harvard Law School.)

[2] Stuart, *American Diplomatic and Consular Practice, op. cit.*, 2nd. ed., p. 233.

[3] *Ibid.*, p. 236.

[4] Deák, *op. cit.*, p. 339.

[5] Sir Cecil Hurst, "Diplomatic Immunities – Modern Developments," *op. cit.*, as cited in Montell Ogdon, *Juridical Bases of Diplomatic Immunity*, (Washington: John Byrne and Co., 1936), p. 204.

traditional nature, i.e. trade and military affairs, the demand for specialists and an increased number of assistants to help the chief of the mission has been inevitable. It is this category of staff, plus such sensitive members as code clerks, which are the center of the controversy. The International Law Commission pointed out the lack of uniformity regarding the status of administrative, technical and even service staff so far as the practice of States is concerned. It is interesting to note that although a stronger case for granting privileges and immunities to such mission members could be made if based on the theory of exterritoriality or representation, the commission did not swerve from its emphasis on a functional basis to privileges and immunities. This necessitated a switch from concentrating on the particular individual in making a determination as to whether privileges and immunities should be extended, to considering the subject "in relation to the work of the mission as an organic whole." [1] Such an approach was not only novel, but the risk was compounded when a majority of the members decided to advocate a "maximalist" position rather than a restricted or "minimalist" one. As a result the majority supported the inclusion of the administrative and technical staff with the diplomatic staff, relegating only the service staff to a lesser status.

This "organic" approach was predicated on the view that many of the administrative and technical staff "perform confidential tasks which, for the purposes of the missions' function, may be even more important than the tasks entrusted to some members of the diplomatic staff." [2] Because of the difficulty in distinguishing between those members who in fact do perform such tasks, and those who do not, the Commission decided that it would be best to provide immunities to all of them.

For the service staff, it was deemed sufficient to grant immunity "only in respect of acts performed in the course of their duties." [3]

Clearly the commission was, and it tacitly acknowledged as much, expanding its work from codification to modification. For while it may be true that no clear cut rule did exist on this matter, it can certainly be argued from our subsequent discussion of the practice of a number of States, that such an expanded view has not been followed. In fact one of the staunchest advocates of this new approach, namely the U.S. did not follow it in its most celebrated cases in the past.

[1] Report of the International Law Commission, Tenth Session, *op. cit.*, p. 23.
[2] *Ibid.*, p. 24.
[3] *Ibid.*

But it is not as clear that the commission was aware of some of the implications of its position. For what has in fact taken place is the emphasis on the rights of the sending State to the disadvantage of the receiving State. Hence, from this development, it is easy to foresee that should any disagreement exist between the sending and receiving State regarding the application of immunities to a mission member whose status is in controversy, it is the sender's view which is bound to prevail. Thus any view which emphasizes the needs of the mission is already arguing on behalf of the sender, for who is better able to judge its needs. It may be that the exigencies of modern diplomacy require such an approach and that such a liberal view has much in it to commend, but it should be accepted only with the clear understanding that if controversies of the kind alluded to do occur, the receiving State has the "cards stacked against it."

Although many delegates opposed this novel approach, their reasons varied. Arab States, such as Tunisia, Morocco and Libya complained of the "crushing burden" it would place on the receiving States.[1] Italy objected that the decision of the commission was *ultra vires*, and Venezuela joined this view and proposed that the entire matter be left to special agreements between States. Portugal contested that a convention which was predicated on a "functional approach" could not logically contain such a provision. Mr. Nameh Zade of the United Arab Republic argued against the article in part because he seemed to interpret article 9 of the Convention in such a fashion that the category of persons in question could not be declared *persona non grata*, and presumably could not be dismissed.[2]

However, the British, and particularly the United States and Soviet delegations supported the Commission, and eventually the liberal version passed by a vote of 54 to 10 with 7 abstentions,[3] although not without some modification. It was declared that immunity from civil and administrative jurisdiction for the administrative and technical staff and their families, provided they are not nationals of the receiving State, only extended to acts performed in the course of their duties.[4] All immunities for the service staff pertained only to acts performed in the course of their duties.[5]

[1] United Nations Conference on Diplomatic Intercourse and Immunities, Committee of the Whole, Provisional Summary Record of the Thirty-Second Meeting, 28 March 1961, A/Conf.20/C.1/SR 32, p. 5.

[2] This, however, seems to be a misreading of intent of the article.

[3] *Ibid.*, A/Conf. 20/C.1/SR. 32–33, *passim.*

[4] Vienna Convention on Diplomatic Relations, *op. cit.*, Art. 37, par. 2.

[5] *Ibid.*, Art. 37, par. 3.

What has been the practice of States on this point? In the United States the Department of State has extended diplomatic privileges and immunities only to "diplomatic officers and subordinate staff of a diplomatic mission." [1]

In the case of Baiz, an American citizen who acted temporarily for the minister of the Republic of Guatemala, and whose substitution the Department of State accepted as "a channel of communication," the Secretary of State's letter to Baiz was produced stating, "It is a common thing to resort to a temporary agency, such as yours, in the conduct of the business of a mission. A foreign minister, on quitting the country, often leaves the affairs of his office in the friendly charge of the minister of another country, but the latter does not thereby become the diplomatic agent of the government in whose behalf he exerts his good offices." [2]

The Government position in the Coplon and Gubitchev case was the same. Gubitchev's claim to immunity was rejected by the Department of State and the court, the former arguing that he was not attached to the Soviet Embassy and had never acted in a diplomatic capacity in the United States. Thus the Court denied diplomatic immunity on the grounds that

> It has long been recognized that the United States will not afford diplomatic immunity unless the person claiming it not only has diplomatic status, but is also in an "intimate association with the work of a permanent diplomatic mission. "1 *Hyde on International Law* Sec. 416 A. The Department of State has had occasion to declare that "under customary international law, diplomatic privileges and immunities are only conferred upon a well defined class of persons, namely, those who are sent by one state to another *on diplomatic missions.*" (The Under Secretary of State to the Turkish ambassador, October 16, 1933, MS Department of State, file 701.09/374, 4 Hackworth, *Digest of International Law*, p. 422).
>
> This principle has been recognized by the Courts of other countries. The courts of England have ruled that in order to establish the protection afforded by diplomatic immunities the evidence must establish actual service as a diplomat, by the one claiming the right. *Crosse v. Talbot*, 8 Mod. Rep. 288 (1724); Widmore v. Alvarez, 2 Stra. 797 (1731); 6 *Halsbury's Laws of England* 512; 30 *Halsbury's Laws of England* 129 ... [3]

The British courts have not really held to the same position. It is true that in *Engelke v. Mussmann* the court said, "By international law ... diplomatic agents of all sorts – the stately ambassador in the restricted sense of the word, the special envoy, the resident minister,

[1] Assistant Legal Advisor to the Department of State, Correspondence, August 9, 1958.
[2] 135 U.S. 403.
[3] *U.S.* v *Coplon and Gubitchev*, 88 Fed. Supp. 915, January 9, 1950.

and the chargé d'affaires" are sent and received with the expectation that they have exemption "from legal process in the courts of the country" which receive them.[1] But in a study by Joyce Gutterridge whose survey of the practices of leading states on this issue is one of the most thorough, she concluded that in Britain, "Members of an embassy or legation *down to its clerical staff* are entitled to diplomatic privileges, and are not subject to the jurisdiction of the civil or criminal courts. Menial servants at an embassy also enjoy a similar immunity, provided they are employed in the minister's or ambassador's household." [2] The author goes on to report that in pre-Hitler Germany, in Austria and in Hungary the position was very similar to that of Britain, but that Switzerland and France have been more conservative, the French Cour de Cassation granting immunities only to those who "form an integral part of the legation and are vested with a public character." [3]

Although not reported in this source the Swiss position might well be represented by *Re The Turkish Inspector of Students*, in which the Zurich Tax Appeals Commission ruled September 12, 1945, that even though the Executive Branch recommended granting immunity, the Inspector of Turkish students in Switzerland was not entitled to it because his functions were not in the same category as a minister's.[4]

In Italy, the survey continues, the Italian practice has become less conservative and in this century the courts have even declined jurisdiction over the Second Secretary of the Swiss Legation to the Vatican who was accused of infanticide.[5]

As for the Soviet Union, the author's findings lead her to conclude that it grants jurisdictional immunity to minor officials and servants.[6] Although Latin American practice varies it generally fits into the same category as the Swiss.[7] The Japanese position may be defined by the Supreme Court's denial of jurisdiction over subordinate officials.[8]

The author suggests the following two proposals, based on her sur-

1 *Engelke* v *Mussmann*, 1928, A.C. p. 450.

2 Joyce A. C. Gutteridge, "Immunities of the Subordinate Diplomatic Staff," *British Yearbook of International Law*, XXIV (1947), 149.

3 S 1938, i 117, cited *ibid.*, p. 153.

4 *Annual Digest*, 1946, Case No. 80.

5 In re Reinhardt, *Annual Digest*, 1938–1940, Case No. 171, cited in Gutteridge, *op. cit.*, p. 153.

6 *Ibid.*, p. 156.

7 *Ibid.*

8 *The Empire* v. *Chang and Others*, *Annual Digest*, 1929–1930, Case No. 205, cited *ibid.*, p. 154.

vey, should guide the decisions of States regarding the position of minor diplomatic officials:

1. The receiving State shall have no claim to exercise jurisdiction over a minor official or servant for any act done by him in the performance of his duty in the service of the mission.
2. As regards all other cases, the receiving State shall exercise jurisdiction over minor officials and servants only in cases in which to do so will not constitute undue interference with the conduct of the business of the mission.[1]

Thus, it is clear that all members of the regular diplomatic staff, regardless of rank, and in many countries, all attached to their missions have been extended diplomatic privileges and immunities. The same could be said of those on special missions who hold diplomatic rank.[2] By the way, it should be noted that the Harvard Law School experts engaged in this study agreed not to attempt "to distinguish sharply between a privilege and an immunity." [3]

WHO DECIDES THE QUESTION OF ENTITLEMENT TO IMMUNITY

It is now in order to raise the question what branch of government decides who is entitled to these immunities. Clearly the Zurich Tax Appeals Commission felt that it was not bound by the federal political department when it recommended immunity be granted on grounds of comity.[4]

In the United States the Department of State makes the determination for the Executive branch. This is implied in the statement of the Assistant Legal Advisor of the Department of State that a State may extend diplomatic privileges and immunities only to those "diplomatic officers and subordinate staff of a diplomatic mission" who are "notified to the host state ... and accepted by it." [5] This was certainly the position of the court in the Baiz case when it ruled that in the absence of any certificate indicating that he had diplomatic status in the eyes of the Department of State that he was not entitled to immunity.[6]

Likewise in *U.S.* v. *Coplon and Gubitchev*, the court ruled "Diplo-

[1] *Ibid.*, pp. 158–59.

[2] Regulation of Vienna, Art. 3; Havana Convention on Diplomatic Officers (1928), Art. 9, as cited in Harvard Law School, *op. cit.*, p. 42.

[3] *Ibid.*

[4] *Annual Digest* 1946, Case No. 80.

[5] Dept. of State, Correspondence, August 9, 1958.

[6] 135 U.S. 403.

matic status is a political question and a matter of state; the findings of the Secretary of State must be accepted unquestioned. The courts of the United States are not alone in applying this rule." The court then cited a number of British, United States, and French cases to support its opinion and concluded that "the decision of the executive department as to whether a person is a member of a foreign mission or of its personnel is conclusive upon the courts." [1]

In his survey on the subject Montell Ogdon writes that if the courts have to decide whether a party before them is entitled to diplomatic immunity, they usually do so "on the basis of the decision of the foreign office." [2]

This is quite in harmony with the opinion of Sir Cecil Hurst who emphatically states, "The final decision rests with the executive government, not with the courts, as to what individuals are entitled to the privilege, and this enables the adjustment in the application of the fundamental principles which are necessary for meeting the new developments, to be made satisfactorily." [3]

The entire subject has been perhaps more thoroughly examined by A. B. Lyons than by any other authority. He ties in this subject with the significance of the diplomatic list, which is examined below, and concludes regarding America and Britain that, "It is the current general practice of English and American courts to accept as conclusive, statements made to them by the Executive as to the existence of certain facts of an international law nature." These include the question of whether a person is entitled to diplomatic immunity.[4] The same has been true for Czechoslovakia and Belgium, but in France the courts have at times ignored the Foreign Ministry and at other times accepted as sufficient administrative decisions of other departments. In Italy the courts have shown a greater degree of independence. Lyons concludes, "For the most part ... the courts in Europe may test any claim for immunity by their own investigation ..." [5]

THE BASIS FOR THE DECISION

A corollary question to which branch of the government generally decides who is entitled to diplomatic status is that of how the decision

[1] Harvard Law School, *op. cit.*, cited in 88 Fed. Supp., 915.
[2] Ogdon, *op. cit.*, p. 203.
[3] Hurst, "Diplomatic Immunities – Modern Developments," *op. cit.*, p. 13.
[4] A. B. Lyons, "The Conclusiveness of the Foreign Office Certificate," *British Yearbook of International Law*, XXIII (1946), 240.
[5] *Ibid.*, pp. 183–210.

is to be made. Is the decision to be based upon the existence of a diplomatic passport, is it to be based upon inclusion on the diplomatic list, is it to be based upon formal presentation of the claimant to the Chief of State or is it to be based on function? We will now examine these possibilities, although some require very little discussion.

The Diplomatic Passport

The question of the significance of holding a diplomatic passport goes right to the "nub" of the Gubitchev case. V. A. Gubitchev was a Soviet diplomatic officer with the rank of third secretary in the service of the Ministry of Foreign Affairs of the U.S.S.R. He was sent by the U.S.S.R. to work in the Secretariat of the United Nations in New York. He had a Soviet diplomatic passport and a diplomatic visa issued by the United States Embassy in Moscow. In correspondence with the Soviet Embassy the United States Department of State rejected the claim of diplomatic immunity. The defendant argued that having a diplomatic passport and visa entitled him to diplomatic status with full diplomatic privileges and immunities. The court ruled,

> The visa which was affixed to the defendant's passport did not of itself constitute a grant of diplomatic immunity for all of his activities in this country. It is provided in the Code of Federal Regulations [Title 22] Sect. 40.4 (a), that such diplomatic visas may be granted to fifteen different categories of individuals. Many of these categories embrace individuals who, it has been universally recognized, do not have diplomatic status or immunity. That diplomatic visas are on occasion granted by the Government of the United States as a matter of courtesy and do not thereby constitute a recognition of diplomatic status has been its proclaimed policy and is set forth in its duly promulgated and publicly published regulations ...[1]

The case of course aroused some controversy, especially between the United States and the Soviet Union. The latter contended forcefully that a diplomatic passport and visa *ipso facto* confers diplomatic status. One might argue that notwithstanding the Department of State's claim to the contrary, its request to the court that sentence be waived, which request was honored, is an implicit acknowledgment that the Soviet Union's position could not be totally ignored. Commenting on the case Deener writes, "Thus while it seems settled as a principle that the consent or acquiescence of the 'receiving' state is a necessary condition precedent to immunity, the attitude of the 'sending' state cannot always be ignored ... There still persists, then,

[1] *U.S.* v. *Coplon and Gubitchev*, 88 *Fed. Supp.*, p. 915.

a problem of clarifying and co-ordinating the procedural requirements for establishing entitlement to immunity." [1]

The United States' court's opinion runs parallel to that of the Zurich Tax Appeals Commission referred to above. In this case the Turkish Inspector of Turkish students in Switzerland likewise held a diplomatic passport but was denied the immunities of a diplomat because his functions did not fall within the diplomatic category. [2]

Interestingly, most writers of the subject of international law do not discuss the significance of the passport, and in correspondence with this writer only one authority addressed himself to it. Bishop states, "Holding a diplomatic passport, and performing some diplomatic functions, does not appear to result in a legal obligation to accord diplomatic privileges and immunities." [3]

So far as the practice of the Department of State is concerned no clear-cut practice in terms of the issuance of passports existed prior to World War I. All government officials were issued the same passport. During the war the diplomatic passport was created. Assistant Secretary of State Adee discussed this new passport in a circular to diplomatic and consular officers. His discussion deserves quoting although it will be noted that his opinion as to the relationship between holding the passport and having diplomatic immunity would certainly not be acceptable to the Department today.

> The issuance of diplomatic passports is, in general, limited in the United States to Foreign Service officers, to other persons in the diplomatic service, and to those enjoying diplomatic status by reason of the office they hold. In addition they are issued as a matter of courtesy to former Presidents, their wives, widows, and unmarried daughters, and to former Vice-Presidents and Secretaries of State, and their wives.
>
> A diplomatic passport serves both as a travel document and as a certification of the official identity of the bearer. It is designed to assure to the bearer the enjoyment of special privileges and immunities accruing to him on account of his official position. The transaction of business of a diplomatic character is therefore expedited, and the officials of the country in which the bearer of the passport is travelling are put on notice concerning his diplomatic status and his right to the enjoyment of the privileges and immunities flowing therefrom.[4]

[1] Deener, "Some Problems of the Law of Diplomatic Immunity," *op. cit.*, pp. 117–18.

[2] *Annual Digest*, 1946, Case No. 80.

[3] William W. Bishop, Jr., Correspondence, May 19, 1958.

[4] Assistant Secretary of State (Adee) to diplomatic and consular officers, No. 611, July 25, 1918, MS, Department of State, file 138/2168a; Department of State, *Compilation of Certain Departmental Circulars Relating to Citizenship* (1925), pp. 76–77, cited in Hackworth, *Digest*, *op. cit.*, III, 452–53. "There are six types of American passports in general use, i.e., regular, special, diplomatic, agency, insular, and service passports. The first four types are issued only in the United States. The fifth is issued in the United States as well as by the chief executives of the insular possessions and the United States High Commissioner to the

In attempting to clarify further the question of which officers of the Government were entitled to diplomatic passports and which were not Assistant Secretary Wright wrote,

I find that the practice of the Department in determining whether officers of the various Departments of the Government shall receive diplomatic or special passports is decided not by the official position occupied by the individual concerned but solely by the character of the duties on which he is to be engaged while abroad. For example, an officer of the Government proceeding abroad on work of an actual or quasi diplomatic nature would receive a diplomatic passport but if his duties did not come within this clearly defined line [!] such officer (even a Cabinet officer or other head of an Executive Department) would receive a special passport.[1]

It will be seen that this does not give a very clear-cut picture since the term "quasi diplomatic nature" is in itself ambiguous. Furthermore, it is not consistent with the statement by Adee some few years earlier. Clearly having the passport or working with the embassy is not always the deciding factor. For example, the military and naval attachés, some members assigned to special missions (as noted above) and the regular ranking diplomats all receive diplomatic passports [2] and are given diplomatic immunities, yet the nature of their work is quite different. On the other hand Treasury attachés, a position established by the Treasury Department in 1919, the title being changed to Customs Attachés in 1923, could not get diplomatic immunities from most states, and hence the State Department did not consider them as having diplomatic status and gave them only Special Passports. But Agricultural Attachés were given diplomatic status.[3] Yet neither of them is defined as a diplomatic officer.[4]

The Diplomatic List

The next aspect that requires investigation is the significance of the diplomatic list. Such lists are drawn up by the foreign office from the names submitted by the heads of the various diplomatic missions.

Philippine Islands to inhabitants of the outlying possessions of the United States who owe permanent allegiance to the United States. The last only is issued by authorized Foreign Service officers abroad. Service passports may be amended by diplomatic or consular officers in such manner as to show that the individual is a national but not a citizen of the United States. Regular passports are issued to persons who prove that they are American citizens or that they owe permanent allegiance to the United States, and who are not entitled to receive special or diplomatic passports." Hackworth, *Digest*, *op. cit.*, III, 445.

[1] Assistant Secretary Wright to Representative Fish, February 16, 1925, MS Department of State, file 138A/166A, cited in Hackworth, *Digest*, *op. cit.*, III, 455.

[2] Stuart, *American Diplomatic and Consular Practice*, *op. cit.*, 2nd. ed., p. 358.

[3] Hackworth, *Digest*, *op. cit.*, IV, 407–408.

[4] Hyde, *op. cit.*, II, 1226.

However, they do not have the same standing in all countries. For example, the Court of Appeals of Paris ruled that although one Drtilik was Chancellor of the Czechoslovakian Legation in Paris he was not entitled to claim diplomatic immunity because his name was omitted from the diplomatic list,[1] and the same view was implied in *In Re Cloete*, although it must be admitted that there were other mitigating circumstances.[2]

The Fall Vitianu case presents, however, an interesting objection to this view where the argument is presented that while no country is required to receive a diplomat, the "reception," and therefore right to diplomatic status, could be implicit from the fact that no objection to the agent's name was made. Hence omission from the diplomatic list would not be decisive.[3]

While this is a novel twist, there is much evidence to indicate that the list itself is not conclusive. This was certainly the position of the court in the famous case of *Engelke* v. *Mussmann*.[4] Lyons points out that in Britain the usual method of verifying a claim to diplomatic immunity by a subordinate member of an embassy or legation is to produce the Foreign Office List or a certificate from the Foreign Secretary certifying that the name appears on the list. Although inclusion on such a published list implies diplomatic immunity, "it is certain that employment alone, even with entry on the list submitted to the Foreign Office, is not sufficient." [5]

And he continues, quoting Halsbury, " inclusion in or omission from the list is not conclusive as to the status of the person claiming privilege." [6]

This also reflected Germany's viewpoint under the Weimar regime. In its reply to the Questionnaire sent out by the League of Nations, it said, "For practical reasons it is open to doubt whether, to avoid all abuses and uncertainty, the enjoyment of privilege can be subject to the condition that the persons' names must figure in a list transmitted to the Minister of Foreign Affairs of the Receiving State." [7]

So far as the United States is concerned the Revised Statutes provide for a list of all employees of an ambassador to be "registered in

[1] *Drtilik* v. *Barbier*, *Annual Digest*, 1925–1926, Case 242.

[2] *Law Times Reports*, LXV (1891), 102–104.

[3] *Schweizerisches Jahrbuch für Internationales Recht*, VII (1950), 146–156.

[4] 1928 A.C., p. 436.

[5] Lyons, "The Conclusiveness of the Foreign Office Certificate," *op. cit.*, p. 236.

[6] Halsbury, *Laws of England*, Vol. VI (Hailsham ed., 1932) cited *ibid.*, p. 279.

[7] League of Nations, "Report to the Council of the League of Nations on the Questions Which Appear Ripe for International Regulation," C. 196 M. 70, 1927 V., p. 1134.

the Department of State and transmitted by the Secretary ... to the marshall of the District of Columbia who shall ... post the same in some public place in his office." [1] This is often referred to as the White List.

But what of diplomatic officers themselves? Once a month the Department of State compiles a list from the various lists of names submitted by the foreign embassies in this country. This list, the so-called Blue List, is that which the officers of the law and others use as a guide to determine who has, as of the moment of issuance, been received by the Department as a person possessed of a diplomatic character.[2] In and of itself, however, such a list is not required by statute and Stuart's reference to the Jules Chaumonet incident seems to contain an error in that he implies that Chaumonet, a butler in the French Embassy, was without immunity because his name was accidently left off the diplomatic list at a time when he was charged with a criminal action. Having been omitted from the diplomatic list (where his name could not possibly have appeared anyhow) and from the list "filed with the United States marshall for the District of Columbia [where it should have appeared as an "employee" of a diplomat] he could not claim immunity according to the laws of the United States." [3] This would appear to mean that immunities exist for ambassadors and other diplomatic envoys and their suite and servants only if their names appear on one of the two lists established by the Department, and this does not seem to be the case.

A similar kind of error has crept into Hackworth's *Digest*. He refers to a problem that developed regarding the wife of a naval attaché of the Spanish Embassy. Someone contemplated legal action against the wife who had separated from her husband, and the Department of Statew as attempting to find out what the Spanish Ambassador considered her status to be inasmuch as her name no longer appeared on the diplomatic list, "a condition which seemed to be necessary to clothe one with diplomatic immunity under the provisions of the United States Code." [4]

In neither of these two cases is any authority, statutory or juristic, cited which could be used to support a contention that the list has standing in law, the significance of which is that omission from such a list prevents an individual from claiming the right to diplomatic or jurisdictional immunities. In fact quite the opposite appears to be true.

[1] *Revised Statutes*, Sec. 4065, as incorporated in 22 *U.S. Code*, Sec. 254.
[2] Stuart, *American Diplomatic and Consular Practice*, *op. cit.*, 2nd ed.; p. 237.
[3] *Ibid.*, p. 237.
[4] MS Department of State, file 701.5211/440, cited in Hackworth, *Digest*, *op. cit.*, IV, 538.

From the Department's point of view the issuance of such a list is undertaken because it is "a usual practice of nations." [1] Both the "Blue" and "White" lists are transmitted to the marshall of the District of Columbia and it has been the opinion of the Department that all those whose names are on these lists are entitled to the immunity prescribed in sections 4063–4065 of the Revised Statutes of the United States.[2] But the Department also has acknowledged that "the general privileges accorded under international law to diplomatic representatives in the United States are not limited to those whose names are contained in the 'Diplomatic List,' but are extended generally to all persons who are officially recognized by the Department of State as attached to a diplomatic mission." [3] It will be recalled that this was the same position put forth by the Department in the Gubitchev case.[4]

Whose name appears on the Diplomatic List is a decision which is made by the Executive branch of a Government and in the United States apparently liberally made by the Department. For example, not only are all the usual high-ranking diplomats' names included in the United States list, but likewise "all *attachés*, including acting commercial *attachés* are acceptable; student interpreters and language *attachés* are specifically included." [5]

Probably one could say this. Inasmuch as the Executive has the sole authority to recognize governments and to receive diplomatic representatives of these governments, any lists of such representatives established for him by the Department of State, would necessarily reflect his decision as to who are the envoys of States who are entitled to diplomatic or jurisdictional immunities. This being an Executive decision and the lists being established by Executive authorization, such lists would have standing before a municipal court as *prima facie* evidence of immunity. However, usually the question of whether an individual has such immunities is determined by a written statement from the Department or by parole by one of its representatives. But to assume that placement of a name on such a list is conclusive would probably not be correct. Rather, if an error were made for any reason and a name appeared which should not have, the position a court would take would probably be similar to that of the Court of Appeals

[1] MS Department of State, file o 26 Diplomatic List/4, cited in Hackworth, Digest, *op. cit.*, IV, 429.

[2] *Ibid.*

[3] MS Department of State, file 701/170, cited in Hackworth, *Digest*, *op. cit.*, IV, 430.

[4] *Supra*, p. 78.

[5] Stuart, *American Diplomatic and Consular Practice*, *op. cit.*, 2nd ed., p. 232; also MS Department of State, file 701.05/126 cited in Hackworth, *Digest*, *op. cit.*, IV, 429.

in the case of *Cloete* where the British Foreign Office said the defendant was not recognized notwithstanding the fact that his name appeared on the Diplomatic List.[1] And in the *Engelke* v. *Mussmann* case the lack of conclusiveness of the list was cited.[2]

Presentation to the Chief of State

The next question is does diplomatic immunity depend upon being formally presented to the Chief of State? This deals with the subject of accreditation which was discussed earlier. Despite the position of the Court of Appeal of Rome in the Worovsky case, which denied Worovsky diplomatic status on several grounds, one of which was the fact that he and his credentials had never been presented to the head of the state,[3] it is not true that only those who are so presented have the immunities. As was noted earlier there is no difference in the immunities to which the various grades of diplomatic officers are entitled and yet the *chargé d'affaires' lettre de créance* is addressed by one foreign secretary to another and he is not presented to the Chief of State.[4] Furthermore it is not possible to say precisely that a diplomat has no immunities until he has been accredited, i.e. received. Some states e.g. Switzerland, extend immunities to the diplomat from the moment he crosses the frontier.[5] Article 22 of the Havana Convention accepts this position also.[6] This is likewise the position presented in Article 16 of the Harvard Law School draft.[7] Of course this is aside from the fact that no one unacceptable to the State could possibly present a valid claim to immunity under any circumstances.

THE MEANING OF FUNCTION

When a court refuses to grant diplomatic immunity to one claiming it on the grounds that he has "not acted in a diplomatic capacity," [8] or when a committee of international law experts reports that function

[1] *Law Times Reports*, LXV (1891), 102–104.

[2] 1928 A.C. 433.

[3] *In Re Serventi*, *Annual Digest*, 1919–1922, Case 211. See dicta by Scrutten L. J. in the Fenton Textile case in which he observed that an agent is entitled to immunity whether or not presented to the King so long as he is a negotiator "about matters of concern" between two states. *Times Law Reports*, XXXVIII (1921), 259.

[4] Hyde, *op. cit.*, II, 1239.

[5] League of Nations, Report to the Council, C 196 M 70, 1927 V, *op. cit.*, p. 248.

[6] Sixth International Conference of American States, adopted February 20, 1928. Most of the Latin American states ratified, but the United States did not.

[7] Harvard Law School, *op. cit.*, pp. 89–90.

[8] Gubitchev case, *supra*, p. 78.

is "la seule base solide" for granting diplomatic immunity,[1] to what kinds of activities are they referring? In these cases and in the many others cited in this study one will not find any discussion of this question. A definition of "diplomatic capacity" might be attempted by listing all positions and functions in which the courts or foreign offices refused to acknowledge it. But in the end this would only tell us what it is not, and in effect this is all we have from such cases and arguments. Most authors do not even deal with the subject, and those that do discuss it briefly either in terms of the relationship of the executive to the judiciary with regard to who decides,[2] or discuss it in terms of the sending State's jurisdiction over the assignment of duties.[3]

The Harvard Law study stresses that customary international law has established no basis for distinguishing diplomatic from non-diplomatic missions based on function.[4] With this the writer is in accord.

Perhaps all that one can determine from an examination of the positions of the foreign offices and courts when they have denied the existence of diplomatic capacity, is that in each case the individual's functions were narrowly defined and his authority limited. The traditional diplomat, such as the regular ambassador will have a broad array of responsibilities, some of which, however, will include the very things that others who are denied diplomatic status are also expected to carry out. His authority will of course be limited, especially today with communication so rapid that he is able to get explicit instructions whenever it appears necessary. But his limitations will be with regard to special problems and not in terms of a narrow range of responsibilities. This was the situation in those cases where the problem arose and diplomatic status was denied, e.g. *In Re the Turkish Inspector of Students*,[5] *Affaire Gravenhoff*,[6] *Taco Mesdag c Heyermans*,[7] etc. We shall discuss later the activities that constitute "function."

One can perhaps sum up the question of how diplomatic status is decided by observing that the decision is usually not based upon one factor alone but upon a combination, which includes holding a diplomatic passport, membership on the diplomatic list as well as functions of the broad nature generally associated with an embassy or legation. If this is a vague definition it is because there has been so little

[1] League of Nations, Committee of Experts, *supra*, p. 69.
[2] Briggs, *op. cit.*, p. 761.
[3] Fenwick, *International Law*, *op. cit.*, p. 466.
[4] Harvard Law School, *op. cit.*, p. 43.
[5] *Annual Digest*, 1946, Case 80.
[6] *Journal de Droit International Privé*, XLV (1918), 1183.
[7] *Journal de Droit International Privé*, XXVI (1889), 618.

agreement or discussion on the subject itself. But it has been shown that each of these alone has been insufficient to determine diplomatic status, although the three together would normally be sufficient to uphold a claim.

RESPONSIBILITY FOR THE PROTECTION OF DIPLOMATS

We arrive now at a discussion of the responsibility of a State for the protection of foreign diplomats. Little really need be said here to add to the lengthy discussion above on the subject of diplomatic immunities. It is clear that protection is incumbent upon the State both from the point of view of providing special protection when necessary, and prosecuting vigorously and swiftly those who would harm any individual entitled to immunity. This is basic in both the common and/or statute law of all states, and the authorities do not disagree on this as a general proposition. One need only recall the views cited in such celebrated cases as *Respublica* v. *Longchamps*,[1] the *Mattueoff Case*,[2] *Triquet* v. *Bath*,[3] and *Barbuitt's Case* [4] to understand the seriousness of the state's obligation in this regard.

Although the diplomat in general is entitled to a greater protection than the average alien [5] some have argued that not all diplomats are entitled to the same degree of precautionary measures in the form of protection. Thus, Fenwick holds, "the degree of its [the state's] responsibility probably varies with the rank of the diplomatic agent concerned.[6] This would not apply, however, to the vigor which the government would be expected to show if the diplomat's inviolability were transgressed or his security endangered.

RESPONSIBILITY FOR THE ACTS OF A STATE'S AGENTS

There are two aspects from which the State's responsibility for its agents' acts may be examined. One is with regard to the status of any negotiation or agreement which such agents enter. Here the picture

[1] Dallas 111.

[2] 10 Mod. 4 (1710), as cited in Briggs, *op. cit.*, p. 763.

[3] 3 Burrow 1748, as cited in Charles C. Fenwick, *Cases on International Law* (Chicago: Callaghan and Co., 1951), p. 36.

[4] *Cases in Equity in the Time of Talbot*, 281, cited in Briggs, *op. cit.*, p. 819.

[5] Stuart, *American Diplomatic and Consular Practice*, *op. cit.*, 2nd ed., p. 233.

[6] Fenwick, *International Law*, *op. cit.*, p. 284.

for the United States is the same regardless of the position held by the agent, i.e., whether he be foreign minister, ambassador or special agent. "What the President accepts as his own is properly negotiated ... what he rejects is destroyed." [1] Generally speaking this would be true for any state insofar as that organ of government is concerned which is empowered to conduct negotiations with other states. Whatever that organ or authority may be the agent's work would have to be acceptable to it. This is the municipal law aspect. Ogdon writes:

> As long as a diplomatic agent does not contravene the laws of the State to which he is accredited no difficulty arises. It may be noted that if he acts contrary to the laws he must do so either as a representative of his government for which that government holds itself responsible, or as an official who acts outside of that category of acts for which his government sees fit to accept responsibility. Any act in pursuance of the instructions sent by a government to its agent, or any act in the discretion of the agent for which his government sees fit to accept responsibility are official acts and are expressive of the will of the foreign government.[2]

But the more significant and complex problem is the responsibility under international law for the agent's acts. There are two possible positions for the agent. Either he is acting within his official capacity, in which case his actions may be authorized or unauthorized, or he may be acting outside of his official capacity, in which case his actions are those of a private individual. If the agent's action is authorized, and such action is a violation of international law, then his state, according to Oppenheim, bears an original responsibility. But, he holds, if the injurious action has not been authorized, then the state's responsibility is only vicarious. This authority maintains that the state's responsibility in either case is the same whether the agent is a high ranking officer, a minor agent or even a private individual. However, a vicarious responsibility can become an international delinquency, just as original responsibility for an injurious act is if the state does not compel its actor to repair the wrong, or if it does not provide appropriate punishment.

If the agent's action is committed in his official capacity, and if it is internationally injurious then it is an international delinquency. But if committed as a private individual there is neither original nor vicarious responsibility. Oppenheim argues that this is true for any diplomatic envoy. Should an administrative officer commit an internationally injurious act without authorization, it is not a state act and thus

[1] Wriston, *op. cit.*, p. 118.
[2] Ogdon, *op. cit.*, p. 221.

not an international delinquency. But, he maintains, there is vicarious responsibility for the state because such acts which are part of official functions are *prima facie* state acts.[1]

Hall is only partially in agreement with this view. He does not discuss the question of responsibility for an agent who is not acting in an official capacity, i.e., when he is acting as a private individual. But when in his official capacity or when fulfilling his functions or powers "a state is responsible for, and is bound by, all acts done by its agents." He disagrees about the responsibility involved if he acts in excess of his powers, however, holding then that "the state is not bound or responsible." [2]

Eagleton does not make a distinction between original and vicarious responsibility. For him "whether the agent acts within or without his competence, whether he be a superior or inferior agent, does not matter if through his act international law is violated." [3]

Perhaps one of the clearest and most thorough discussions of one aspect of this subject is that by Meron. In his study of the responsibility for unauthorized acts he concludes that very few court decisions have ever reflected the view that states are not responsible for the *ultra vires* acts of their officials. In one such case (Tunstall Case) Secretary of State Bayard denied the United States was responsible when a deputy sheriff in New Mexico shot and killed a British subject after catching him while the man was attempting to flee a court order. Bayard held that the act was not a government act, and that it could not be considered as coming under the rule of *respondeat superior* since this does not include acts outside the scope of agency.[4]

The other significant case along this line was the Sea Fisheries-Behring Sea Case, in which Attorney-General Griggs of the United States took approximately the same position vis à vis the seizure by United States officials of arms aboard a foreign vessel at sea.[5]

Most cases support a different conclusion, however. The consensus as Meron sees it is as follows: "If an official purports to act within his apparent authority, the State is responsible even if the official has exceeded his competence; provided, of course, that the act, if author-

[1] Oppenheim, *op. cit.*, 8th ed., chapter III, *passim.*

[2] Hall, *op. cit.*, 8th ed., p. 378.

[3] Clyde Eagleton, *International Government* (3rd ed.; New York: The Ronald Press Co., 1957), p. 89.

[4] *Papers Relating to the Foreign Relations of the United States* [1885], p. 451 (1886), cited in Theodore Meron, "International Responsibility of States for Unauthorized Acts of Their Officials," *British Yearbook of International Law*, XXXIII (1957), 91.

[5] *Official Opinions of the Attorneys-General*, XX (1900), 64, as cited in Meron, *op. cit.*, p. 91.

ized, would be internationally wrongful." [1] Meron raises an important question. He asks where does an *ultra vires* act of an official end and a private act of an official begin, i.e., can *ultra vires* acts of officials (for which there is state responsibility) be distinguished from private acts of officials (for which there is no state responsibility)? In answer he refers to Dunn, "States must assume the liability for 'misuse of governmental power' by their officials regardless of the latters' rank or status and regardless of the motivation of the act ..." [2]

There have been two important international conferences which have addressed themselves *inter alia* to this topic. And it is interesting to note that they took exactly opposite positions on the question. The League of Nations Meeting of the committee of Experts for the Progressive Codification of International Law, which was held in 1927, approved a Sub-committee report which proposed the following: (1) A distinction should be made between acts done within the competence of office and those which go beyond this. (a) In regard to competent acts the State must assume responsibility, and if a foreigner suffers damage the State must provide compensation. This is so because officials fulfilling their duties must obey the commands of the State. If international law is infringed the State is responsible "since the infringement must arise from the command being wrongful, either as going beyond the rights of the State or as failing to satisfy a duty owned by the State ... (b) "*If the act of the official is accomplished outside the scope of his competence,* that is to say, if he has exceeded his powers, we are then confronted with an act which juridically speaking, is not an act of the State." [3] Clearly this view is at variance with that of most other authorities including the report of the Hague Codification Conference of 1930. Probably the reason for this is that the Rapporteur, M. Guerrero, assimilated the responsibility of the state for its agents' actions under international law to that of its agents' actions under municipal law. It is doubtful that agency is comparable in these two different situations.

Briggs argues that even though it is true that a State appoints its agents and confers authority upon them, "principles of international law impute to the State responsibility for certain acts and omissions of those agents ..." [4]

When the Hague Codification Conference was held in 1930, its Third

[1] Meron, *op. cit.*, p. 94.
[2] Dunn, pp. 133–134, as cited *ibid.*, p. 111.
[3] League of Nations, Report to the Council, C 196, M. 70, 1927 V, *op. cit.*, p. 97.
[4] Briggs, *op. cit.*, 2nd ed., p. 616.

Committee took a position in direct opposition to that of the League's Committee of Experts. It very carefully and concisely examined the subject and reported its interpretation of a state's responsibility as follows:

> Article 7: International responsibility is incurred by a State if damage is sustained by a foreigner as the result of an act or omission on the part of the executive power incompatible with the international obligations of the State.
>
> Article 8.1: International responsibility is incurred by a State if damage is sustained by a foreigner as the result of acts or omissions of its officials acting within the limits of their authority when such acts or omissions contravene the international obligations of the State.
>
> Article 8.2: International responsibility is likewise incurred by a State if damage is sustained by a foreigner as a result of unauthorized acts of its officials performed under cover of their official character, if the acts contravene the international obligations of the State.[1]

There is probably one other effort by a group of scholars on the subject of state responsibility which should be mentioned here, and that is the work of the Harvard Law School which also took place about this time. In Article 18 the committee specifically approached the question of the state's responsibility for diplomatic and administrative agents abroad. It read: "A receiving State shall not impose liability on a person for an act done by him in the performance of his functions as a member of a mission or as a member of the administrative personnel." The comment on this Article was as follows:

> Willful disregard of the criminal law of the receiving State by a member of a mission is not presumably an act within the scope of his official functions. If it were it would be attributable to the sending State, and would be a matter for diplomatic reclamation with the receiving State. If, however, it is not within the scope of his official functions there is personal responsibility for the act, but in the absence of renunciation or waiver, the receiving State would have no jurisdiction over the person for such an act.[2]

This is the kind of situation to which Oppenheim alluded when he held that the state's vicarious responsibility would become an international delinquency if the state did not take appropriate action with regard to the official who committed the injury.

The rapporteur in charge of the report on state responsibility was Edwin Borchord. It was through his influence that the view was adopted that the state's responsibility would differ in degree depending upon the rank and position of the state official concerned.[3] This idea

[1] Third Committee of the Hague Codification Conference of 1930, cited *ibid.*, p. 695.
[2] Harvard Law School, *op. cit.*, p. 99.
[3] Meron, *op. cit.*, p. 100.

is strongly disputed by Meron who believes that from the point of view of logic and of practice such distinction in responsibility based on rank is neither practiced nor desirable.[1]

FUNCTIONS OF A DIPLOMAT

We may now turn our attention very briefly to the functions of the regular diplomatic envoy. Oppenheim lists three essential functions – "negotiation, observation, and protection." [2] The first refers to both the daily kind of discussion along the general lines which his government has authorized, concerning matters of mutual interest between the home state and the receiving state, and the special efforts authorized in bilateral or multilateral conferences. The second refers to the gathering of data and impressions on almost every conceivable subject, e.g., political stability of the present government, agricultural and industrial output, population trends, military preparedness, diplomatic agreements with other states, etc.

In paragraph 3 of article 3 of the United Nations Conference on Diplomatic Intercourse and Immunities, held in Vienna in 1961, the need to gather such information only by "lawful means" is stressed. This, as a generalization, would undoubtedly be accepted by all States. However, there was no discussion at this conference of the meaning of this term. The receiving State would generally be considered as having within its province the right to make such a determination. Nevertheless, it is clear that disagreements may very well arise here, for some States will take a much more restricted view regarding the rights of a member of a mission to gather information, even through conversations with its citizens.

The third refers to the protection of the citizens of one's home state presently located in the country. This will take the form primarily of advising them on any matters pertinent to their stay in the country, of making inquiries for them regarding matters of personal interest to them, and of offering diplomatic aid to the extent permitted by international law and authorized by the home government, should a denial of justice or other difficulty arise. On infrequent occasions the diplomat will perform similar duties for aliens of other states if authorized to do so by both his government and the alien's when, for some reason, usually due to a break in diplomatic relations, no accredited diplomats from the alien's state are present.

[1] *Ibid.*, p. 98.
[2] Oppenheim, *op. cit.*, 8th ed., p. 785.

The question of whether or not a diplomatic mission should also engage in consular functions was discussed at some length at the 1961 Vienna Conference on diplomacy. Although the International Law Commission did not recommend that such functions could be assumed, there was some feeling, especially on the part of the Italian delegation, that consular functions would have to be consented to on the part of the receiving State. Others, such as the Soviet Union, United Kingdom and Malaya, with slight variations in view, argued for the position, which was finally adopted, that the Convention should not be "construed as preventing the performance of consular functions by a diplomatic mission." [1]

These are approximately the same duties mentioned by Childs who refers to them as "the four basic phases" of "all American Foreign Service officers." [2] There are, of course, numerous miscellaneous tasks that may be assigned to or requested of them from time to time.

The International Law Commission gave a more extensive list of functions than those referred to by either Oppenheim or Childs. In article 3 of their draft they referred first, and most obviously, to the function of representation. It is the mission which represents the sending State to the receiving State and in large measure the two Governments are in contact with each other only through their missions. This applies both to the day to day activities which require communication between the two States, and to any extraordinary, sometimes crisis, situations which may arise. This is not to say that special missions may not be sent out from time to time, but an analysis of their functions will be undertaken later.

To this list one other function was added as a result of suggestions by the Philippine representative to the Sixth Committee of the General Assembly and by the delegate from Czechoslovakia.[3] It was proposed that diplomatic missions should aid in "promoting friendly relations between the sending State and the receiving State, and developing their economic, cultural and scientific relations." [4] Clearly such a view is reflective of attitudes of recent times regarding the purposes of foreign policy, and it is interesting to observe that such a proposal should have come from two States with such divergent ideologies.

[1] United Nations Conference on Diplomatic Intercourse and Immunities, Provisional Summary Record of the Fourth Plenary Meeting, 10 April 1961, A/Conf.20/Sr. 4, p. 3–10.

[2] J. Rives Childs, *American Foreign Service*, (New York: Henry Holt & Co., 1948), p. 64.

[3] United Nations Conference on Diplomatic Intercourse and Immunities, Guide to the Draft Articles on Diplomatic Intercourse and Immunities Adopted By the International Law Commission, 25 Jan. 1961, A/conf.20/8, p. 11.

[4] *Ibid.*, article 3.

The work is quite involved, as Oppenheim points out, because the permanent ambassador "represents his home state in the totality of its international relations not only with the state to which he is accredited, but also with other states. He is the mouthpiece ... of his state ... to the state to which he is accredited, [and] ... receives communications from the latter [for] his home state. In this way not only are international affairs between these two States fostered and negotiated but such international affairs of other States as are of general interest to all or a part of the members of the Family of Nations are also discussed." [1]

It is clear that these functions can not be neatly separated and, in fact, are highly intertwined. In order to be successful in performing his duties the diplomat must make the acquaintance of a large variety of people and know how to "draw them out" with regard to those things in which his government is interested. This is one of the most difficult and important parts of his assignment and the skill and ability with which he and his subordinates do this work will often distinguish between those who are doing a good job and those who are not. But his task is not finished here. He must also make his reports honestly and without yielding to the temptation to "present his activities in the best light," or "to draft reports of developments in a way which he considers may best please those at home instead of reporting the situation as it exists, however distasteful it may be to those in power." [2]

Of course to be able to fulfill his task appropriately it is assumed that the agent must have a minimum of restrictions on his travel. Fifty years ago this necessity would have been so obvious as to hardly merit comment. Except for fortified areas, diplomats had the opportunity to move about freely as their work required. The only general exception to this was during time of war.[3] However, just prior to and especially subsequent to World War II restrictions on travel have considerably grown, and in most instances seem to be politically inspired rather than to have any genuine basis in security matters.

This problem was broached at the recent diplomatic convention in Vienna, and it seemed to be widely accepted that the emphasis should be on freedom of movement rather than restrictions. One problem that did arise in this regard was raised by Mr. Kahamba of the Congo (Leopoldville), who pointed to the difficulty of transportation in some

[1] Oppenheim, *op. cit.*, 8th ed., p. 434. For a similar view see Mathews, *American Foreign Relations*, *op. cit.*, p. 399.

[2] Childs, *op. cit.*, p. 74.

[3] Hyde, *op. cit.*, II, 1263.

countries because of the nature of the terrain. Hence aircraft were commonly relied upon, and in this instance specific controls on the part of the receiving State had to be understood. This could mean controlling the use of airports and establishing the routes.[1] Article 26 was unanimously adopted but provided for the right to prohibit entry into certain zones established for "reasons of national security."

It might be well here to mention one other characteristic which may be considered valuable in helping the diplomat to perform his functions satisfactorily. This is the ability to appreciate the differences in culture between the diplomat's state and that of the state to which he has been accredited. Childs quotes Lord Malmesbury significantly on this point.

> Never ... attempt to export [your country's] habits and manners, but ... conform as far as possible to those of the country where you reside – ... do this even in the most trivial things – ... learn to speak their language, and never ... sneer at what may strike you as singular or absurd. Nothing goes to conciliate so much, or to amalgamate you more cordially with its inhabitants, as this very same sacrifice of your national prejudice to *theirs*.[2]

DIPLOMATIC AGENTS BELOW THE RANK OF AMBASSADOR

There remains one further question to ask ourselves in this analysis of the role of the regular diplomatic agent, and that is whether there are different rules that pertain to diplomatic agents below the grade of ambassador, or whether what has been said of him applies as well to all regular agents.

The present ranking of diplomatic envoys is the result of the agreement reached among the major West-European States at the Congress of Vienna in 1815, supplemented by the further agreement at the Congress of Aix-la-Chapelle, November 21, 1818. The United States has accepted this classification.[3] At the earlier Conference the agreement was that "Diplomatic agents are divided into three classes: that of ambassadors, legates, or nuncios; that of envoys, ministers, or other persons accredited to sovereigns; that of chargés d'affaires ac-

[1] United Nations Conference on Diplomatic Intercourse and Immunities, Committee of the Whole, Provisional Summary Record of the Twenty-Fourth Meeting, 21 March 1961, A/Conf 20/C.1/SR 24, p. 9.

[2] Childs, *op. cit.*, p. 73.

[3] Moore, *op. cit.*, IV, 430–31; *Official Opinions of the Attorneys-General*, *op. cit.*, VII, 210–211.

credited to ministers for foreign affairs. Ambassadors, legates, or nuncios only have the representative character." [1]

Throughout much of the nineteenth century it was accepted that those representatives in the first grade had a special status which afforded them nothing more in the way of immunities, but something "extra" in the way of privileges. Because of the additional privileges, and consequently prestige, the United States began to appoint diplomats of the first grade at the end of the century.

It is maintained by some that in the democratic state with an elected executive sovereignty rests with the people.[2] Thus a diplomat from a state like the United States does not stand on an equal basis with other diplomats who represent a monarch. It was to this opinion that Attorney-General Cushing addressed himself in a note to Secretary of State Marcy, May, 1855.

> If by usage in Europe the ambassador enjoys higher privileges because of his pretended or putative direct relation to the sovereign, we may with right demand the concessions of those privileges for the representatives of the popular sovereignty of a republic not less than of the regal or imperial sovereignty of a monarchy ... We acquiesce in what is a matter of no account, the classification of ministers arranged at the Congress of Vienna and Aix-la-Chapelle ... but, in doing this, we relinquish no rights ... Of course we can by no means admit that ambassadors, and they only, have a representative character. Whatever in Europe may be the arbitrarily assumed relationship of any ... minister to the sovereign of his country, all ministers, duly appointed and commissioned by the constitutional authorities, are alike the direct "representatives" ... of the United States.[3]

Moore is in agreement with this. Regardless of whether the ambassador is "the personal representative of his sovereign, or, in the case of a republic, of the whole people of his country,... [he] is accorded special distinction. Regarded as the equal of the head of the State to which he is accredited, there is asserted in his behalf the right to be treated accordingly." [4]

Hill, in pointing out that the distinction between ambassadors and diplomats of lesser rank was made "as a special benefit to monarchies," supports the Attorney-General, and calls the distinction "obsolete." Now, he argues, it is assumed that the diplomat speaks "not for a

[1] Moore, *Digest*, *op. cit.*, IV, 430. The class of ministers-resident was provided at Aix-la-Chapelle, and they are also accredited to sovereigns.

[2] Hyde, *op. cit.*, 2nd ed., p. 205.

[3] *Official Opinions of the Attorneys-General*, *op. cit.*, VII, 210–211.

[4] Moore, *op. cit.*, IV, 740.

personal sovereign, but simply for his government," and this be so whether he be called chargé or ambassador.[1]

Hyde, however, takes the view that the Ambassador does have an advantage which lesser diplomats do not have. "The right of access to the head of the State to which he is accredited, and that without delay, gives to an ambassador the opportunity to exercise his diplomatic functions with a facility not possessed by an officer of lesser rank." [2]

Others disagree and present what would seem to be the sounder view. Satow states that the special privilege of seeing the head of the state at any time is not an actuality since the occasions when he can do so "are limited by the etiquette of the court or government to which he is accredited." [3]

Hall is inclined toward the same view holding that the entire classification has "little but ceremonial value" because modern day conditions are such that diplomatic agents are not given an opportunity to talk with anyone other than those charged with the responsibility for foreign relations.[4]

Oppenheim supports this position and states that the special privilege of negotiating directly with the head of the state has "little value nowadays, as all states have, to a certain extent, constitutional government, and this necessitates that all the important business should go through the hands of a Foreign Secretary." [5]

Thus it may be assumed that an ambassador of a republic has the same standing as one from a monarchy, and that there is really no significant difference in the privileges or immunities of the various diplomatic grades.

SUMMARY

The status of the diplomatic agent under international law has had a long and much discussed history. It has not been the purpose of this writer to make a detailed analysis of the development of the subject, but rather to single out those aspects that would enable us to obtain a better understanding of the status of the special agent.

[1] David Jayne Hill, "Classification of Diplomatic Agents," *American Journal of International Law*, XXI (1927), 738.

[2] Hyde, *op. cit.*, 1st ed., I, 782–783.

[3] Sir Ernest Satow, *A Guide to Diplomatic Practice* (3rd ed.; London: Longmans Green and Co., 1932), I, 154.

[4] Hall, *op. cit.*, 8th ed., p. 356.

[5] Oppenheim, *op. cit.*, 8th ed., p. 777.

The acceptability of a diplomat is generally considered to be a decision which the receiving state is privileged to make. States have not always followed the practice of determining this matter before the diplomat is sent and, in fact, the United States did not do so until it began to assign the rank of ambassador at the end of the nineteenth century. Whether the receiving state has been notified by the sender or not, it is agreed that the latter must be willing to assign a different agent if the former decides that the person who was originally chosen is undesirable. On a number of occasions the United States has had to accept such a demand by other states even though the President felt the reasons for the rejection were based on false information and misunderstanding.

Agents who are accepted carry with them letters of credence which indicate the rank and general nature of the assignment. Such a letter is presented in a highly formalized ceremony at which time the diplomat and the Chief Executive, to whom the letter is given, exchange hopes for continued, or improved diplomatic relations. Many states maintain that from this moment on the agent has diplomatic status. Others insist that he has such from the moment he crosses the receiving state's border.

Just what this status entails is a matter of incomplete agreement, although there is probably more harmony among states on the subject of diplomatic status than on many others. In brief we can say that it is accepted that the diplomatic officer has inviolability, that this applies to himself, his official papers and his official residence. Other members of his residence and mission are likewise considered inviolable, but there is some disagreement as to who they are. Apparently the Swiss and French are more restrictive in their views regarding who is so entitled, whereas the Americans, British and Italians are more liberal. The minimum would seem to be members of his immediate family and those in the mission who are assigned duties upon which the mission is dependent for its effective operation.

This immunity is not only with regard to criminal and civil suit, but also pertains to his right to be free from subpoena, from taxes, except those levied for local services, and from requirements levied by the national government on its citizens, e.g., conscription, requirement to vote, etc.

The reason why this inviolability exists is not a matter of complete agreement among scholars. It is like the question of sovereignty. The existence of sovereignty and the effects of it upon the individual are obvious. But the reason that this is so varies with different students of political science. Some have suggested that inviolability exists because the diplomat stands in the place of his chief of state who, as a sovereign is not subject to the laws of the foreign state. Others argue that it is based upon the concept of exterritoriality – a myth which conveniently removes the diplomat from the jurisdiction of the host state. Still others base inviolability upon function and maintain that inviolability should only exist to the extent necessary to enable the agent to represent satisfactorily his state. This is perhaps becoming the more popular theory and carries with it the belief that the very extensive immunities which existed in the past, so extensive that whole sections of a city would be "off-limits" to the host state, are no longer acceptable, and that immunities should exist only where necessary – *ne impediatur legatio*. Some have argued that immunity is only for private acts, that official acts are beyond the jurisdiction of the host state inasmuch as the latter are expressions of sovereignty over which the host has no jurisdiction.

Generally speaking the branch of the government which decides the question of who is entitled to immunity is the executive. This is particularly true for the Anglo-Saxon countries. In countries like Germany and France the courts have been more reluctant to accept the statements of the Foreign Office as conclusive. The same is true for Italy. Generally speaking then, in European countries the courts tend to make such determinations with a greater degree of independence from the foreign office than is traditionally true in the United States or Britain. Yet there would seem to be good grounds for arguing in support of the latter's approach rather than the former's. As Sir Cecil Hurst has put it the need is for flexibility in determining exactly who should receive immunity and the executive branch is in the best position to supply it.

Indications by the Executive of who is entitled to immunity are generally made in the form of the diplomatic list and the diplomatic passport. But they do not provide conclusive evidence. It is possible to be on the list or to have a diplomatic passport and get no diplomatic status. Deener has very correctly pointed out that the significance of the diplomatic passport has not been definitely established. But its standing and that of the list would seem to be a matter well within the domestic jurisdiction of any state. In other words the "Gubitchev-kind-of-problem" need never have occurred if the United States had statutes that clearly established the significance of such a passport in this country's eyes. Inasmuch as there are six different kinds of passports in use in the United States there is no reason why it is necessary to give a diplomatic passport to one who is not entitled to immunities. If the Department of State had given Gubitchev a passport other than diplomatic then the matter would have come to a head between the Soviet Union and the United States before an incident occurred requiring some determination on this issue. It should also be remembered that the controversy between the two states dealt with the charge of espionage – a situation which was not exactly conductive to a dispassionate analysis of the problem.

So far as the basis of immunity is concerned the concept of function has received increasing attention from courts and scholars. As explained above it has generally been translated as significant work carried out as a member of a diplomatic mission. But the question what is, or is not, a diplomatic function, is extremely difficult to answer, and no scholarly or juridical opinions exist to aid one in this matter.

In regard to the responsibility a state must assume for its agents' actions, there is no disagreement that the responsibility is complete if the injury occurs as a result of an authorized act. Some, perhaps the majority, seem to argue that there is a responsibility also for unauthorized acts, acts that exceeded the competence of the agent. This is what Oppenheim calls vicarious responsibility. The questions of greatest disagreement are: (1) to what extent is a state responsible for acts of minor agents and, (2) is the state at all responsible for acts of a private nature. The problem has generally arisen because the tendency has been to define the responsibility by analogy with the state's responsibility for its agents' acts in a domestic situation. But this is a very poor way of trying to clarify the matter. States generally have been very slow to assume responsibility for injury to their residents. In the United States, for example, the Federal Tort Claims Act was not passed until 1946. Acceptance of international responsibility for the acts of state agents has had a much longer history, and it cannot be established by analogy from the traditions of municipal law.

The concept of sovereignty has implied that the government of a state may determine what the rights of its citizens are within its borders, and except for modifications of this view which have been raised in recent years, notably the concepts of human rights that are implicit in the international trial at Nuremberg and especially those discussed in the United Nations debates, this traditional view still has wide acceptance. But even here, it should be noted, the rights of aliens within the state are not a subject which may be determined solely by the host state. The home state of the alien has some right to act in behalf of its citizens abroad. Thus States must show a willingness to assume responsibility, many authorities maintain, for the acts of major and minor agents.

This chapter has also indicated that agents of lower rank are entitled to the immunities of the ambassador and will normally receive his privileges. For those who are not considered to have diplomatic status but who are nevertheless assigned to work with a diplomatic mission, it may be argued that their immunities will simply be jurisdictional rather than diplomatic.

CHAPTER VI

STATUS OF MISCELLANEOUS AGENTS UNDER INTERNATIONAL LAW

One other category of officials merits brief attention before our discussion turns to the special executive agent, the subject of concern in this study. This is a broad, rather amorphous category which includes those sent to attend *ad hoc* international conferences, delegates and officers of regular international organizations, judges of international courts and members of special technical commissions representing states and public international organizations.

This is by no means a new category, but what is new is the great increase in the number of individuals in this category, as well as the increase in the use of such agencies. Shortly after World War I the number and variety increased to the point where a prominent international lawyer could write, "... the new problem which confronts the international lawyer, arising from changing habits of life, is that of the protection to be accorded to the multifarious agents representing the increasing ramifications of governmental interests abroad. Existing classifications are insufficient." [1]

INTERNATIONAL CONFERENCES

Agents sent as delegates to *ad hoc* international conferences or congresses are quite common. The status of such agents is a matter of some dispute between the authorities. Hyde maintains that because an agent is authorized to attend such a conference and perhaps even to sign a convention which results from its deliberations, "does not necessarily indicate that the delegate is regarded by the state appointing him as a diplomatic officer, or as one entitled while engaged on his mission, to the privileges of such an officer. The view of his own country respecting his status is to be derived from the form or language of his commission ..." [2]

[1] Clyde Eagleton, "The Responsability of the State for the Protection of Foreign Officials," *American Journal of International Law*, XIX (1925), 312.

[2] Hyde, *op. cit.*, I, 719-720.

Oppenheim, on the other hand, argues that such envoys "are not, or need not be, accredited to the State on whose territory the Congress or Conference takes place, but they are nevertheless diplomatic envoys, and enjoy all the privileges of such envoys as regards exterritoriality and the like which concern the inviolability and safety of their persons and the members of their suites." [1]

This is very similar to the position of Loewe and Rosenberg in their commentary on the German Criminal Code regarding agents at international conferences. It is the opinion of these authors that when state agents appear at international conferences they are entitled to be treated as exterritorial persons. "Alle Vertreter fremder Staaten auf internationalen Kongressen und Conferenzen und fremde Mitglieder zwischenstaatlicher Abordnungen mit repraesentativem Charakter als Exterritoriale zu behandeln sind." [2]

Van Vollenhoven is likewise sympathetic to this attitude and refers with apparent approval to Lord Birkenhead's view that such negotiators and representatives are entitled to diplomatic prerogatives.[3]

Sir Neville Bland points out that in Britain the diplomatic status of delegates to international conferences is provided for by statute and is not a part of the common law.[4] He has in mind here such Acts as the Diplomatic Privileges (Extension) Act of 1944 which provides in section 3, paragraph 1:

> Where a conference is held in the United Kingdom and is attended by representatives of His Majesty's Government in the United Kingdom and the government or governments of one or more foreign sovereign powers [the Secretary of State shall compile a list of those entitled to diplomatic immunity] and every representative of a foreign Power who is for the time being included in the list shall, for the purpose of any enactment and rule of law or custom relating to the immunities of an envoy of a foreign Power accredited to His Majesty, and of the retinue of such an envoy, be treated as if he were such an envoy, and such of the members of his official staff as are for the time being included in the list shall be treated for the purpose aforesaid as if they were his retinue.[5]

INTERNATIONAL ORGANIZATIONS

Referring to those who may be identified as international organization officials, e.g., the chief officers of the secretariat of the United

[1] Oppenheim, *op. cit.*, 8th ed., I, 775.

[2] Loewe und Rosenberg, *Die Strafprozessordnung und das Gerichtsverfassungsgesetz* (20th ed.; 1956), II, 73.

[3] C. Van Vollenhoven, "Diplomatic Prerogatives of Non-Diplomats," *American Journal of International Law*, XIX (1925), 473.

[4] Sir Neville Bland, correspondence, August 5, 1958.

[5] Diplomatic Privileges (Extension) Act, 1944.

Nations, Kunz likewise argues that "a uniform and general law of privilege and immunities for international officials is a task; but at the present time [1947] it seems that no such general customary international law has yet come into existence." [1]

The Convention of Contingents of the Panama Congress of 1826 contains one of the earliest examples of granting diplomatic immunity to non-diplomatic international functionaries. According to Article 15 of the Convention the members of the *Comision Directiva* "were to enjoy all the immunities and exemptions of a diplomatic agent, wherever [they] reside." [2] Similar provisions were made for the Central Commission for the Navigation of the Rhine, the European Danube Commission, the International Congo Commission (the first to receive diplomatic prerogatives by international agreement, under the Treaty of Berlin, 1878), the International Finance Control Commission of Greece as well as the judges of the Permanent Court of Arbitration.[3]

The 1907 Hague Convention gave the members of the Permanent Court of Arbitration "diplomatic privileges and immunities [when] in the exercise of their duties." Hyde points out that "Such provisions ... purport to confer ... certain rights possessed by a public minister without suggesting that the former is in any sense a diplomatic representative of the State appointing him, or that he is engaged in any diplomatic service in its behalf. It must be clear that general agreement to clothe an administrative officer with diplomatic privileges and immunities does not necessarily indicate that the individual is regarded as possessed of diplomatic character." [4]

Article 7, paragraph 4 of the Covenant of the League of Nations provided that "'Representatives of the members of the League and officials of the League when engaged on the business of the League shall enjoy diplomatic privileges and immunities.'" [5]

One may say, therefore, that by 1920 there was a beginning, but by no means an extensive one, of the practice of granting special privileges to functionaries of international organizations. And in those cases where privileges and immunities existed they were always based upon specific agreements.

During the inter-war period the practice was greatly extended, al-

[1] Kunz, *op. cit.*, p. 854.
[2] *Ibid.*, p. 828.
[3] *Ibid.*, pp. 828–829; Lawrence Preuss, "Diplomatic Privileges and Immunities of Agents Invested with Functions of an International Interest," *American Journal of International Law*, XXV (1931), 696–697.
[4] Hyde, *op. cit.*, 2nd ed., II, 1232–33.
[5] Preuss, *op. cit.*, p. 699.

though the United States continued to take "a negative attitude on the basis that under international law diplomatic privileges were due only to members of national diplomatic missions.[1]

Various organs of the Inter-American system have also followed the League practice as has the United Nations. Article 105 of the United Nations Charter provides: "(1) The Organization shall enjoy in the territory of each of its members such privileges and immunities as are necessary for the fulfillment of its purposes. (2) Representatives of the members of the United Nations and officials of the Organization shall similarly enjoy such privileges and immunities as are necessary for the independent exercise of their functions in connection with the Organization."

So far as officials of the United Nations are concerned their immunity can be waived. Section 2 of the United Nations General Convention gives to the Secretary-General the authority and duty to do so for any official "in any case where, in his opinion, the immunity would impede the course of justice and [it] can be waived without prejudice to the interests of the United Nations. Waiver of immunity of the Secretary General is the right of the Security Council." [2]

Many of the charters of the Specialized Agencies contain such provisions e.g. the International Labor Organization, the former United Nations Relief and Rehabilitation Administration, the Food and Agriculture Organization, the International Bank and the International Monetary Fund, the United Nations Education, Scientific and Cultural Organization, etc.[3]

The Statute of the International Court of Justice provides diplomatic privileges to the judges, "when engaged on the business of the Court." [4] This status was also provided by Holland for the Judges of the Permanent Court of International Justice. Kunz reminds us that these judges are neither representatives of states nor officials of an international organization. But he is quite firm in his belief that at least the higher officers must have immunity.[5]

The first General Assembly approved on February 13, 1946, a convention, which it proposed the members ratify, dealing with the diplomatic status of the members.[6]

[1] Hackworth, *Digest*, *op. cit.*, IV, 419–23; Kunz, *op. cit.*, pp. 829–30.
[2] *Ibid.*, p. 861.
[3] *Ibid.*, pp. 832–35.
[4] Article 19.
[5] Kunz, *op. cit.*, pp. 852–53, 856.
[6] United Nations General Assembly, First Session, Document a/43, Annex 22.

The United States Congress had anticipated such a need and passed enabling legislation, December 29, 1945. Under Title 1 – International Organization Immunities Act, Sec. 7(a) the law provides, "Persons designated by foreign governments to serve as their representatives in or to international organizations and the officers and employees of such organizations, and members of the immediate families of such representatives, officers and employees residing with them, other than nationals of the United States, shall, insofar as concerns laws regulating entry into and departure from the United States, alien registration and fingerprinting, and the registration of foreign agents be entitled to the same privileges, exemptions and immunities as are accorded under similar circumstances to officers and employees respectively of foreign governments and members of their families." [1]

Section 7 (b) provides that "Representatives of foreign governments in or to international organizations and officers and employees of such organizations shall be immune from suit and legal process relating to acts performed by them in their official capacity and falling within their functions as representatives, officers, or employees except insofar as such immunity may be waived by the foreign government or international organization concerned." [2]

Section 3 allows officers and employees of such organizations, their families, suites and servants to enter their personal belongings free of customs duties and internal revenue taxes.[3]

In Britain the International Organizations (Immunities and Privileges) Act, 1950, gives to representatives of any international organization of which the United Kingdom is a member, to the members of any committees of such organizations and to the "high officers" and "persons on missions" of such organizations the same immunity from suit and legal process, inviolability or residence and exemption or relief from taxes as would normally be extended to any duly accredited diplomatic envoy "of a foreign sovereign Power." [4]

The Canadian Government has also passed legislation which provides immunities for delegates, officials, and experts of the United Nations. Article IV of the Privileges and Immunities (United Nations) Act of 1947 provides that the representatives of the members to the various United Nations organs enjoy the traditional immunities of diplomats, e.g. personal inviolability, inviolability of papers, ex-

[1] Public Law 291, 79th Congress.
[2] *Ibid.*
[3] *Ibid.*
[4] 14 Geo. 6, Ch. 14, Schedule, Part II.

emption from restrictions and regulations generally dealing with immigration and aliens and other general privileges dealing with baggage, etc.[1]

Certain immunities and privileges are also provided for the officials of the organization, e.g. immunity from national service obligations, from immigration and alien regulations, privileges of the port with regard to personal belongings, etc. Experts who are hired by the United Nations or its agencies receive those privileges and immunities conceived as "necessary for the independent exercise of their functions." [2]

What is the position of experts hired by the Organization? Kunz writes:

> A special position is that of international experts, technical counsel, members of a consultative commission, appointed by an international organization, but not working under its control. They were, under Article VII, paragraph 4, of the Covenant mostly excluded from diplomatic privileges and immunities ... Sections 22 & 23 of the United Nations General Convention grant now to "experts on missions for the United Nations" such privleges and immunities "as are necessary for the independent exercise of their functions during the period of their missions." [3]

On what basis are these officers of international organizations granted an immunity which formerly only diplomatic representatives of states held? Kunz rules out reasons of representation and state responsibility and reciprocity, and maintains that "function is the true basis." It derives, he believes, from "the immunity of international organizations themselves." [4]

Preuss holds that it is a matter of "... the necessity of protecting the common interstate interests with which [public international organizations] are charged." [5] However, he argues, whatever the extent of their benefits, they exist "only by virtue of express treaty provision or by the concession of the states in whose territory they act. Any further claims to diplomatic treatment rest upon extremely tenuous legal grounds." [6]

Although there is no solid agreement on the extent of the diplomatic immunities for international officials, Kunz reports that many authorities feel that it covers the officials' "effects, papers and correspondence and those of his family living under his roof." The League

[1] Revised Statutes of Canada, 1952, IV, chapter ccxix, Article IV, 4433.
[2] *Ibid.*, Articles V and VI, pp. 4434–4435.
[3] Kunz, *op. cit.*, pp. 853–54.
[4] *Ibid.*, p. 854.
[5] Preuss, *op. cit.*, p. 694.
[6] *Ibid.*, p. 695. See also Van Vollenhoven, *op. cit.*, p. 473.

of Nations *modus vivendi* of 1926 contained this stipulation.[1] The United Nations General Convention provides that the Secretary-General and the Assistant Secretaries-General, their wives and minor children have full diplomatic privileges. Their private suite and servants are not included. So far as lesser officials are concerned the Secretary-General is empowered to determine who shall be covered. He has included all staff members except those recruited locally and paid on an hourly rate.[2]

There has been much disagreement over what the position of the private suite and servants should be but, inasmuch as no United Nations cases have arisen, no juridical interpretation has been made.

So far as the duration of these immunities is concerned there is no reason to question that they remain as long as the officials are in the exercise of their office.[3]

INTERNATIONAL COMMISSIONS

There are, of course, many special missions on which governments send official representatives. The status of such representatives is generally determined by the participating States. Eagleton maintains that commissioners "do not possess diplomatic prerogatives . . . unless specifically invested" with them. "When one of the British Commissioners to the United States sent under the Jay Treaty provisions was prosecuted before a criminal court in Philadelphia, his government did not complain, while the American Commissioners to England under the same treaty applied for and were refused diplomatic privileges." [4]

The grounds for refusal of the British Foreign Office was that the American Commissioners, Gore and Pinckney, had no "letters of credence to the King [nor did they], possess the character of diplomatic officials. Hence they were denied any immunities." [5] It should be remembered that this opinion followed on the heels of the American revolution and subsequent loss to Britain of the colonies. Hence the court's tendency would very likely be an extremely narrow one which

[1] Kunz, *op. cit.*, p. 856.

[2] *United Nations Journal*, No. 54, Supplement A-A/P, L (December 9, 1946), as cited *ibid.*, p. 859.

[3] Kunz, *op. cit.*, p. 854.

[4] Moore, *Digest*, *op. cit.*, IV, Sec. 623, cited in Clyde Eagleton, "The Responsibility of the State for the Protection of Foreign Officials," *American Journal of International Law*, XIX (April, 1925), 303.

[5] Foster, *op. cit.*, pp. 194–95.

in fact has not been followed. Foster suggests that the basis of the "diplomatic courtesies" which have been extended is comity.[1]

Eagleton states that "commissioners do ... receive a special protection, even though it does not amount to diplomatic privileges ..." [2] The problem that needs to be resolved, he argues, is that of "measuring the responsibility of a state for the protection of the various sorts of commissioners who are sent to it. It is impossible to establish from practice." The problem stems from a lack of a sufficient number of examples "from which a practice could be educed." [3] This is an area in which there has been no real agreement in practice or theory, and yet it would seem that some degree of responsibility is necessary; but "how much, or who belong to the group, is still an unsettled question." [4]

Hall takes a similar stand. He maintains that commissioners "do not represent their government, [nor are they] employed in such functions as to acquire diplomatic immunity. They are, however, held to have a right to special protection, and courtesy may sometimes demand something more. It would probably be correct to say that no very distinct practice has been formed as to their treatment, contentious cases not having sufficiently arisen." [5]

The question arises whether all commissioners may be considered as meriting the same treatment. Secretary of State John W. Foster in discussing this matter in instructions issued to Mr. Heard, Minister to Korea, pointed out that "commissioners have often, from the foundation of the Government, borne commissions signed by the head of the Government, and have been accredited and received as full envoys." [6] Other commissioners, however, "have at times been appointed on the certification of the Secretary of State and without diplomatic capacity. The title is vague, and only the language and purport of the incumbent's commission and credential letters can determine whether it possesses a diplomatic character ..." [7]

A Department officer at a later date in a discussion of the status of the Reparation Commission established after World War I noted that

[1] *Ibid.*
[2] Eagleton, *op. cit.*, p. 303.
[3] *Ibid.*
[4] *Ibid.*, p. 307.
[5] Hall, *op. cit.*, p. 371. Van Vollenhoven is also of this opinion, *op. cit.*, p. 473.
[6] Hyde, *op. cit.*,, 1st ed., I, 719.
[7] Mr. Foster, Secretary of State, to Mr. Heard, No. 151, Diplomatic Series, October 31, 1892, MS Instructions Korea, I, 414, as cited in Moore, *Digest*, *op. cit.*, IV, 440.

the Government of the United States did not object in principle to granting reciprocal privileges but that diplomatic privileges and immunities were granted by statute to ministers of foreign states or princes received as such by the President and that the statute would hardly cover representatives of the Reparation Commission. Additional legislation to secure such privileges for them, it was said, would therefore be necessary and, while it was not possible to propose such legislation at this time, the matter would be favorably considered later.[1]

Thus the United States was not willing to consider the commissioners *per se* were entitled to regular diplomatic immunities.

Hershey accepts this view but emphasizes that if the commissioner has "a mere technical or administrative character" he is definitely not entitled to diplomatic privileges and immunities.[2] Hyde adds to the list of exceptions "commissioners appointed to fulfill judicial functions through service on mixed claims commissions, ... or courts of arbitration ..." [3]

Satow is probably in the middle in this controversy. Though his view is not as clearly stated as one would wish, he appears to be of the opinion that such agents get some of the privileges and immunities but not all that the regular diplomat is entitled to.[4]

The scholars involved in the Harvard Research in International Law support this position. Although they are aware of the difficulty of expounding a definitive rule, they hold that "the members of non-diplomatic missions, such as frontier commissions, or agents sent abroad for purposes of an administrative or technical character, are entitled by international law to a special protection and consideration, the limits of which are not determined with precision." [5] But this same source acknowledges that

> Customary international law has established no stand by which diplomatic missions may clearly be distinguished in all cases from non-diplomatic missions on the basis of differences in their respective functions. The expansion of the activities entrusted to diplomatic missions and the growth in recent decades of new types of state agencies operating on foreign territory have tended to obscure the distinction between diplomatic and non-diplomatic functions ... It appears to be the practice of states to accord the benefits of diplomatic privileges and immunities to the members of missions whose heads have been invested by their governments with a diplomatic rank and title recognized in international intercourse.[6]

[1] MS Department of State, file 701.0611/79, as cited in Hackworth, *Digest*, *op. cit.*, IV, 420–421.

[2] Amos S. Hershey, *Essentials of International Public Law and Organization* (New York: The Macmillan Co., 1927), pp. 411–12.

[3] Hyde, *op. cit.*, 1st ed., I, 722.

[4] Satow, *op. cit.*, I, 174.

[5] Harvard Law School, *op. cit.*, p. 44.

[6] *Ibid.*, p. 43.

SUMMARY

A brief section has been included in this study on agents other than the regular diplomat and special executive agent. In this miscellaneous category are three main sub-groups, agents sent by states to attend *ad hoc* international conferences, officers and delegates of international organizations, and members of international commissions established for such purposes as delimitation of State borders, development of technical information, determination of peace terms, etc.

Although agents who attend international conferences are given credentials entitled *pleins pouvoirs*, some authorities, such as Hyde, insist that this does not mean that they have a diplomatic character. Hence these authorities would extend very limited privileges. Oppenheim and others, however, feel that they are diplomatic envoys and are therefore entitled to inviolability. The British have gone so far as to grant them this status by statute.

It would certainly seem desirable to do so inasmuch as historically even diplomatic missions were of an *ad hoc* nature. And furthermore, to make it possible for "conference diplomats" to achieve the results which their states must have desired when they established the conference, one would have to grant them, their papers and the subordinate members of their mission inviolability.

Although international organizations have a fairly long history, the record of establishing immunity for the participating officials has not been consistent. But, throughout the nineteenth and twentieth centuries the custom grew of providing that the officers of the organization would have diplomatic immunities. The two large international organizations of this century, the League of Nations and the United Nations, each provided for immunities for its secretariat. However, the United Nations General Convention goes even farther than the League did by granting those privileges and immunities which are necessary to perform their functions to technical experts and others employed by the organization.

Of course officials of such organizations are entitled only to those privileges and immunities which the member states are willing to grant. And it is clearly necessary where such agreements are not considered self-executing, as in the United States, for the members to pass enabling legislation within their states so that the courts, police and administrative authorities will know to what extent privileges and immunities have been authorized.

As regards technical commissions, arbitration courts, etc., there is much disagreement. Where there is a special agreement establishing their status there is no difficulty, where none such exists many authorities hold that they are entitled to nothing more than the courtesies established by comity. Others insist that they do have a status which entitles them to some immunities and special protection but the exact amount or nature of these has not been established by custom or widespread agreement.

CHAPTER VII

STATUS OF THE SPECIAL AGENT UNDER INTERNATIONAL LAW

Special agents are individuals sent abroad by Governments on a specific assignment of limited duration. The nature of the assignment may or may not be similar to some aspect of the work normally assigned to a member of a regular diplomatic mission. There are four subdivisions of the category of special agents in foreign affairs. The agent may be a public or a secret agent. If secret his status may or may not be known by the receiving State. If public he may or may not have been given diplomatic rank. We shall not attempt, however, to examine these latter two categories of public agents separately.

SPECIAL SECRET AGENTS

So far as secret agents are concerned they may be further divided into two subdivisions, those officially admitted as agents by the State to which they are sent, and those admitted by the State without realization of the fact of their being secret agents. The former are thus secret agents insofar as third States are concerned, the latter are secret agents insofar as receiving States are concerned.

The true identity of the latter agents not being known to the receiving State they are in the same category as aliens. Thus they have "no recognized position whatever according to International Law." [1] Furthermore, this agent is in "the same position as any other foreign individual living withhin the boundaries of a State. He may be expelled at any moment if he becomes troublesome, and he may be criminally punished if he commits a political or ordinary crime." [2] The cogency of this argument is so obvious as to require no further elaboration.

With regard to the former category, those secret agents who are received as such, the position is somewhat different. Inasmuch as their true character is known to the host state they can be given special

[1] Oppenheim, *op. cit.*, 7th ed., I, 490.
[2] *Ibid.*, p. 491.

consideration. However, the very secrecy of the mission will necessarily bar such an agent "from the full enjoyment of the privileges and immunities" of one who is publicly accredited.[1] This is obvious, for were it not so his true character would be revealed and hence the chances for the successful completion of his mission destroyed. He will receive, at best, only those considerations

> which are consistent with the maintenance of secrecy, that is to say [he will enjoy] inviolability and the various immunities attendant on the diplomatic character insofar as the direct action of the State is concerned. Thus his political inviolability is complete; and it may be presumed that no criminal process would be instituted against him where the state charges itself with the duty of commencing criminal proceedings. On the other hand, in all civil and criminal cases in which the initiative can be taken by a private person he remains exposed to the action of the courts; though it would no doubt be the duty of the government to prevent a criminal sentence from being executed upon him by any means which may be at their disposal ...[2]

Foster seems to disagree with this position, but he is not explicit. Referring to such agents, sent by the United States, he reports that they have usually been "without any diplomatic standing."[3] He does not indicate if he believes that this was the result of their not being given any by the United States or if it was because the receiving State felt that such a status was not inherent in their position.

Eagleton, on the other hand, supports Oppenheim and Hall in arguing that secret agents must be granted "a special protection" because they have a "public character." In fact, he argues, the same position is held by "envoys of a *de facto* government [and] agents of a state which refuses recognition to the state to which [the agent] is sent ..."[4]

SPECIAL PUBLIC AGENTS

Although it would be possible to discuss special agents without diplomatic rank separately from those with such rank, and in fact there may even be good reasons to do so, nevertheless, so little is known about the whole category that it seems wiser to treat them as one. In the conclusions some observations will be presented about distinguishing between the two. All that need be said here is that of the two, those without diplomatic rank probably outnumber those who have received it. The reason for this assumption is that the practice of

[1] Hall, *op. cit.*, 8th ed., pp. 370–71.
[2] *Ibid.*; see also Moore, *Digest*, *op. cit.*, IV, 427.
[3] Foster, *Practice of Diplomacy*, *op. cit.*, p. 198.
[4] Eagleton, *op. cit.*, p. 300.

using such agents has probably been greater on the part of the United States than any other country, and by far the greater number of them has not been given diplomatic rank. It is assumed that this is not so of agents of other States, i.e. that they generally carry diplomatic rank. But too little is known of the practice of other States with regard to this question to warrant any firm conclusions.

The status of this category of agent has been given a degree of attention by the International Law Commission. It assigned to Professor A. E. F. Sandström the task of drawing up a draft on "Ad Hoc Diplomacy" which dealt, *inter alia*, with the subject of special missions.[1] These special missions are considered to exist when "a special diplomatic assignment" abroad is given to "a diplomatic officer" "who does not belong to [the] permanent mission accredited" from his own country. They are also characterized "as performing temporarily an act which ordinarily is taken care of by the permanent mission." [2] Paragraph five of this Report states, "The head of a special mission is also generally, but not always, a diplomatic officer by profession." Just what the significance of this statement is is not clear. Whether a diplomatic agent is a career officer or not is of no import in international law. If, however, the statement may be taken to mean that sometimes the head of a mission has no diplomatic rank it is of great importance. There is no indication in the Rapporteur's Report that he recognized the existence of these two categories of agents, and therefore no attempt is made to indicate whether they would hold a different status under international law. But somewhere in the Introduction or Commentary it would have been wise to indicate that there are two different categories, and perhaps some views presented thereon. In the Twelfth Session of the International Law Commission several members referred to agents without rank, hence it would seem that they had such agents in mind when they considered the Rapporteur's draft. But again no effort to distinguish between the two appears.

The Establishment of Special Missions

Special agents do not get letters of credence. They often do, however, get special letters of introduction to those authorities, generally the Chief Executive, to whom their mission takes them. Sometimes it has

[1] United Nations General Assembly, International Law Commission, 12th Session, "Ad Hoc Diplomacy," 11 March, 1960, A/CN.4/129.

[2] *Ibid.*, para. 4 and 5.

been necessary to telegraph their letters of authorization. In some instances where American agents were concerned the "Department of State ... merely telegraphed [the necessary information] to the Foreign Minister of the country to which the envoy was [sent]." [1]

Although letters of introduction and other credentials may serve as an entré to those officials whom the special agent is sent to see, it is quite clear that such papers are not always necessary. If the agent is an unknown and little or no publicity has been given to the mission, the credentials will probably be necessary. But if the agent's relationship to the Executive is well established he may not have any papers of introduction or, if he has them, he may not be expected or required to show them.

Colonel House received letters of introduction to the President of France and the King of England as well as to the Kaiser from President Wilson. Harry Hopkins likewise received one for King George VI and for Premier Stalin.[2] The same was true of Sumner Welles' trip to European capitals in 1940 and of Wendell Willkie's visit to England and Russia on his world tour in 1942.[3] House and Hopkins did not always show their letters, but because of the lack of formality of such missions and the non-existence of any established procedures for the presentation of such letters, it was not really necessary to present them.

It seems clear from the above that a form of the *agréation* is sometimes followed. At least it can be seen that in most instances the receiving State was notified of the missions. This being so the possibility of refusing to accept the agent would be inherent in the power of the receiving State. Although he cites no specific cases Rivier takes the same position.

> Si ces agents sont introduits officiellement auprès du gouvernement, ce n'est pas au moyen de lettres de créance, mais par de simples lettres de recommandation ou provision en général, et à défaut d'obligations particulières, le gouvernement est libre de ne les point accueillir.[4]

In Sandström's Report to the International Law Commission he points out quite appropriately that a form of the *agréation* is followed in sending special agents. But the difference in the practice followed

[1] Hackworth, *Digest*, *op. cit.*, IV, 413–14.

[2] The Diary of Edward M. House, February 12, 1915, VI, 34, Yale University Library (hereinafter cited as "House Diary"); Sherwood, *op. cit.*, pp. 232, 321.

[3] Louis Koenig, *The Presidency and the Crisis*, (New York: Kings Crown Press, 1944), p. 24; *New York Times*, August 22, 1942.

[4] Alphonse Rivier, *Principes du Droit des Gens*, (Paris: Librairie Nouvelle de Droit et de Jurisprudence, 1896) I, 156.

between regular and special agents, he notes, is that when a regular diplomatic mission is established no mention is made of the persons who will constitute the mission. Although the Rapporteur does not indicate why, it is clear that the reason is that the mission, being permanent, is expected to continue even after the initial agents are no longer a part of it. However, with regard to the special mission, its establishment is generally synonomous with that of the agent who is sent, and in all probability will terminate with the cessation of his functioning.[1]

At the Commission's 565th meeting Sir Gerald Fitzmaurice likewise took the view that an agreement exists in the establishment of such missions that they must be mutually acceptable.[2] It was, however, argued that it is perfectly reasonable to assume that a State may agree to accept a special mission, but that it may not necessarily be willing to receive a particular special agent. This could develop as a result of a disagreement at the outset, or because the agent's name, for one reason or another, was not revealed until after an agreement had been reached regarding the establishment of the mission. Thus it was generally agreed by the members of the ILC that acceptance of the mission and a form of the *agrément* were necessary i.e. that they could be withheld.[3]

Several other factors can be adduced from this. First, just as the receiving State does not have to accept the establishment of the mission nor the agent, so likewise could it object to a certain category or class of individual. Mr. Bartos of Yugoslavia said his country had not permitted men from the military services of West Germany to enter his country on a mission which had an acceptable objective.[4] Though the draft report contained no such provision it seemed like a logical extension of the above principles and therefore brought forth no protest.

Second, if a State had the right to refuse to accept an agent, it likewise should have the right to declare him *persona non grata* even if the decision had originally been to accept him. Almost all delegates at the ILC meeting accepted the view that the receiving State had the right to declare a special agent *persona non grata*.[5]

1 "*Ad Hoc* Diplomacy," A/CN.4/129, *op. cit.*, p. 5.

2 Yearbook of the International Law Commission, 1960, vol. 1, Summary Records of the Twelfth Session, A/CN.4/SER. A/1960, p. 261.

3 *Ibid.*, pp. 271–2.

4 *Ibid.*, p. 274.

5 *Ibid.*, pp. 273–75; "Ad Hoc Diplomacy," A/CN.4/129, *op. cit.*, art. 3.

Third, the very nature of a special mission is such that frequently the sending State may want its agent to travel to more than one State. This would be particularly true if the objective of the mission was of an exploratory nature e.g. fact-finding. The question arose at the ILC meeting whether one of the receiving States could object to the agent, even though it accepted the purpose of the mission, on the grounds that he had visited some other State. Delegates from several States, notably Yugoslavia and the Soviet Union, took the view that objection by receiving States on this matter should be valid, whereas others, notably Mexico and, interestingly, Iran argued against this. Mr. Matene-Daftary, from Iran, pointed out that exceptionable situations such as the Arab-Israel conflict could not be used to derive a rule which if applied, would make "the very institution of *ad hoc* diplomacy ... meaningless." [1]

Other agents have received letters that are most unusual. For example, Edmund Roberts was appointed by President Jackson in 1832 to act as a roving envoy in the region of the Indian Ocean in order to get commercial rights with the various local authorities. He was given "blank letters" and was authorized to make one out to the Emperor of Japan if he found the prospects of opening trade favorable.[2] As was mentioned earlier, James Blount's letter carried with it the statement that his authority was paramount to that of the regularly accredited agent, Stevens.[3]

Averell Harriman, who was sent on a special mission to England in 1941, carried a letter of introduction to Prime Minister Churchill in which the President referred to Harriman as one in whom he was "'reposing trust and confidence [and who will] act as my personal representative in all matters relating to the facilitation of material to the British Empire and to expedite the provision of such assistance by the United States.'" [4]

Another unusual letter was that given to Byron Price by President Truman. Price was sent to Germany as Truman's "personal representative in charge of public relations between American occupation forces and the German people." [5] In his letter was the statement, "You are hereby authorized to visit any place you deem necessary for this purpose." The letter continued, "At the end of your assignment, the

[1] Yearbook of the International Law Commission, 1960, *op. cit.*, vol. 1, p. 273.
[2] Flanders, *op. cit.*, pp. 181–82.
[3] Wriston, *op. cit.*, p. 293.
[4] *New York Times*, March 18, 1941.
[5] *Ibid.*, August 31, 1945.

duration of which you yourself will determine, I request you to submit to me your report and recommendations." [1] This is one of the most far-reaching grants of authority any agent has received so far as is known to this writer, and exceeds in scope even that of Robert's described above.

Another mission which was unusual and in which the agent carried a letter different from others was that of Robert H. Jackson. He was "designated to act as the Representative of the United States and as its Chief of Council in preparing and prosecuting charges of atrocity and war crimes against such of the leaders of European Axis Powers and their principal agents and accessories as the United States may agree with any of the United Nations to bring to trial before an international military tribunal ..." [2]

It should be pointed out that there is no significant difference between the letters given to special agents without diplomatic rank, and those given to such agents with rank. For example, Myron Taylor who held the personal rank of ambassador had one similar to Hopkins.

Beginning in 1940, Taylor was President Roosevelt's representative to the Vatican. This was one of the most controversial of missions. When Taylor held his first audience with the Pope, a ceremony which was very similar to that followed by the regular diplomats was adopted. He presented a letter in Roosevelt's handwriting which defined his mission. In this letter Roosevelt wrote, "I shall be happy to feel that he may be the channel of communication for any views you and I may wish to exchange in the interest of concord among the peoples of the world." Taylor's own letter contained the same idea with the further request that he pass on all pertinent information which he considered would serve the best interests of the United States.[3] One may note that the expected performance here is identical to that of the regular diplomat.

Frank Corrigan had the rank of Envoy Extraordinary and Minister Plenipotentiary.[4] His letter informed him that he was to work with representatives of Costa Rica and Venezuela in tendering "'good offices to the Governments of Honduras and Nicaragua with the object of facilitating a pacific solution of the controversy which has arisen between them over the definition of their common boundary.'" [5]

Edwin W. Pauley also was given the rank of Ambassador as the

[1] *Ibid.*
[2] Executive Order No. 9547, *Federal Register*, X, 4961.
[3] *New York Times*, February 28, 1940.
[4] Hackworth, *Digest*, *op. cit.*, IV, 414.
[5] MS Department of State, file 715.1715/930, cited *ibid.*

personal representative of former President Truman. His mission took him to Moscow as the American representative of the Allied Reparations Commission. The President's letter informed the bearer that he was designated

> to act as my personal representative, with the rank of ambassador, to represent and assist me in exploring, developing and negotiating the formulae and methods for exacting reparations from the aggressor nations in the current year. In this matter you will represent me in dealing with the other interested nations ... I wish you to represent the United States and me personally, as a member of that commission. In all matters within your jurisdiction you will report to me personally and directly.[1]

It will be observed from those cases cited that the phraseology and the uses of the letters given to special agents varies considerably, but in establishing the purpose and the powers of the agent the letters are not significantly different and in this respect are very similar to letters of credence given to the regular agent and signed by the President. In fact on one occasion when the President was reported to have been reluctant to authorize the mission personally, the agent refused to accept the assignment until he did so in a letter.[2]

Privileges and Immunities

Probably the most important aspect of any attempt to evaluate the international law status of special agents would be the extent to which, if any, they are entitled to the privileges and immunities accorded to regular diplomats. There has, unfortunately, not been a degree of attention paid to this matter sufficient to provide a well-established consensus. What is required, therefore, is an examination of the opinions of foreign offices, decisions of municipal courts, and opinions of scholars. Some of these opinions and decisions are vague, others are presented clearly but lack supporting evidence. In the latter category, of course, much of the discussion is normative.

The uncertainty of the picture of the special agent has been lamented by several authorities over many years. As far back as 1927 the United States Department of State replied to the League of Nations' survey on "Questions Which Appear Ripe for International Codification" that "it might be well to give particular attention to the

[1] *New York Times*, April 28, 1945.

[2] *Ibid.*, January 23, 1947. The agent was Herbert Hoover who was sent on an economic mission to Europe. Hoover was one agent who was reported never to have accepted any pay for his special missions.

situation of representatives on special missions or representing their country at a Congress or Conference." [1]

Writing shortly after this Sir Cecil Hurst pointed out that so many special missions had been created since World War I that it was becoming increasingly difficult to determine who were and who were not deserving of diplomatic status. Attached to his observation was a warning that "a large increase in the number of persons entitled to diplomatic immunity is an evil from the point of view of the local administration ... Its duty to its own nationals obliges it [the State] to refrain from acquiescing in any undue growth in the number of those who are acknowledged to be entitled to the privilege." [2] This stress upon the administrative difficulties and the problems of justice to one's own citizens which have to be faced when a large number of envoys seek the privileges and immunities of a diplomat is frequently made. It was in fact the very issue alluded to by the Swiss government in its reply to the League of Nations questionnaire on "Questions Ripe for Codification" when it said that the large number of agents claiming immunities stems from the liberal issuance of diplomatic passports.[3] But Hurst's would appear to be a view which places the cart before the horse. Although it cannot be denied that if the number who are entitled to such consideration is large there may well be a corresponding increase in the problems of local courts and public authorities. This is not and should not be, however, the criterion upon which the decision to the question of who is entitled to privileges and immunities rests.

More recently David Deener has touched upon this problem also. In his analysis of the Department of State's position in the Coplon and Gubitchev case he points out that there still exists "a problem of clarifying and co-ordinating the procedural requirements for establishing entitlement to immunity. Other continuing problems revealed in postwar court decisions concern variations with regard to the particular categories of personnel entitled to immunity, and also with regard to the degree of immunity [to be] accorded." [4]

Perhaps the most recent statement regarding this difficulty is that of Clyde Eagleton written shortly before his death. Eagleton was a very keen observer of international affairs and aware of the growing complexity which they had assumed. It is perhaps only natural that

[1] League of Nations, "Report to the Council," C 196.M.70 1927 V. *op. cit.*, p. 248.
[2] Hurst, "Diplomatic Immunities – Modern Developments," *op. cit.*, p. 5.
[3] League of Nations, "Report to the Council," C 196.M.70. 1927 V. *op. cit.*, p. 248.
[4] David R. Deener, "Some Problems of the Law of Diplomatic Immunity," *American Journal of International Law*, L (1956), 117–18.

he should have referred to one of the major reasons why special agents have become increasingly used in recent years, and to have stressed that states have been reluctant to agree on their status.

> The increase in the number and type of national agents abroad produces a disinclination on the part of states to extend further the peculiar privileges of a diplomat; it is often true that an agent sent by a state on a specific mission performs more important functions than the agent accredited as a diplomat. On the whole, the tendency seems to be to decrease the privileges as well as the number of those to whom these privileges belong – though increasing activity constantly swells the number.[1]

Foreign office views – So far as the foreign offices are concerned, the information which has been uncovered leads one to conclude that they are generally reluctant to go on record in favor of granting any specific immunities or privileges. This is readily understandable. Until states are able to get fairly widespread agreement at closed meetings on what they are willing to grant other states regarding unsettled issues of international law, they are going to be very cautious in their discussion of such issues. And what they are willing to grant usually is closely related to what they think they will receive in the way of considerations. Hence these unsettled issues are often a matter of negotiation in which each party endeavors to obtain at least a modicum of advantages for itself.

Nevertheless a number of foreign offices have, through correspondence or in other ways, provided some indication of their governments' position regarding the status of the special agent. Almost all of them indicated that they do not believe special agents *per se* have the status of a diplomatic envoy. Thus, consideration given to them beyond that accorded to any foreign visitor would have to be provided on an individual basis and extended on the basis of reciprocity.

When the Swiss government replied to the League of Nations questionnaire referred to above, it ventured the opinion that it would be desirable to examine the status to be given to those agents "who, though not actually holding permanent credentials like diplomatic agents, nevertheless have a diplomatic standing and may accordingly claim diplomatic perogatives [*sic*] independent of any treaty." [2] Unfortunately the reply contained no inkling by example or definition of whether the government was speaking of the whole category of special

[1] Clyde Eagleton, *International Government* (3rd ed.; New York: Ronald Press Co., 1957), p. 147. It will be seen that the data gathered in this study do not completely support this conclusion.

[2] League of Nations, "Report to the Council," C 196.M.70. 1927 V. *op. cit.*, p. 248.

agents or whether it had in mind only those who are on official state missions of a temporary nature.

The German reply, on the other hand, was much more traditional. After supporting the need to study this problem it suggested that the question of what persons have privileges and immunities and to what extent the immunities would exist "must be decided in each particular case." [1] More recently the German ministry of Justice reiterated its belief that a general rule of international law does not exist which grants immunities to special agents. It admitted the right of exterritoriality would exist under special circumstances, e.g. when he travels with his Chief of State or represents his State during ministerial visits.

> Eine allgemeine Regel des Völkerrechts, die den privaten Sonderbeauftragten des fremden Staatsoberhaupts *schlechthin* diplomatische Vorrechte gewährt, dürfte nicht bestehen. Jedoch wird ein solcher Sonderbeauftragter nach allgemeinen völkerrechtlichen Grundsätzen als Exterritorialer anzusehen sein wenn besondere Voraussetzungen vorliegen, so wenn er im Gefolge des Staatsoberhaupts reist oder wenn er als Vertreter des fremden Staates bei Ministerbesuchen oder bei Staatsbesprechungen auftritt.[2]

Further correspondence with the German government has revealed that no decisions or informal agreements have ever been reached in or by the Foreign Office. However the Chief of Protocol was willing to offer a personal opinion. He felt that the use of special agents has not become a practice sufficiently widespread to warrant a conclusion that a custom was growing regarding the status of the special agent. (Presumably he is here referring only to German use and reception of them.) And he further concluded that there has not arisen a large enough number of critical problems to have created an extensive literature.[3]

Of course there are many examples of special missions of one or more persons sent for different purposes, often along commercial lines, in which the status of the agents is specified by agreement between the sender and receiver. Thus, Oppenheim points out, agents who are not diplomatic representatives, who are sent to "transact business in a foreign state are occasionally granted a degree of diplomatic immunity. This has been the case, for instance, with various Trade Delegations acting on behalf of the Soviet Government." [4] This practice has been a fairly common one but it does not indicate anything other

[1] *Ibid.*, p. 135.
[2] Ministry of Justice, German Federal Republic, Correspondence, April 21, 1958.
[3] Chief of Protocol, German Federal Republic, Correspondence, September 16, 1958.
[4] Oppenheim, *op. cit.*, 8th ed., I, 827.

than that States, on occasion, have been willing to bestow a privileged status on non-diplomats. Such a practice has by no means yet become universal and it would be unwise to generalize from these special agreements.

Although the British have been willing to conclude such agreements they would probably be the first to deny that it represents any established practice. In correspondence with the writer the British Foreign Office indicates that special agents (not covered by written agreements) do not have the character of accredited diplomats and are not a part of the category of persons considered entitled to diplomatic privileges and immunities by the courts or granted such by statute. Therefore, the government states, "it follows that the nature and extent of the facilities to be accorded to them cannot be expressed with any certainty.[1]

The picture painted by the Embassy of the Republic of China did not contain any developed or detailed examination, but implicit in their statement was likewise the viewpoint that such agents did not have any rights that are based upon international law.[2] The same may be said of the French government's position.[3]

Officials of the Soviet Union have stated their position quite frankly. "Soviet law and regulations do not contain any general provisions concerning the status of 'special agents' of Chiefs of States." [4]

It may be noted here that in correspondence and discussion with officials of foreign governments they have insisted that their Executives would not lightly bypass their foreign service career officers. This is probably correct but one would also have to acknowledge that the practice of such Executives has not been given any thorough study by foreign scholars. Hence the possibility is raised that it may have existed to a greater extent than is realized. For example, one would have to investigate the numerous missions of Sir Stafford Cripps of England to India in April, 1942, to the United States, September, 1948, and to Italy, April, 1949. Likewise the mission of Lord Philby. Also that of Leon Blum to the United States in March, 1946, and Jean Monnet to the United States in March ,1946, March, 1948, May, 1953 and January, 1958. Admittedly they may not all reflect missions comparable to

[1] British Foreign Office, Correspondence, September 4, 1958.

[2] Embassy of the Republic of China, Washington, D.C., Correspondence, September 4, 1958.

[3] French Embassy, Washington, D.C., Correspondence, October 13, 1958.

[4] Embassy of the Union of Soviet Socialist Republics, Washington, D.C., Correspondence, November 3, 1958.

those under discussion here, but they indicate that other states do use special missions, some of which may be similar to those of concern to this study.

The position of the United States on this subject needs the most careful consideration. More than any other state it has used special agents. Its common use of them can probably be partly attributed to our Constitutional requirements which place more restrictions upon the Executive's choice of regular diplomatic envoys than are generally found in other states. It probably also is partly the result of the "Topsy-like" way in which our foreign service grew. The use of special agents has increased the President's freedom of action and one would expect, therefore, to find our Executive relying upon it fairly often.

So far as American agents are concerned the Department of State's position is that they have no right to expect privileges or immunities under international law. "In the absence of treaty or other international agreements, the United States has no general expectation that a foreign government will accord diplomatic privileges and immunities to a person who may be denominated a 'special agent of the President.'" [1] And what of the status of agents who come to the United States from abroad? The position would be the same – they would not be accorded diplomatic privileges and immunities "in the absence of statute or treaty or other international obligation." [2]

Secretary of State John Quincy Adams in a note to Mr. Aguirre of Buenos Ayres dated August 27, 1818, stated with regard to this very issue, "No person has ever presented himself from your Government with the credentials or commission of a public minister. Those which you have exhibited give you the express character of agent only, which neither by the law of nations nor by those of the United States confers the privilege of exemption from personal arrest." [3] Secretary of State Blaine in instructions to Totten, April 12, 1881, took the same view. "A 'political agent' sent as such by a Foreign Government to the United States, is not to be regarded as [*sic*] a diplomatic character, even though he is at the same time consul-general." [4]

Further indication that at least in the United States the special agent may not generally receive the privileges and immunities of the regular agent is found in the statement by Under Secretary of State

[1] Department of State, Correspondence, August 9, 1958.

[2] *Ibid.*

[3] MS Notes to Foreign Legations, II, 327, cited in Moore, *Digest, op. cit.*, IV, 441.

[4] Francis Wharton, *A Digest of the International Law of the United States* (Washington: Government Printing Office, 1886), p. 625.

Polk to the Attorney-General regarding the claim of diplomatic status by one Ludwig C. A. Martens of the Russian Soviet of Federated Socialist Republics. "It appears that although the right of legation is accorded full Sovereign States and may be, in a limited sense, accorded to Semi-Sovereign States ... a deposed Sovereign or a community recognized as a belligerent can act only through political agents, who are not entitled to diplomatic privileges." [1]

If these agents cannot lay claim to the privileges and immunities of a diplomat, does it follow then that they will be considered as nothing more than visiting aliens? In other words do the foreign offices conclude that inasmuch as such agents are not entitled to diplomatic status that they may expect no special consideration? Clearly this is not so. From the British point of view and reflective, therefore, of their practice,

Certain facilities can be afforded by the appropriate administrative authorities within the limits of their administrative authority, as and when occasion arises. In practice these facilities might include the grant of material privileges and exemptions (other than those needing the sanction of statutory authority) to a extent regarded as necessary in the particular circumstances to enable the agent to discharge his functions. The question of immunity from jurisdiction would be, however, for the courts themselves to decide should the need to do so arise.[2]

For the Republic of China the treatment provided special agents is not predicated so much on a functional basis, although this may very well enter into the decision in an indirect way, as, apparently, on the basis of the considerations others will give to Chinese agents. "On the basis of reciprocity, the rights and privileges enjoyed by foreign special agents in the Republic of China are similar to those which are accorded special agents of the Republic of China in the United States." [3]

The Canadian Department of External Affairs apparently takes the same approach. It replies that there are no regulations covering such missions but that the government attempts "to be guided by international usage." [4] In further correspondence with the writer the government has stated that

the special agent would be granted a diplomatic or at least a courtesy visa. If he enters Canada on a diplomatic visa he will be accorded the same treatment as that given to persons of diplomatic rank, i.e., he will not be subject to customs

[1] MS Department of State, file 701.611/648, cited in Hackworth, *Digest*, *op. cit.*, IV, 415

[2] British Foreign Office, Correspondence, *op. cit.*, To be noted here is the emphasis on the functional approach, discussed above.

[3] Embassy of the Republic of China, Correspondence, *op. cit.*

[4] Canadian Department of External Affairs, Correspondence, March 10, 1958.

and immigration inspection. The same privileges are accorded to holders of courtesy visas as a matter of grace.[1]

The government further stated

that any special agent representing the head of a foreign state would receive every proper courtesy during his stay in Canada. In short, we can foresee no difficulty in assuring such an agent of a status analogous to that of a diplomatic envoy on an administrative basis, once he is issued with an appropriate visa.[2]

When special agents are sent to France "the usual practice is to grant to [them] during their stay in France, the status of diplomatic envoy, provided that the latter has given its agreement." Presumably this means that when a state sends such an agent to France, the agent will receive diplomatic status if his state so wishes. Once again the basis for such treatment is "international courtesy, and under conditions of reciprocity ..." The French government assumes that any such agents she sent abroad "under the same conditions would receive ... the same privileges and immunities." [3]

The United States position seems to parallel that of the British. It does not reflect a concern for reciprocal treatment, although this, perhaps, would not be overlooked, nor does it suggest the significance of function only. Rather it places its position on a combination of the latter plus that of representation. The Department of State's reply to the question of what it would expect in the way of considerations for American agents and what it would accord others was, "The United States would expect that such a person, when within the jurisdiction of a foreign state, would be accorded courteous treatment taking into consideration the personality of the 'agent' and the nature of the 'mission' upon which he is engaged." The same courtesy would be extended "to special agents of foreign governments." [4]

The Soviet Union, though it has made no provision by statute for special executive agents, does nevertheless give them full consideration. Referring to American agents such as Hopkins and Averell Harriman the Soviet Government said:

When such "special agents" ... arrived in the U.S.S.R. the Soviet authorities proceeded from the fact that they enjoy privileges and immunities, similar to those of a diplomat, with regard to entering and leaving a country, inviolability of the person as well as privacy of personal papers, luggage and resi-

[1] *Ibid.*, September 25, 1958.
[2] *Ibid.*
[3] French Embassy, Correspondence, October 13, 1958.
[4] Department of State, Correspondence, August 9, 1958.

dence. "Special agents" as representatives of Chiefs of States were accorded appropriate honorary privileges. They were not included in the list of the Diplomatic Corps.[1]

This is perhaps one of the most forthright statements that any of the governments provided and makes crystal clear just what status special agents have had in the Soviet Union.

The German Foreign Office writes that should the question of treatment of special agents arise, it would take the position *with all due emphasis* that the agent be accorded as a matter of international courtesy privileges and immunities to the extent necessary under the circumstances of the case.

Solange sich daher die von den einzelnen Staaten geübte Praxis noch nicht zu einem allgemein anerkannten völkerrechtlichen Grundsatz verdichtet hat, würde das auswärtige Amt – sollte ein praktischer Fall dringlich werden – sich mit allem Nachdruck dafür einsetzen, das dem "special agent" Immunität und Privilegien in dem nach Lage des Falles erforderlichen Umfang auf Grund der international üblichen Courtoisie gewährt werden.[2]

Although many of the prominent writers of international law spend much time discussing the status of delegates to international congresses and conferences, the letter continues, they tend to ignore the status of special agents. If one accords immunities and privileges to such delegates it would only seem right, the writer maintains, to provide the same treatment to personal agents.

Wenn man, wie es diese Schriftsteller tun, den Delegierten bei internationalen Konferenzen und Kongressen Immunitäten und Privilegien zubilligt, wird man nach meiner Auffassung die persönlichen Abgesandten wohl gleich behandeln müssen.[3]

This letter, possibly more than those of any of the other government officials, gets at one of the most significants aspects of the use of special agents – their relationship to the Executive. The official notes that inasmuch as the person is chosen as a special agent by the Chief of State, it is a clear indication that he enjoys a position of special confidence in the carrying out of a mission for his superior. This should then give him a very high position, one which by far exceeds that of even a foreigner of distinction. "Damit erhält er *eo ipso* einen sehr hohen Rang eigener Art, der weit über die Bedeutung des Ranges hinausgeht, den ein einfacher 'étranger de distinction' geniesst." [4]

[1] Embassy of the Union of Soviet Socialist Republics, Correspondence, *op. cit.*
[2] Chief of Protocol, German Federal Republic, Correspondence, September 16, 1958.
[3] *Ibid.*
[4] *Ibid.*

The German government revealed that there is, if the case so warrants, a device which makes it possible to facilitate border crossing by prominent foreigners into the Federal Republic. All diplomatic representatives of the Republic abroad are empowered to issue to such travelers recommendations for border crossing which involves a preferred treatment so far as border crossing formalities are concerned, e.g., passport, inspection, car inspection, clearance of goods for levying of duties.

Decisions of courts – Let us turn now to those views expressed in court decisions. It is to be expected that there would not be a large number of cases dealing with the subject due to the care which agents would normally exercise in their activities as well as to the fact that their missions are usually brief, allowing little time for problems which might be associated with residence. Although they do not deal with the special agents who are the subject of inquiry of this study, the cases are concerned with special missions and are of value because of the analogy they present to executive special agents.

One case of which we may take note because of its interest as well as its applicability was *Taco Mesdag* c *Heyermans*. In this case the defendant was the official representative of the Dutch government for the fine arts section of the Brussels International Exposition of 1897. The plaintiff had entered a picture in the Exposition and after acceptance the defendant ordered it to be removed. To the suit for damages the defendant pled diplomatic immunity based upon the fact that he was a government agent and upon the laws of Belgium, which forbade any action against agents of foreign governments without fulfillment of certain specific procedural requirements. The Court of Brussels having upheld the defendant the appellant appealed to the Cour de Cassation, May 23, 1898. This highest court overruled the lower court's decision accepting the argument that agents who are purely administrative, whose powers are narrowly limited, and whose missions are more in the nature of applying and fulfilling instructions than of deliberating and advising, are not clothed with diplomatic immunity.[1]

In the *Affaire Gravenhoff*, the defendant, after expulsion from France, returned to Russia which, at the time, was under the Kerensky regime. He was sent by the latter to France as a delegate of the Russian Ministry of Commerce. In this capacity he carried a diplomaticpassport and visa, the latter signed by the French Embassy in Petrograd and

[1] Heyermans, *op. cit.*, p. 618.

countersigned by the French Foreign Office in Paris. When he was arrested on grounds of a violation of the expulsion order he pleaded lack of jurisdiction by the Court on the grounds of diplomatic immunity. The tribunal ruled that he had no such immunity because the mission itself was not one in which the inherent rights of a diplomatic mission existed, "attendu que la simple mission de delegué du Ministère de commerce russe, qu'il y a lieu de tenir pour constante, ne saurait conférer au prévenu les privilèges de ladite immunité, comme en bénéficient notamment les chargés d'affaires dûment accrédités." [1]

In the Fenton Textile Association case a different kind of problem was considered. Britain had granted *de facto* recognition to the Soviet Union and had signed a Trade Agreement with her on March 16, 1921. This agreement contained a definition of the status of the Russian members of the trade mission while in Britain and specifically mentioned immunity from arrest and search. Krassin, who was the chief official of the mission, became involved in a civil suit. He maintained that his status provided immunity from civil process. Upon inquiry the court learned not only of his position but also that the Foreign Office even discussed other matters with him in addition to those concerning his mission. It also was informed that his name had not been carried on the diplomatic list due to the lack of full recognition of his government. The court ruled that neither the agreement nor the discussions of various matters between Krassin and the Foreign Office conferred diplomatic immunity, and that his capacity was "insufficient to carry with it immunity accorded to accredited and recognized representatives of foreign States." [2]

Despite the decision it is interesting to take note of the dicta of Lord Justice Scrutten who sat on the case. His views, if followed, would surely have altered the position the Court took in this and other cases. "It is sufficient to say that so long as our government negotiates with a person as representing a recognized foreign state about matters of concern as between nation and nation, without further definition of his position, I am inclined to think that such representative may be entitled to immunity ..." [3] Here again there is the argument that negotiation, i.e., function is the crucial factor.

It plays the same importance in the *Turkish Inspector of Students* case. In this case the Tax Commission of Switzerland argued that "the

[1] *L'Affaire Gravenhoff, op. cit.*, p. 1183.

[2] *Fenton Textile Association Ltd.* v. *Krassin and Others, Times Law Reports*, XXXVIII, (1921), 259.

[3] *Ibid.*

quality of ... a special representative is to be recognized only when the functions with which the person concerned is entrusted by the foreign State fall within the category of functions of a minister or consul." [1] The Commission seemed to say that although the Inspector would not have his claim for immunity supported by it, he could present a case with the probability of success if he did perform duties and functions akin to those of a diplomat (or apparently even a consul!).

Recently the United States Court of Appeals for the District of Columbia had to deal with this general problem. Trost, an Assistant Commissioner for Shipping and Immigration of the Royal Yugoslav Government was a member of an agency with which the United States government had no connection, the Interallied Shipping Pool. He put forth a claim of diplomatic immunity as a bar to a suit for possession of his rented premises. The Court, denying his right to diplomatic immunity, held, "The generally accepted limitation to the rule of diplomatic immunity is that it extends only to ambassadors or ministers who are the representatives of one state to another." [2] Citing the decision in *U.S.* v. *Deutsches Kalisyndikat Gesellschaft*, the court continued, "[diplomatic] immunity has not been extended to ... any officers, agents or employees of a foreign sovereign ruler or sovereign state other than those entrusted to negotiate between foreign states such as ambassadors and other diplomatic representatives of the foreign state. *It has never been held that everyone acting on behalf* of a foreign state enjoys immunity from suit."[3]

The most recent case, and possibly the one in which the question of immunities for those other than the regular diplomat was most thoroughly discussed is *U.S.* v. *Coplon and Gubitchev*.[4] In situations like this where the claim to diplomatic immunity is raised, the court noted that it can accept it only if warranted by express treaty provisions, or if the party is a member of a permanent diplomatic mission. The Court quoted Halsbury as its source of authority in the matter and thereby implicitly ruled out the possibility of a claim to diplomatic immunity based solely on function. Thus it rejected Gubitchev's claim to diplomatic status on the grounds that

he was on a mission of a non-diplomatic nature. The Soviet Union itself has recognized that its personnel on missions of a non-diplomatic character may

[1] *Re the Turkish Inspector of Students*, Case No. 80, *Annual Digest* (1946), p. 177.
[2] *Trost* v. *Tompkins*, 44 A 2d, 226, October 11, 1945.
[3] *Ibid.*, my emphasis.
[4] 88 Fed. Supp. 915.

acquire diplomatic privileges and immunities only by express treaty provisions and attachment to a permanent diplomatic mission ...

Where "a person is sent by a foreign government as a special diplomatic representative for a temporary purpose, without being authorized or received by the Sovereign as an ambassador or public minister, recourse must be had to the terms of the special agreement governing his mission and the extent of diplomatic privileges determined therefrom as a question of fact."[1]

Opinions of scholars – From the scholars who have touched upon this subject, and unfortunately few have made any careful analysis of it, have come several interesting points which merit examination. Those who have written, however, have not attempted to buttress their positions with any documentation or reasoning assiduously developed from theoretical principles. Some have taken a more forthright position than others. Most have approved of giving certain special considerations to these agents in some cases tantamount to limited privileges and immunities.

Raoul Genet has taken as firm a position as any in his interpretation of their status. Although they may be assigned different kinds of missions, he says, "they have no diplomatic status."

Les agents privés d'un chef d'Etat, comme ceux envoyés dans des intentions de politique personnelle ou dynastique, ou encore pour le règlement d'affaires personnelles, ne pourront jamais revêter le charactère public; ils ne relèvent à aucun titre du droit diplomatique.[2]

This is all Genet provides in his commentary but it is a position with which most other scholars are in accord. Many of them, however, have given some additional thought to the considerations to which special agents might be entitled. For the moment let us merely examine their viewpoints on the status of such agents as they perceive it.

Joseph Kunz agrees that special agents are not diplomats and "enjoy, therefore, no diplomatic privileges and immunities. ... The practice of States has developed no particular rules, as far as special privileges to be granted to them are concerned." [3]

Over a century ago Von Martens took the same stand although it is not clear whether he had the same kinds of agents in mind. He referred to "Agents of private affairs" (a rather strange title) as "agents [who] carry with them no credentials but letters of recommendation," a description which would certainly fit the special executive agent. But he gave as examples "agents resident, counsellors of legation, and titular

[1] 6 Halsbury's Laws of England, 509, cited *ibid.*

[2] Raoul Genet, *Traité de Diplomatie et de Droit Diplomatique* (Paris: Revue Générale de Droit International Public, 1931), I, 83.

[3] Joseph Kunz, Correspondence, April 14, 1958.

agents," examples which seem to imply a somewhat different category of persons. At any rate, he held that they "are all excluded from the rank, title, and privileges of ministers," and added in a telling and amusing note, "If sometimes, in little states, they are indulged with immunities of jurisdiction, or of imposts, we ought not, on that account, to look upon such immunities as their due." [1]

It is interesting that about 100 years later Sir Cecil Hurst wrote in the same vein. He did not feel that even to the extent that a practice existed by which such agents got special considerations, that this gave them an entitlement to immunities. Any special facilities could only be accorded on the basis of courtesy, he believed. Sir Cecil was one of the few who discussed this in conjunction with a particular special agent in mind, an agent who was an outstanding representative of this category, and whom he knew personally – Colonel House.

> Des affaires plus modernes établissent que le simple délégué d'un gouvernement étranger qui réside sur le territoire d'un autre pays n'a pas droit aux immunités ... les agents non-officiels des gouvernements étrangers n'ont aucune prétention de droit aux immunités diplomatiques. Si des facilités spéciales leur sont accordées, c'est une affaire de courtoisie et non pas de droit.
>
> Il n'est pas probable que les gouvernements des pays qu'a visités le Colonel House pendant la guerre de 1914–1918 auraient essayé de le soumettre à leur juridiction; néanmoins cette immunité aurait eu pour fondement la courtoisie et non point le droit puisque le Colonel House n'était pas un représentant officiel des Etats-Unis.[2]

All of these views are very much in harmony with that of Bishop who points out that "even holding a diplomatic passport and performing some diplomatic functions does not appear to result in a legal obligation to accord diplomatic privileges and immunities." It is therefore his opinion that special agents "are *not* as a matter of international law right (and duty) entitled to diplomatic status with the accompanying privileges and immunities ... These seem to result only from being sent as a diplomatic representative, and *received as such.*" [3] It is clear that Bishop places his emphasis on the Executive's right to make the determination, although he feels that the opinion of the sending state as well as of the receiving state must be taken into consideration. Clearly this would be the case for the regular envoy as well. All members of the diplomatic corps can only receive their privileges and immunities in this way.

According to Calvo, because they are not a part of the diplomatic corps

[1] G. F. Von Martens, *The Law of Nations*, trans. William Cobbett (4th ed.; London: William Cobbett, 1824), p. 209.

[2] Sir Cecil Hurst, "Les Immunités Diplomatiques," *Recueil Des Cours*, XII (1926), 154–55.

[3] William W. Bishop, Jr., Correspondence, May 19, 1958.

agents sent abroad "pour régler certaines affaires particulières de l'État ou d'un souverain" do not enjoy any of the immunities of the mission.[1]

Sir Neville Bland (author of Satow's *Guide to Diplomatic Practice*) has communicated his position, and although he was a member of Her Majesty's Government and, therefore, perhaps should not be included here, his views were solicited and offered on a personal basis. These views appear to have been derived after much deliberation, and therefore merit careful consideration.

Though legal immunities of diplomatic agents are established in the common law, and their privileges by statute or by administrative act, the immunities and privileges of other specified classes of individuals (officials of international organization, delegates to conferences, etc.) are provided for by statute, but outside those classes, there is no obligation, other than that of courtesy to grant any special consideration to foreign visitors, however eminent.[2]

The similarity of this to the Foreign Office statement cited above [3] is obvious. And, of course, it was intended to reflect the British position. Hyde, on the other hand, reflects the United States position and the similarity of this with that of the British will be apparent.

From Hyde's viewpoint it is not a question of whether such agents are entitled to immunities based on whether they are or are not diplomats. The non-diplomats may likewise have jurisdictional immunities. This will be true because they fall into one of two categories. On the one hand some, such as attachés, will have them because of their close association with a diplomatic mission. Others, not associated with such missions, will likewise have these immunities, but in their case "it is to conventional arrangements rather than to a practice as yet assignable to the law of nations pertaining to diplomatic usages that must be ascribed such concessions as have been yielded." [4] So far as the United States is concerned, this author states, such agents have "not been clothed with a diplomatic character." This has been true even with regard to "commissions sent to investigate political conditions in foreign States."[5] Foster,[6] Corwin,[7] and Stuart [8] are all of the opinion that these agents have no diplomatic status.

[1] M. Charles Calvo, *Le Droit International Théorique et Pratique* (Paris: Librairie Nouvelle de Droit et de Jurisprudence, 1896), III, 192.

[2] Sir Neville Bland, Correspondence, August 5, 1958.

[3] *Supra*, pp. 123, 125

[4] Hyde, *op. cit.*, 2nd ed., II, 1233.

[5] *Ibid.*, p. 1231. As Appendix A indicates, this is an error.

[6] Foster, *The Practice of Diplomacy, op. cit.*, p. 198.

[7] Edward S. Corwin, *The Constitution and What It Means Today* (11th ed.; Princeton: Princeton University Press, 1954), p. 115.

[8] Graham H. Stuart, *American Diplomatic and Consular Practice* (2nd ed.; New York: D. Appleton Century Co., 1952). p. 147.

Oppenheim presents a somewhat more detached analysis, along the same lines, however. He says there are two kinds of special agents, public and secret. The former may be sent "for a permanency or for a limited time only. They may be sent by sovereign states, states under suzerainty and insurgents who have received belligerent status." Regardless of this, Oppenheim argues, "they are not invested with diplomatic character." [1] As this authority points out, states that fall into the last two categories have no other way of conducting personal political negotiations than by public or secret agents.[2]

At this point he goes somewhat farther than the others and concludes that although such public agents do not enjoy diplomatic privileges and immunities, "they have a public character, being admitted as public political agents of a foreign State, ... but no distinct rules concerning special privileges to be granted to such agents seem to have grown up in practice.[3]

Only one authority has approached the question from the point of establishing a test. It will be recalled that this test is one to which the court in *Trost* v. *Tompkins* referred. Ogdon raises the problem of how the question of whether a person is to be dealt with as a diplomatic officer can be resolved. He proposes that to be entitled to immunity "he must be concerned with the work of the head of the mission or the channel of communication with the government to which he is accredited." [4] This certainly would not necessarily omit the special agent. From the discussion and development of his subject as it appears in his study, it is difficult to believe that Ogdon would accept such a conclusion, however, regarding the special agent.

Bluntschli also belongs in the category now under discussion and agrees with the aforementioned scholars. Persons who have been authorized by a state or agency in order to execute certain official duties are not *bona fide* agents. They have no immunities and get only the privileges agreed upon. "Aber auf Exemption von der Gerichtsbarkeit und auf Exterritorialität haben solche Personen keinen Anspruch, wenn nicht und so weit nicht durch besondere Verguenstigung des besendeten Staates ihnen solches verstattet worden ist." [5]

Some authorities have made observations which appear to this

[1] Oppenheim, *op. cit.*, 2nd ed., I, 489.
[2] *Ibid.*
[3] *Ibid.*
[4] Ogdon, *op. cit.*, p. 204.
[5] J. C. Bluntschli, *Das Moderne Völkerrecht der Civilisierten Staaten* (Nordlingen: H. Beck, 1878), p. 155.

writer to be more liberal in their interpretations of the status of special agents, or feel that the trend is moving in such a direction as to entitle them to greater consideration. Bishop refers to what he believes is a trend "toward recognition of limited immunities, clearly distinguished from diplomatic immunities and confined chiefly to exemptions relating to official acts and official archives, which should be accorded to miscellaneous agents of one state found in the territory of another. This does not yet appear to have developed into any clear customary rule of International Law, but agreements, local statutes, and the practice of executive agencies indicate a willingness to give a special position to such foreign government employees." [1]

Because this category of agent is so varied in membership it always is difficult to be sure whether those scholars who make observations upon the status of its members all have in mind the same type of agents It is clearly possible that if an attempt were made to indicate precisely who should be on the list there would be differences of opinion. For example, Bishop referred to these people as government employees, which seems to imply that he has in mind those in the various administrative agencies of government. And yet in correspondence with this writer he clearly considers the agents with which this study is concerned to be properly included.[2] Certainly it is to be lamented that in this as well as many other subjects in law and in the social sciences the terminology is so imprecise.

It is not an ambiguity that has recently come to light, however. As far back as 1888 Heffter pointed to the same problem. He noted that that nothing was as indeterminate as the legal status of agents or special representatives who are sent to a foreign state without being characterized by diplomatic title. He established three categories of such agents: (1) agents who conduct private business such as negotiating loans and administering foreign possessions, (2) secret agents, and (3) agents without diplomatic power who are sent because conditions do not permit official exchange of representatives or because their duties are very specific. Agents in the first two categories, he believes, cannot demand diplomatic privileges. But agents in category three do have a right to diplomatic immunity, although it is not customary to give them complete rights to exterritoriality. He points out that their lack of permanency should not be a bar to immunity

[1] Bishop, *International Law*, *op. cit.*, p. 457.
[2] Bishop, Correspondence, *op. cit.*

inasmuch as the diplomatic agents of earlier times were likewise not permanent ones.[1]

It is interesting that Heffter should consider agents who negotiate loans or administer foreign possessions as being in a category which does not warrant diplomatic immunity. Perhaps the greater extent to which such practices occur today would alter his thinking. But it is even more interesting that he should point out that because some missions are not permanent we have come to think of them as inferior to regular ones which are permanent. Thus we conclude that temporary missions are not entitled to full diplomatic status without realizing that such missions were the normal practice during much of the past, and in fact are very commonplace today.

One authority who has corresponded with this writer believes that it is possible that customary international law would "in part ... apply to special agents." However, the requirements which he suggests would probably remove them from the category we have been studying. He believes that they would be covered by international law if they "are identified to the local foreign ministry [which is quite likely for most of these missions], and are included in the diplomatic list overtly or by implication [which is not likely]." [2] He continues:

> in part such agents are presumably covered by national legislation which prohibits various acts that contravene diplomatic privileges and immunity, but this again would depend upon identification in the diplomatic list ... To some extent the nature of the legal status also would depend upon the nature of the advance arrangements with the local government concerning the diplomatic activities of the special agent.[3]

Implicit in Plischke's statement, it would seem, is the view that the special agent does not come under customary international law unless he is put on the diplomatic list or unless some special arrangements are concluded between sending and receiving states. If the latter were the case he obviously could receive any considerations which the states involved desired to give him. If the former were the case his placement or not on the diplomatic list would depend upon his status, and thus we appear to have completed a circle.

In all fairness to Professor Plischke, however, we must note that one of the prominent reports on the subject of diplomatic immunities does not help to clarify the picture either. We refer here to the Harvard Law

[1] August W. Heffter, *Das Europäische Völkerrecht der Gegenwart auf den bisherigen Grundlagen* (Berlin: H. W. Müller, 1888), pp. 455–56.

[2] Elmer Plischke, Correspondence, May 20, 1958.

[3] *Ibid.* This reflects France's view.

School study discussed above. One of the primary reasons why some confusion exists is the lack of agreement on what constitutes a diplomatic agent. The study takes cognizance of this problem while at the same time it attempts to discuss the status of such agents. The category is broadened beyond the traditional conception by defining a mission as consisting of "a person or group of persons publicly sent by one state to another to perform diplomatic functions" [1] and a "member of a mission" as a "person authorized by the sending states to take part in the performance of the diplomatic functions of a mission." [2] But what are diplomatic functions? The "Comment" to Article 1 (b) says,

> Customary international law has established no standard by which diplomatic missions may clearly be distinguished in all cases from non-diplomatic missions on the basis of differences in their respective functions. The expansion of the activities entrusted to diplomatic missions and the growth in recent decades of new types of state agencies operating on foreign territory have tended to obscure the distinction between diplomatic and non-diplomatic functions.[3]

This being so, the scholars conclude, it makes no sense to attempt to determine status by function. Hence, they are of the opinion that a sounder basis for determining diplomatic status "must rest upon purely formal grounds." These formal grounds consist of investing the agent with some traditional diplomatic rank. This certainly would get away from the aspect of function as the determining factor. But the problem is not solved for the solution is, by this suggestion, thrown back upon the sending state. But the Gubitchev case indicates that the sending state cannot have the final word. Furthermore, are those who are given diplomatic rank and title to have diplomatic status? And what criterion should the sending state use in making the decision? To the first question the scholars reply not necessarily, for the receiving state can "refuse *agréation* or to acquiesce in the attachment of members in the personnel of accredited missions ... persons whose functions depart too widely from those traditionally considered to be appropriate to diplomatic activity." [4] The argument would appear to have swung full circle again for it is clear now that function will be if not the determining factor certainly of major importance. There is a further weakness in this proposal in that it suggests that the question of who gets diplomatic status should be settled by negotiation. "The

[1] Harvard Law School, *op. cit.*, Article 1 (b), p. 43.
[2] *Ibid.*, Article 1 (e), p. 46.
[3] *Ibid.*, Article 1 (b) Comment, p. 43.
[4] *Ibid.*, Article 1 (b), Comment, p. 44.

limits of the class can best be determined by agreement of the states concerned, doubtful cases being decided as they arise." [1]

It would appear, therefore, that the authors of the above study have relied upon the functional theory more than they have acknowledged or are aware, and that for whatever reasons they would not prefer an attempt to be made to establish a rule but would allow the states to make their own determinations of who gets immunity. Thus they are willing to accept the possibility, nay the probability, that great variation and confusion may continue to exist.

A further word on the question of the basis for immunity is found in Article 18 of the same work. Here again we have implied, at least, that function in a broad sense is a determining factor.

> Insofar as the member [of a mission] acts in his official capacity, his immunity confounds itself with that of the sending State, and depends, not upon the person of the representative, but upon the intrinsic nature of the act performed. ... Immunity for official acts ... applies to all public acts, by whomsoever performed, and to all State agents whether diplomatic or otherwise.[2]

We might conclude from the above, then, that special agents may or may not have diplomatic status depending upon the wishes of the sending and receiving states, and that if the former desires the agent to have same it should provide the agent with one of the traditional diplomatic grades. But if the receiving state determines, on the basis of function, that said agent should not be given diplomatic status it need not accept him in that capacity. Furthermore, whether he has diplomatic rank or not he is still entitled to immunity for his official acts.[3]

Many of the authorities referred to, though of one opinion on where the special agent stands, are of another opinion as to the treatment he is actually and/or ought to be given. So far as the practice of states is concerned, Kunz points out that even if there are no rules of law regarding such agents,

> there may be rules of "courtoisie internationale" which are not legal but conventional norms, but also strictly observed between States. In addition, political considerations will often [encourage] the foreign State, accepting such special agents with no diplomatic character, to grant them a far-reaching protection and privileges.[4]

[1] *Ibid.*, Article 1 (e), Comment, p. 46.

[2] *Ibid.*, Article 18, Comment, p. 99.

[3] *Ibid.*, Article 1 (g) gives to even "administrative personnel" a special status "because of their public character." *Ibid.*, p. 49.

[4] Kunz, Correspondence, *op. cit.*

Bland, too, emphasizes that the basis for special consideration would be courtesy. It is the "administrative machinery" which, in practice, can arrange for "material facilities." "Immunity from the jurisdiction is not so easy to guarantee, since only the courts can decide whether it can be considered applicable to any particular case." [1] But, as we have shown, the Courts in Britain usually accept the Foreign Office position.

There are apparently four grounds upon which an argument is raised in behalf of giving these agents special privileges. One is that notification to the receiving country of such a mission entitles the agent to special consideration. In fact von Martens goes even farther and notes that there are times when a sovereign may need to resort to such missions, possibly because secrecy is required, or for some other reason. "If the court to which he is sent be informed of the object of his mission he ought to be granted all the inviolability [which would be] due to him as a minister ..." [2]

Although Plischke does not go so far as to define the status of the agent, he does believe that customary international law would generally apply to him, basing this in part on identification in the diplomatic list (discussed above), and in part on "the nature of the advance arrangement with the local government concerning the diplomatic activities of the special agent." [3]

A second basis for granting special consideration to these agents is presented by Oppenheim. He argues that public special agents have a public character and therefore "inviolability of their persons and official papers ought to be granted to them." [4] The question again could be raised whether Oppenheim, in such a forthright statement, is referring to the same kinds of agents as is this writer. It is assumed that he is.

A third basis takes us again to Plischke who argues with eminent soundness that any man who enjoys an intimate kind of relationship with the President, a relationship such as Colonel House had with Woodrow Wilson, Harry Hopkins had with Franklin Roosevelt, or Averell Harriman had with Harry Truman is "likely to enjoy far greater diplomatic status, privileges and immunities even than the ordinary resident diplomat, because the special emissary more directly and personally represents the President of the United States and therefore the receiving government is inclined if not morally obligated

[1] Bland, Correspondence, *op. cit.*

[2] Von Martens, *op. cit.*, p. 266.

[3] Plischke, Correspondence, *op. cit.*

[4] Oppenheim, *op. cit.*, 2nd ed., I, 489. In the 8th edition he says they are inviolable, p. 860.

to extend extraordinary status and courtesy." [1] This is certainly a point well made and from the point of view of behavior and not of rights probably paints a very accurate picture. It not only is substantiated quite well in the private remarks of the German Foreign Office official referred to above, but is essentially what a number of consuls and diplomats indicated was their belief in personal talks with the writer.

The fourth reason, and the one most popularly supported is based on the functional approach. For Calvo, special agents who are sent abroad "pour régler certaines affaires particulières de l'État ou d'un souverain," are not part of the diplomatic mission and thus have no diplomatic immunities. Yet, he argues, they are entitled to "les droits et les facilités qui leur sont necessaires pour remplir leur mandat spécial." [2]

Deener reminds us that in some states the domestic law "permits privileges and immunities only to those persons sent and received as diplomats proper." In such situations, he suggests, it might be difficult to extend any privileges at all. However, where this is not the case, one could argue that approaching the matter on a functional basis, an agent would be entitled to certain privileges.

> On this basis, you might make a case that a special agent, sent to perform ambassadorial functions, should be accorded some privileges that normally would attach to an ambassador ... If an agent were sent and received with full knowledge of both parties that he was to perform diplomatic functions, it seems to me that the sending state would have a good case in asking that certain diplomatic privileges be accorded the agent, and, possibly, the receiving government would attempt to accord such privileges as it might be able to under its own domestic law. [3]

He really combines the functional approach with the first – the need to notify the receiving state of the mission. From both of these bases of argument it would seem that a good case could be made for giving the special agent immunities.

Bishop is another authority who points to the functions of the agent as providing the reason for being entitled to special consideration. He notes that special representatives are likely to receive the same treatment as a diplomat especially "when traveling on a diplomatic passport of the sending state." He suggests that,

[1] Plischke, Correspondence, *op. cit.*
[2] Calvo, *op. cit.*, III, 192.
[3] Deener, Correspondence, *op. cit.*

at the very least ... such a special representative will receive ... as good treatment as that required in international law for a diplomatic officer in transit through, or visiting in, a third State to which he is not accredited. Instead of diplomatic immunity, I believe such a special representative would be entitled, as a matter of international legal right ... to immunity from having to answer for official acts and immunity of official archives.

Thus, he concludes, the agents would probably be entitled only to "functional immunity" of the archives, and "to some extent non-liability for official acts ..." [1]

Corwin, Stuart and Wriston should probably also be mentioned here. Although none of them really discusses the international law aspect of the problem each is of the opinion that if the "true" identity of the agent is known he will be accorded "the same privileges and immunities" as are shown to public ministers.[2] Wriston goes so far as to make it a statement of fact that American agents have received diplomatic immunity, but unfortunately offers no documentation.

Probably the one person more than any other who has given careful thought to the status of the special agent is Siegmund Kauffmann. In a very scholarly article written in Germany just before the rise of Hitler, Kauffmann examines the status of the non-diplomat, a category obviously larger than that of the special agent herein of concern.[3] He points out the fact that international relations has become much more complex than it was before and hence what might be considered purely political representation in the traditional sense is no longer sufficient. For this kind of representation which was typical before World War I did not require any specialized knowledge. Today, however, diplomatic relations *per se* have assumed a highly technical character. Thus, the diplomat alone cannot carry out the full task of representing his state to another and frequently is in need of a technician who knows a special subject matter better than he. This technical expert is rarely given a diplomatic rank. In order for any non-diplomat to discharge his functions properly ,Kauffmann argues, he must have a special position. To be able to do his job, therefore, the principle *officium ne impediatur* must be considered as basic to his position. (For that matter Kauffmann believes that the same principle is the basis for the regular diplomat's status.)

[1] Bishop, Correspondence, *op. cit.*

[2] Stuart, *American Diplomatic and Consular Practice*, *op. cit.*, p. 147; Corwin, *The Constitution and What It Means Today*, *op. cit.*, p. 115; Wriston, *op. cit.*, p. 299.

[3] Siegmund Kauffmann, *Die Immunität der Nicht-Diplomaten; ein Beitrag zur Kodifikation des Völkerrechts*, (Frankfurter Abhandlungen Zum Modernen Völkerrecht," Hft. 33 [Leipzig: Robert Noske, 1932]).

Although he agrees that other theories have been highly desirable, the need for unimpeded function he considers to be the only sound one. However, he does not believe that any privileges beyond that permitted by this principle could be supported by international law for any non-diplomat. Any privileges which extend beyond this are, to him, clearly a matter of international courtesy. "Es bleibt somit, mit noch viel zwingenderen Gründen als bei den Gesandten, für die Begründung des Genusses der Immunitäten der Nicht-Diplomaten die Theorie des 'ne impediatur legatio' allein übrig." [1] Kauffmann's examination of the problem takes him into an examination of how the principle should be applied, the nature of the immunities, and those who are entitled to them.

> Es mag bemerkt werden, dass bei der Gewährung von Immunitäten an nichtdiplomatische Personen dem Prinzip der "Einschrank" Rechnung zu tragen ist. Denn einmal zeigt sich ein immer stärkeres Anwachsen der Zahl der für die Immunitäten in Betracht kommenden Personen. Es kommt noch hinzu, dass immer mehr das Territorialitätsprinzip betont wird, das nach Möglichkeit alle im Territorium sich befindlichen Personen von der Staatsgewalt erfasst wissen will.[2]

Insofar as the nature of the immunities is concerned he examines them with regard to those traditional immunities of the regular diplomat which could be relevant to the non-diplomat. Thus, following the principle of *officium ne impediatur* he concludes that the non-diplomat ought to get immunities from the jurisdiction of the civil courts, immunities from criminal courts, immunities from being summoned as a witness, immunities from the jurisdiction of administrative organs, and immunities of officers' archives, correspondence, etc.[3]

The author goes so far as to suggest that the wife and child ought not to be entitled to any immunity except with regard to any immigration and residence restrictions generally applicable to foreigners. At the end of this very interesting study the author presents a draft convention on the immunity of non-diplomats. One interesting point raised here is the proposal that agents operating with *de facto* recognized governments must have credentials. All other agents may have these credentials, but if they do not they should carry an official letter indicating the nature and purpose of the mission.[4]

In such a study we have probably the most thorough examination

[1] *Ibid.*, p. 65.
[2] *Ibid.*, p. 5.
[3] *Ibid.*, *passim.*
[4] *Ibid.*, *passim.*

of the problem that exists without, however, any effort at a comparative national study, and without an attempt at documentation by court cases. It is essentially a theoretical study of the propositions that exist for immunities, with a well reasoned argument in favor of extending many of these immunities to a new group who are becoming more and more numerous and more and more necessary, "der Nicht-Diplomaten."

When the Special Rapporteur on the subject of *ad hoc* diplomacy for the ILC approached the question of privileges and immunities, he took the view that the provisions which were put forth in the 1958 draft on Diplomatic Intercourse and Immunities for permanent missions were applicable to special missions, with only slight changes. Thus articles 4–9, and 11 of his draft are all directly based on the provisions set forth for the permanent agent.[1] It does not seem necessary to review them here since we discussed them in detail in the previous chapter. Suffice it to point out that the proposed immunities are broad with regard to the archives, premises, the person of the agent and his property, his staff and his and their families.

The basis for these immunities, as argued by the Rapporteur, is function, a view that conforms to the position taken on behalf of immunities for the permanent diplomatic agent. However, as with the regular agent, the representative character of his position is likewise important and in fact was mentioned by one of the members of the ILC when he addressed himself to this subject. That they deal with and represent governments, the Cuban delegate said, "could not possibly be denied." [2]

Freedom of Movement and Communication

There does not appear to be any discussion of this problem in the literature except for that introduced above regarding regular diplomatic missions. Yet clearly as with such missions, freedom to travel within the host State, and to communicate with one's own Government is extremely important for special missions. Any restrictions on travel should be kept to a minimum and, with the exceptions to the use of radio revealed at the 1961 Vienna diplomatic conference, none at all should prevail with regard to communications. Article 4 of the Sandström draft provides that "full facilities" shall be accorded for the

[1] "Ad Hoc Diplomacy," A/CN.4/129, *op. cit.*, p. 14–15.
[2] Yearbook of the International Law Commission, 1960, *op. cit.*, p. 262.

performance of the mission.[1] With some missions the need to travel would be most important, and in fact if the agent is to go to more than one State so might the right to communicate speedily and without surveillance. This would be true especially if the decision to go to several other States, or if the content of the discussions to be undertaken in any of these other States in any respect hinges upon the outcome of the agent's activities in the first.

Responsibility for the Protection of Special Agents

A question to which we may now turn our attention is what, if any, is the responsibility of the host state for the protection of special agents? In part the answer to this may depend upon whether one considers he is entitled to diplomatic status. If we assume, in light of the evidence and arguments introduced, that he is not so entitled is there no special responsibility of the state for his protection? This very question was posed by Eagleton several decades ago. He refers to "the multifarious agents representing the increasing ramifications of governmental interests abroad," and suggests that "the position of the commissioner, the consul, and the agent whose character is not recognized, need clarification." He further suggests that some differentiation must be made "so far as the protection due them in accordance with the importance of their work is concerned." [2] It seems strange that he would even imply that this problem of protection should be at all related to the "importance" of the work. How such a determination could be made he does not say, but the influence of Borchard's position regarding the responsibility of states for their agents' acts would seem to be evident. And as with Borchard's proposition, the wisdom of trying to determine the responsibility by rating the importance either of the mission or of the category of the mission is highly questionable. Nevertheless he presents in this piece evidence of careful deliberation of the matter. He suggests that there is a scale of protection starting from the average foreign visitor to the Chief of State or his ambassador. With regard to the average foreigner he believes that the state is only restricted by the need to assure that the alien gets the same quality of procedural protection as the national. But, for the foreign official, certainly a higher degree of protection than that shown to the average alien is to be expected. At the top would be the diplo-

[1] "Ad Hoc Diplomacy," A/CN.4/129, *op. cit.,*, p. 14.

[2] Eagleton, "The Responsability of the State for the Protection of Foreign Officials," *op. cit.*, p. 312.

mat who "may claim the utmost inviolability, as well as immunity from the operation of municipal law ... [However] between the diplomat and the individual [the rights and duties of States] are not at all well established." [1]

He goes on to point out that special visitors are entitled to and have received a special protection, but the question of the extent of this protection for different categories of individuals, and the possible indemnities that may be due them have not been examined and therefore have not been classified and defined.[2] Although the tendency has been toward greater restrictions on the granting of protection, he believes, a new problem is growing that is in need of attention. As relations between states grow more technical various facets of foreign relations are entrusted not to the Ambassador but to special agents. His view is that "these new agents, though they are not given diplomatic credentials, deserve special protection ... but the protection which they deserve is simply that which is necessary to enable them to discharge their functions, and need not include exemption from territorial jurisdiction except for such acts as are done upon the order of their government." [3]

Oppenheim and Kunz are also in accord with the view that these agents are entitled to special protection. It will be recalled that Oppenheim believes that since such political agents are admitted publicly they have a public character. Both of these scholars agree, therefore, that they are entitled to a "special protection." [4] Again the primary reason is that a public agent of this kind is engaged on an important mission which he may not be able to carry out unless such protection is provided.

Rivier points out that the state doesn't have to accept such a mission, "mais du moment qu'il les accueille, ils sont ses hôtes, et il leur doit tout au moins la sécurité nécessaire à l'accomplissement de leur mission." Acceptance, therefore, implies the obligation to provide such protection.[5] Again the emphasis on the minimum security necessary to carry out their functions.

There have been two important cases in which the issue of protection arose regarding special agents. In one the facts and results were

[1] *Ibid.*, p. 309.
[2] *Ibid.*, p. 310.
[3] *Ibid.*, p. 313.
[4] Oppenheim, *op. cit.*, p. 489; Kunz, Correspondence, *op. cit.*
[5] Rivier, *op. cit.*, I, 156.

such that the Soviet Union and Switzerland were unable to carry out diplomatic relations for some time thereafter.

In November, 1922, the First Lausanne Conference was held. It was an attempt to conclude peace between Greece and Turkey. The major problems dealt with the new borders of Turkey, the disposition of the Aegean Islands and the capitulations which Turkey had been forced to accept in the past. The Conference broke up and met again in April of the following year. Less than a month later, on May 10, a Swiss citizen, Conradi, fired at, and killed, the Russian unofficial observer to the Conference, Mechelav Vorovsky. The case went to court and Conradi was acquitted in November. When the Swiss Government refused to step in and take a stand to punish Conradi the Russian Government issued a violent protest. The matter was extremely heated due, in part, to Conradi's confession that the assassination was part of a general plot to kill Bolshevik leaders. Switzerland, however, refused to accept the Russian complaint that she was responsible for providing extra-precautionary measures for Russia's special representative on the grounds that "Vorovsky had not been invited to the conference and when he appeared was definitely excluded." [1] (Again we get the picture that even with special agents the *agréation* plays a part.) Switzerland's position would therefore be that her responsibility exists only when such agents are accepted.

The second affair which occurred in which the problem of protection arose was likewise a dramatic one. This was the Corfu incident of 1923. After World War I the boundary between Greece and Albania was in dispute. The Conference of Ambassadors (of the major powers) had been established to work out such problems, and it sent a commission into the disputed area to try to resolve the difference. One of the members of the commission was an Italian, General Tellini, who, along with four members of his staff, was assassinated August 27. Two days later the new Fascist government of Mussolini issued an ultimatum to Greece which Greece did not fully accept. Forty-eight hours later Italy severely bombarded the island of Corfu, after which it was occupied. Greece appealed to the Council of the League of Nations in September. The Council proposed a solution but the Italian government refused to accept the League's jurisdiction. Then the Council turned its proposals over to the Conference of Ambassadors which adopted them. Greece was held responsible because of insufficient protection and Italy finally abandoned its occupation. Being desirous of a thorough

[1] *New York Times*, May 11, November 17, 22, 1923, as cited in Stuart, *op. cit.*, p. 235.

examination of the legal aspects of the case the League Council submitted to a committee of prominent jurists the question of the responsibility of states for the protection of foreign agents. On March 13, 1924, the Council unanimously adopted the reply:

> The responsibility of a State is only involved by the commission in its territory of a political crime against the persons of foreigners if the State has neglected to take all reasonable measures for the prevention of the crime, and the pursuit, arrest, and bringing to justice of the criminals. The recognized public character of the foreigner and the circumstances in which he is present in its territory, entail upon the State a corresponding duty of special vigilance on his behalf.[1]

Here we find unanimous support for the thesis that a state does owe a special degree of protection to foreign agents even though they may not be regular diplomats.

It was probably with just such an incident and reply in mind that the Harvard Law School study also emphasized the obligation of special protection to these agents. It proposed that,

> the members of non-diplomatic missions, such as frontier commissions, or agents sent abroad for purposes of an administrative or technical character, are entitled by international law to a special protection and consideration, the limits of which are not determined with precision.[2]

Responsibility for the Acts of the Special Agent

Much of the discussion presented in the previous chapter regarding state responsibility for actions of its own officials would be pertinent here. It will be recalled that Oppenheim held that a state had an original responsibility for any authorized or commanded action it gave to any agent or even private individual, and that it had a vicarious responsibility for any unauthorized injurious action by any of the above.[3] To some extent this was likewise the view presented by Hall and Eagleton.[4] It will likewise be recalled that Borchard's view that a state's responsibility varied with the rank of the official was adopted by the scholars of the Harvard Law School study, but apparently this view has not been widely supported by scholars or by tribunals.[5]

Meron, who is quite critical of any attempt to make such a distinction argues that:

[1] World Peace Handbook (World Peace Foundation), Appendix III, cited in Eagleton, "The Responsibility of the State for the Protection of Foreign Officials." *op. cit.*., p. 307.

[2] Harvard Law School, *op. cit.*, Article 1, Comment, p. 44.

[3] *Supra*, p. 88.

[4] *Supra*, p. 88.

[5] *Supra*, p. 90.

> Practice shows that the defense of respondent States based on the inferior rank of the acting official was often rejected. [A series of cases then follows.] From the more recent arbitrations it appears clearly that the rank of the official is irrelevant to the determination of the responsibility, and that the only pertinent considerations are "the character of the acts alleged to have resulted in injury to persons or to property, or the nature of the functions performed whenever a question is raised as to their proper discharge." [1]

If this view were adopted, the state would have to accept responsibility for even a private individual's acts, and this is Oppenheim's contention also. One will likewise find this same thought expressed in Article 10 of the Hague Codification Conference of 1930. The view presented there is very much in line with Oppenheim's "vicarious responsibility" theory.

> As regards damage caused to foreigners or their property by private persons, the State is only responsible where the damage sustained by the foreigners results from the fact that the State has failed to take such measures as in the circumstances should normally have been taken to prevent, redress, or inflict punishment for acts causing the damage.[2]

Eagleton may also be cited as concurring with this view. He has expressed concern that this rapidly increasing tendency to use special agents has not been getting proper attention and believes that even though such agents are not given diplomatic credentials, "they should not be held responsible personally under local laws for acts done under governmental authority ..." He points out that military and naval officers would generally not be so considered and sees no reason why the special agent should not be treated on the same basis.[3]

There have been several cases which were concerned with lesser agents of the state. In the *Quintanella Case*, the United States was held responsible for the action of a deputy sheriff of Texas. The sheriff had arrested Quintanella, an alien, and then the latter was found dead shortly after. No evidence existed indicating investigation and prosecution on the part of the Texas authorities.[4]

In the *Massey Claim Case*, Nielsen, writing for the Commissioners of the United States-Mexico General Claims Commission, stated, "I believe that it is undoubtedly a sound general principle that, whenever misconduct on the part of any such persons, whatever may be their

[1] Massey (*U.S.* v. *Mexico*, 1927), *U.S.-Mexico, Opinions 1927–8*, p. 228, cited in Meron, *op. cit.*, p. 98.

[2] Minutes of the Third Committee, 1930, V. 17, p. 237, cited in Briggs, *op. cit.*, p. 711.

[3] Eagleton, "The Responsibility of the State for the Protection of Foreign Officials," *op. cit.*, p. 313.

[4] *Annual Digest*, 1925–26, Case No. 163.

particular status or rank under domestic law, results in the failure of a nation to perform its obligations under international law; the nation must bear the responsibility for the wrongful acts of its servants." [1]

Although circumstances existed which could be construed as mitigating the responsibility of Mexico, the Commission in the *Margaret Roper Case* found Mexico guilty for the death of United States seamen. These men were fired at by a Mexican policeman who apparently did not intend to injure them but whose warning shots nevertheless led to their death. Lack of prosecution on the part of the Mexican authorities was again held up as a factor in Mexico's disfavor.[2]

Apparently such commissions have ruled that having the capacity of only an administrative official does not remove the state's responsibility. In the *William Way Claim* the Commission pointed out that even though he was only an administrative officer, there wasn't any point in trying to distinguish between officers of different rank in determining the state's responsibility for their acts.[3]

From these cases it is apparent that the question of responsibility based upon diplomatic status, has not been involved. This was specifically the point at issue in the suit against the Danish Consul at San Francisco. The Consul moved to dismiss the suit on the grounds that it was against him in his official capacity. The Court determined that, "in actions against the officials of a foreign state not clothed with diplomatic immunity, it can be said that suits based upon official authorized acts, performed within the scope of their duties on behalf of the foreign state, and for which the foreign state will have to respond directly or indirectly in the event of a judgment, are actions against the foreign state . . ." [4]

Functions of the Special Agent

Probably little need be said here inasmuch as Appendix A to this study reveals how varied the use of special agents has been. There is no reason why a special agent of the Executive cannot be given any mission which a diplomatic officer of the government might be assigned. Most missions have probably had an economic basis and have dealt with opening or improving trade relations, or arranging to pro-

[1] United States (Massey Claim) v. Mexico, cited in Briggs, *op. cit.*, 2nd ed., p. 683.

[2] *Annual Digest* 1927–28, Case No. 150.

[3] *William Way Claim*, United States-Mexican Claims Commission, 1928, as cited in Wesley L. Gould, *An Introduction to International Law* (New York: Harper Bros., 1957), pp. 525–526.

[4] *Lyders* v. *Lund* 32 F (2d) 308, as cited in Hackworth, *Digest op. cit.*, II, 470.

vide military materials. Others have had primarily political overtones such as arranging for the establishment of diplomatic recognition. Still others have been essentially fact-finding missions which attempt to assess economic or military conditions within a state. And others have been primarily designed to promote good will between the sending and receiving states.

Those missions which are sent to represent the Chief Executive at coronations, funerals, and other solemn state affairs are generally quite formal and the members usually have the highest diplomatic rank. On the other hand, those sent to obtain information, which was the objective of many of the agents sent during World War II, are usually quite informal and the agents often have no diplomatic rank. And, of course, some will be sent because of their specialized training to attend international conferences of some kind.

It will be noted that there is great similarity between the kinds of things the regular diplomat may be expected to do and those which the special agent may be assigned. In fact it is perhaps true that the only area of activity which may and usually does differ between the two is with regard to looking after and advising nationals of the home state, a responsibility which may constitute a sizeable portion of the regular envoy's duties. Other than that and other than the fact that their reports will usually go directly to the Executive and not through foreign office channels, special agents may be charged with and may perform functions similar to that of any regular envoy.

This same viewpoint may be found in the Special Rapporteur's Report on Ad Hoc Diplomacy for the ILC. Particular mention is made of the fact that special agents are often chosen because the nature of their assignment requires a special competence not found in the permanent mission. In a discussion on this point at the Twelfth Session of the ILC, one of the members expressed the opinion that their tasks are so varied they are called upon to "negotiate, act in a representative capacity and, if necessary, even protect nationals," though the latter seems highly unlikely.[1]

Perhaps one important difference between the regular and special agent with regard to function is that so long as diplomatic relations are maintained a regular mission must not be interrupted, i.e. there must be continued representation. Such a responsibility does not pertain to the special mission, which can and may start and stop its function if need be.

[1] Yearbook of the International Law Commission, 1960, *op. cit.*, p. 263.

SUMMARY

The category "special agent" covers many different kinds of agents. Commissioners, arbitrators, technical experts, etc., of states all would be included. And it is quite probable that those who have written about such agents have had at least some of the above types in mind. But the only agent with which this study is concerned is the one sent abroad by the Executive or chief cabinet officer. What he will do, where he will go and the length of time he will be away, is generally up to the discretion of this official. Although no state has engaged in the practice of using such agents to the extent the United States has, the number has been sufficiently large to require careful attention. When propositions are made concerning the status of special agents, the executive special agent should be included wherever appropriate. Of course, as has been pointed out above, even the classification special agent includes several types. Because agents with diplomatic rank are accorded the same status under international law as the regular diplomat, and because secret agents are at best similar to other special agents only to a very limited extent, the only executive agent who has been deemed sufficiently important to study is the one without diplomatic rank who is sent on a public mission.

There has been no general agreement among states or scholars concerning the status of this kind of agent, and in fact very little discussion. It has seemed wise to examine him from five different points of view: (1) the means by which his presence and activity is made known to his host, (2) the question of whether he should or does have privileges and immunities, (3) the question of whether his host state is obligated to show a special degree of protection beyond that to which any foreign visitor is entitled, (4) the responsibility which his state must assume for his acts, and (5) the nature of his functions. It will readily be seen that 2, 3, and 4 are the most significant aspects of such an analysis.

The agent is generally given a letter of introduction which indicates the nature of the mission, its author, and the identity of the bearer. There is no special form and it is doubtful if such a thing as protocol has developed on this matter. The Executive may take pains to indicate that he has great confidence and trust in the agent and to express hope that the host will feel free to reveal his convictions to him fully and honestly. Some agents have been permitted great latitude with regard to how their letter should be used. Others have had their instructions very carefully spelled out. Some have been permitted a large measure of discretion in terms of how they should proceed. Others have had directions which allowed little exercise of independent judgment. When agents and their relationship to the Executive are well known it has not even been necessary for the agent to exhibit his letter. (In fact Hopkins is reported as not having had to show even his diplomatic passport on his first trip to the Soviet Union.)[1] In this respect perhaps more than any other, the difference between these letters and the letter of credence of a regular diplomat can be seen. At no time would even a well-known diplomat be permitted to forego the reception ceremony. And of course the two presentations will generally be quite different, the one being a formal ceremony and the other an informal meeting.

Insofar as privileges and immunities are concerned very few would propose that special agents have a diplomatic character. It is a question that has been raised many times but not very often discussed. Several authorities are of the opinion that the question of their status is a problem partly because some states have granted them what is tantamount to a diplomatic character. It is proposed that this not be done because of the inconvenience that accrues when too many foreigners have such status within a country. The question of convenience, as important as that may be to local administrators and other authorities would hardly seem to be the best grounds upon which such a determination should be made.

There have been no court cases which deal with the kind of special agent of concern to us. One can therefore only make some tentative assessment of their status before the courts by extension from those cases which do exist. In France, Belgium, Switzerland, Britain and the United States, the courts have denied the existence of diplomatic immunity to special agents on the grounds that they do not have a diplomatic character as such, that they are not a part of a diplomatic mission, and that the executive branch has not granted them such a status (although in one case in Switzerland it appears that this was the government's intention). In only one case, *Re the Turkish Inspector of Students*, was there an indication that if the agent's functions had been those traditionally undertaken by a diplomat he might have been granted immunity. In other cases, including the famous Gubitchev case in the United States, the question of function was not considered of sufficient importance to merit being the deciding factor.

[1] Sherwood, *op. cit.*, p. 321.

Although many scholars concur that special agents do not have a right to immunity, they believe that agents frequently get this consideration on the basis of courtesy. It is interesting to note here the discrepancy between what the scholars consider to be the proper basis for the granting of diplomatic immunity and that which the courts have used whenever the matter has arisen. The scholars emphasize that immunity is based on function, the courts agree that function is important, but emphasize that immunity is primarily based on the agent's being received as a diplomat. Yet the scholars acknowledge that special agents do not have a diplomatic character, although on the basis of function they should be entitled to it. One scholar, Bishop, points out what he considers to be a change in attitude along this line, citing as his support the fact not only that such agents are increasing in number but also that more and more of them are being covered by special agreements which grant them immunity. It would seem that if the trend to use these agents continues, as well it might, then at least a limited protection will have to be guaranteed.

Another authority has suggested that it is possible that such agents already have limited immunity especially if they receive a diplomatic passport and are carried on the diplomatic list. It is quite possible that they do get such a passport but they are probably not put on these lists. But it is doubtful that one could maintain that either or both of these conditions is sufficient to bestow immunity.

All do agree, however, that the special agent is entitled to special consideration and that this implies the utmost courtesy in treatment, including privileges usually accorded a diplomat. Some go even farther and suggest that he is entitled to at least a degree of immunity sufficient to permit him to fulfill his mission successfully. They are not all in agreement as to why this is so, some suggesting it is because his host has been notified of his coming (and presumably acquiesced), others propose that it is because he is a public agent. Several suggest that his special treatment should be based upon the functions he performs, which are similar to the diplomat's, and a few point out that his close relationship to the Executive entitles him to this consideration. The latter observe quite aptly that whether or not he is entitled to special treatment he undoubtedly will get it, perhaps even to a greater degree than the regular envoy because of his standing with his chief.

The foreign offices have been most reluctant to indicate just what special considerations they will grant the agent, although all have been quite clear that he is not by right entitled to any privileges or immunities. However, all have indicated that upon the basis of courtesy, and some have added reciprocity, they will and do extend special considerations to ensure the success of the mission. In fact a member of the German Foreign Office has offered as his personal view that inasmuch as delegates to international conferences are nowadays always granted diplomatic immunities, special agents ought to receive the same consideration.

The British Foreign Office states that it will give courteous consideration to the special agent but is restricted from extending any immunities since this is for the courts to decide. This is contrary to the findings of Lyons who has found that in both the United States and Britain the courts will decide immunity on the basis of the "suggestion" (in the United States) or the Foreign Office statement.[1] It is highly unlikely that the Foreign Office would not exert itself, and strenuously if necessary, on behalf of an agent if an action were brought against him in court. This type of action could have been taken against Harry Hopkins, for example, when he left London without paying his hotel bill at the Claridge.[2] He paid it many weeks later but it cannot be seriously assumed that the British government would have allowed a suit for recovery to be instituted, or that if it were, the government would not have filed a statement asking for dismissal on the grounds of immunity. Unfortunately, from the point of view of clarification of this issue, no such action has ever taken place.

So far as protection is concerned, all authorities who have discussed this agree that the agent should get special consideration. One has proposed that the extent of the protection should depend upon the importance of the agent, but this would appear to be hard to determine and undesirable to follow. Certainly when the Tellini affair arose the League of Nations did not propose any distinction other than that any special agent was entitled to a greater degree of protection than the average alien. This would surely be supported by all authorities.

The question of responsibility is not one that meets with as great consensus, however. There is no disagreement that a state is responsible for all authorized acts of its agents, and this is as true whether he be a diplomat or a non-diplomat. This is really the most important aspect of the question. Whether the state is also responsible for unauthorized acts and how the line can be drawn between *ultra vires*

[1] Lyons, "Conclusiveness of the Foreign Office Certificate," *op. cit.*, pp. 116–147.
[2] Sherwood, *op. cit.*, p. 321.

action and private action is a matter of disagreement. It would seem necessary, and this is becoming the more acceptable viewpoint, for the state to assume some responsibility; otherwise the host state and its subjects are placed at a serious disadvantage. This responsibility may, perhaps, go no farther than assuring either punishment or compensation for injury, but that would seem to be at least the minimum. At this point it should also be added that it would seem that under no circumstances has the home state the right to disavow responsibility on the alleged grounds that the actions of a special executive agent are not actions of a state agent. Further discussion of this point will be presented in the conclusions.

As for functions it has already been indicated that no significant difference exists here between the special and regular agent. The former may be assigned any task given to the latter, and although it would not be customary for him to provide the usual services of preparing visas and the like or to help the agents' nationals regarding problems incurred from residence abroad, the major reason for not doing so would be lack of familiarity with the regulations and not necessarily lack of authority. It is conceivable that even these functions could be fulfilled by someone given authority paramount to the regular envoy as was true with James Blount. Regarding functions therefore, it may be assumed that there is no significant characteristic distinguishing the special agent.

CHAPTER VIII

CONCLUSIONS

MUNICIPAL LAW ASPECT

Historical Development

The use of special agents in international relations can undoubtedly be traced back many centuries. In fact, before the practice of establishing permanent missions began, the diplomatic envoy in ancient Greece and Rome, and later in the Middle Ages in western Europe, was a temporary agent. Because he was an official agent of the Executive or ruling organ he was probably comparable to the special agent of modern times who goes abroad with diplomatic rank. Yet there were undoubtedly others who were sent without title quite possibly on what amounted to secret missions. Lawrence gives Louis XI credit for being the first to use the special agent in a fashion similar to those who fill this role today. Louis, who reigned from 1461–1483, a forerunner in ideas of the Sun King, Louis XIV, was one of the first to create a modern state under centralized (and absolutist) authority, a ruler interested in internal reform and external relations. In addition to traveling much himself he also sent many agents abroad in an informal capacity. Lawrence writes, "Louis XI de France introduisit la coutûme d'envoyer des personnes d'un rang inférieur, appelées 'agents,' pour traiter des affaires sans représenter la personne. Sa diplomatie agissait souvent dans l'ombre." [1]

Centuries later with the development of the new world and the breaking away of the colonies from England, the practice was established in this country and grew rapidly. Both World Wars have helped to emphasize the reliance upon their use, and the current President has continued in the tradition. In numbers and variety of such missions the United States probably has no equal.

[1] T. J. Lawrence, *Les Principes de Droit International*, trans. Jacques Dumas and A. De-Lepradelle (5th ed.; London: Oxford University Press, 1920), p. 304.

Possible Reasons for the Use of Special Agents

Because there has been no historical treatment of the subject one cannot go beyond making some assumptions as to the reasons special agents have been used in many countries. One is probably safe in stating as a generalization that there may be several advantages in using such agents. First may be cited the desire for secrecy. This should not be taken to mean secrecy in the sense that no one except the author of the mission knows of his mission. Secrecy may be understood to include also those missions in which the existence of the mission is publicly known and possibly the itinerary also. But the true nature of the mission may not be, nor the position taken by the government, nor the information obtained. This especially depicts the kinds of missions often undertaken by Colonel House and Harry Hopkins. When such agents report their findings they will generally not be made available to the public, nor even to the legislative body, nor possibly to the foreign office. In this way the possibility of "leaks" of the information can be avoided.

Furthermore, using such agencies may be desirable because it removes the problem of having to go through the multitudinous channels of the bureaucracy. The usual procedures not only produce delay but may be subject to examination and questioning by the various officials within the foreign office. In the end the questioning and doubting may either result in revision or cancellation of the plan.

Then, too, one can hypothesize that executives may turn to the use of these agents, at times, because the nature of the mission is such that the agent's special training or contacts will enhance the probability of its success. Certainly this must have played heavily in the reasons that Jean Monnet was dispatched to the United States several times in the post-World War II period.[1]

One might also surmise that an Executive will use a special agent because that particular person holds the confidence of the leader in a way in which no regular diplomat does. And this may be an extremely important factor in deciding whom to send. It may not be a question of specialized training but rather a faith in the person's judgment and point of view. This was the belief of Blair Bolles who felt that in Harry Hopkins the President had a feeling of "fidelity, understanding, and common sense rather than expert knowledge of foreign affairs." [2] This

[1] March 21, 1948; June 4, 1953; January 31, 1958.

[2] Blair Bolles, "Who Makes Our Foreign Policy?" *Headline Series 62* (New York: Foreign Policy Association), 1947.

is exactly the same point of view voiced so many times by those who were interviewed by this writer.[1]

There is one final reason which may entice a state leader to use a special agent. Because the agent may not be an officer, and usually would not be if he were a part of the American practice, but often may be on intimate terms with the Executive, the head of the government to which he is sent may feel much more inclined to frank and full discussion than he would if he felt his statements were going to be circulated through the official channels of a foreign office. As a result of the special kind of relationship between the agent and his Chief of State and the agent and the foreign host, the agent may come to play an extremely crucial role in the relations between the states, and in effect may become an advisor to the leaders of both. This becomes very obvious when one reads accounts or transcripts of the conversations between Colonel House and Viscount Grey of Britain or between Hopkins and Churchill during World War I and II, respectively.

United States Usage

For the above reasons, then, agents have been used by leaders of different countries. But this does not complete the picture for the United States. Other factors must be considered. The first agents were used in the Revolutionary period before there was a Constitution, e.g., Silas Deane and Arthur Lee, 1775. Others continued to be used during Washington's administrations. The reasons are quite apparent. In the first place there was no other way of conducting foreign relations in the early period. Not even a rudimentary foreign service existed. And furthermore those Americans who did have contacts abroad had to be used. Franklin and Jefferson, for example, were extremely effective because of their popularity in Paris. And, of course, much need for secrecy existed in order to obtain support for the struggling nation.

The Constitution itself presented certain problems. The President could not appoint any officer without Senate approval. Even if relations between the President and the Senate were good the problem of delay while the Upper House investigated and debated was always there. In addition there was the possibility of rejection. When political parties were created the problems regarding appointments increased. Here lay the seeds of partisan politics. A President who had incurred

[1] Eleanor Roosevelt, July 27, 1955; Samuel Rosenman, August 23, 1955; Oscar Cox, April 2, 1956; Benjamin Cohen, April 3, 1956; Phillip Young, April 4, 1956; Bernard Baruch, April 5, 1956; Isador Lubin, April 6, 1956.

the wrath of the opposition might find his nominees subjected to public attack and vituperation. These factors would naturally create a desire on the part of the President to find a way of circumventing the requirements and overcoming such obstacles without violating the Constitution.

His need to find a solution was increased as the country grew and the ceaseless struggle for power and freedom of action between the two branches also grew. By the middle of the nineteenth century Congress had very definitely developed its prerogatives over the creation of diplomatic posts as well as the appointments thereto. Inasmuch as the President could not create the posts nor appoint to those created without Senate approval, his hands would have been effectively tied without the possibility of using special agents. This possibility was enhanced, although not made possible by the existence of the contingent fund, a fund put at the disposal of the President without requiring itemized expense vouchers as an indication of its proper use. In 1946 Congress did restore the President's right to create diplomatic posts by removing the restrictions of the 1855 statute.

With regard to international conferences and organizations the Congress has here too passed measures restrictive of the President's freedom to extend or accept invitations, and to appoint the delegates from this country. This is not to say that in all of these matters the President has felt constrained to interpret his rights in such a fashion as to eliminate all freedom of action along such lines. As we have noted he has not always sought approval for extending or accepting an invitation to an international conference. Nor has he completely refrained from creating diplomatic posts and appointing to them, as Coolidge's appointment of a minister to the Irish Free State in 1927 would indicate.[1] As for delegates to international organizations the President has accepted in almost all instances the Congressional requirements regarding appointments. It should be noted that although Congress has kept for itself a right to have a veto on appointments to most of the United Nations agencies, the President was given some latitude regarding some of them.[2]

The question of the President's right to appoint such agents and to give some diplomatic rank has very definitely been resolved. Each branch has the inherent right to create agencies which it believes are necessary to carry out its authorized powers – in this case the Execu-

[1] *Statutes at Large*, XLIV, 1180.
[2] See Appendix B.

tive's right to negotiate with foreign powers. And that he may give diplomatic rank without violating the constitutional provision that appointment to office requires Senatorial approval is also quite clear. Such agents' appointments are not to office because they are temporary, their performance transient and their duties limited.

Problems That May Result from Using Special Agents

There are many problems that have arisen or may arise as a result of using special agents. First of all there is always the possibility of misrepresentation of the situation. This may take two forms. If the agent is not careful and discreet he may give the impression that he is authorized to do more than he actually has been. Speaking in the name of the Executive he may imply acquiescence to a committment that he has not had a right to make. Or if there is no question of a committment then he may wrongly give the impression of agreeing to ideas or proposals. The problem is not so much one of the legal position the state would be in if any decision were reached between the agent and his host as it is a problem of a misunderstanding that can arise. In other words the Executive's right to disavow the agent always exists whether he be a regular official or special agent. That the state may not be officially obligated to anything (although responsibility for damage might exist) without the Executive's approval is clear, but is not the real problem. If the agent believes that because he has a close personal relationship with the Executive he knows his mind well and will be supported in the actions he takes, he may be more indiscreet than he would or could be if these actions were reported to the foreign office where one or several superiors would become aware of them.

The second kind of problem of this nature may arise *despite* the caution of the agent. The party or parties of the foreign government with whom the agent is in contact may conclude that they have a direct and sympathetic approach to the Executive, which in fact may be very misleading. The belief that they have the "inside track," that the matter will not come under the scrutiny of the foreign office, the legislature or the public, the lack of realization that the Executive may not be able to fill their requests even if he is sympathetic, in short the possibility of misinterpretation is grossly magnified – and with this may come a strain in relations of serious dimensions.

Problems from United States Practice

The complexity and possible dangers in the practice can be compounded if it becomes abused. Because the practice has become so well established in the United States, because it does not fit into the traditional aspects of checks and balances, there is little likelihood that any branch or group will attempt to keep informed of what is going on. This lack of scrutiny, this lack of concern may lead to an increasing extension of a practice that within limits can have great value if not overdone. It seems to this writer that this is what did happen with regard to a number of the missions sent during the latter part of World War II and thereafter. They appear to represent examples of taking advantage of the practice and unnecessarily using special agents. Some of these have been included in Appendix A. Many others were not included of this same nature simply because the Appendix was intended only as a representative sample of the kinds of missions American Presidents have established. But it should be clear even from this abbreviated list that some of these missions were of questionable value, e.g., General Fleming's European tour to study housing and road construction, July, 1945; Maury Maverick's and Patrick McDonough's trip to the Pacific and Far East to study small business conditions, December, 1945; Donald Nelson's trip to China to study production problems, September, 1944.

What may result from this practice especially if it is engaged in very often? First there is a possibility of a strain in relations between the Executive and the foreign office. This can take on serious proportions. For example there is no doubt that this was a problem that the Department of State and the President had when Woodrow Wilson almost literally by-passed Bryan and then Lansing, the Secretaries of State, by his use of Colonel House. When the Secretaries found out things after they had been completed or decided upon, sometimes getting this information from sources other than the President, the feelings that resulted did not make possible harmonious relations between the Department and President.[1] The same thing happened in World War II when Ambassador John Winant wrote a pathetic cable to Harry Hopkins indicating his concern that he was being by-passed by the British government. Due to the fact that Hopkins had great influence with the President and that Lendlease Administrator Averell Harriman reported directly to Hopkins, Winant complained that he was ill-informed of what was taking place.[2]

[1] "House Diary," *op. cit.*, June 4, 1915, VI, 156.
[2] Hopkins MSS, October 16, 1943, Franklin D. Roosevelt Library.

Exactly the same kind of concern was expressed in an interview with Dean Acheson who said that the use of such agencies had a bad effect on morale and furthermore was administratively unwise. If the practice were engaged in while he was Secretary of State, he said, he would protest strongly.[1]

This leads to another problem that arises when special agents are used. Generally the agent sends his report or goes directly to the President with it. Rarely is this report disseminated among others in the State Department and hence the information, which might be of great value to others in important positions never gets to them, or else they may receive the information when it is no longer of value. Although this direct reporting may be of advantage in preventing "leaks" of information that should be kept secret, it also has the disadvantage of permitting policy to be formulated with incomplete data and possibly without proper co-ordination or consideration. This is generally one of the main problems of administration in the Department of State anyway, and the use of special agents must aggravate the problem considerably.

Critics' Views

Feelings outside of government circles regarding the use of these agents must also be considered. Usually generally public reaction will develop only with regard to some outstanding mission or well-known persons. That is to say, we may not expect a public reaction whenever such agents are used but only when some crisis occurs. Hopkins and House were the subject of attack because their names were linked to crises.

Much of the public criticism, however, will be of a somewhat different nature. We refer here to the arguments of scholars based on constitutional issues. These scholars' objections seem to indicate a feeling that the Constitution is being violated in spirit or word, or that even if no violation occurs the practice is inherently dangerous.

Despite the widespread use of these agents, for a long time many prominent members of Congress argued against its constitutionality. Since World War II, however, that has not been the approach that Congressional critics have taken, but rather theirs has been based on the use of specific men for specific purposes. Hence, for example, Congress has attempted to restrict the President's latitude of action by insisting that appointment of our delegates to most of the United

[1] April 2, 1956.

Nations agencies be subject to Senatorial approval thereby preventing the President from appointing special agents in situations he might normally have used them.[1] This has given the Senate the opportunity to block appointment of some of the appointees and has revealed that the attitudes of Senators often have run parallel in such cases to that exhibited when appointments to Cabinet or traditional diplomatic posts were being considered. Stuart reminds us that numerous appointments have been bitterly attacked and presents a list of such names.[2]

Aside from the reason that certain agents may be considered as misfits for their assignments, the basis for attacking the President's use of them, generally speaking, will be the individual Senator's attitude toward the President. In other words, much of the criticism that has been leveled at the President can probably be laid to partisan politics. If the Executive is disliked, if he has strong opposition for any reasons, the opportunity to attack him particularly when he uses special agents is exceedingly tempting.

Thus we can say that Congressional opposition, when it occurs, is more likely to be specific to the relations the President has with members of Congress and is not based on party doctrine. Presidents from all of our parties have used such agents and criticism has come from all parties. And interestingly, some critics have "reformed" and become supporters. Senator Lodge, a critic of Wilson's use of special agents in the Reparations Commission established after World War I, nevertheless was quite willing to serve in the same kind of capacity at the disarmament conference of 1922. John Quincy Adams noted even in his day that these attacks on the President's actions were not based on doctrine but on attitudes toward the Executive.[3]

Supporters' Views

The experience of Tracy Lay in the Foreign Service leads him to conclusions which seem sensible and worthy of repeating. He notes the frequent controversies that have arisen "over these seeming evasions of Constitutional obligation," and concludes that the power to negotiate is the basis for the President's freedom in this matter. Such representatives, he states, are not

[1] See Appendix B.

[2] Stuart, *op. cit.*, pp. 135–136.

[3] Charles F. Adams (ed.), *Memoirs of John Quincy Adams Comprising Portions of His Diary from 1795 to 1848* (Philadelphia: J. B. Lippincott and Co., 1874–1877), IX, 131.

in the Constitutional sense public ministers, although they have frequently exercised the powers of an ambassador or minister. They may become an essential instrument for the carrying through of negotiations in which the element of secrecy is a factor of success. The fact is generally recognized that "the employment of such agencies is a necessary part of the proper exercise of the diplomatic power which is entrusted by the Constitution with the President ... The precedents also show that the Senate, though in session, need not be consulted as to the appointment of such agents or as to the instructions which the President may give them." [1]

Lay concludes that, "without such authority our foreign relations would be so embarrassed with difficulties that it would be impossible to conduct them with safety or success." [2]

The Writer's Opinion

These agents have undoubtedly been of great assistance to their Executives, especially in the United States. At the same time it is probably true that much of the information they gather is not circulated among the appropriate officials of the government and it should be. Perhaps one could say then that in terms of morale, efficiency, and the diffusion of authority usually considered essential in a democracy the use of an agent is not always wise. But in these times, and particularly during crises the burdens of office may become severe. Through the use of a special agent the government may be able to operate with greater insight and speed. Although there may be certain dangers involved to democratic and efficient government, it is doubtful, particularly for the United States, whether a "legalistic" approach would be a realistic approach. Restrictions upon the President in the name of democratic government might in the long run produce dangers to its security and well being that would be neither warranted nor wise.

INTERNATIONAL LAW ASPECT

As for the international law aspects of the study a number of points should be summarized. In the first place not very much has been written on it and for this reason it will be of great interest to students of the subject to learn the results of the United Nations' inquiry and especially any convention which may be brought forth.

[1] Senate Document 231, 56th Cong., 2nd Sess., part 6, p. 387, as cited in Lay, *op. cit.*, pp. 45-46.

[2] *Ibid.*

Ambiguity of the Term "Special Agent"

The lack of attention to and critical analysis of the subject is apparent even with regard to the use of the term "special agent." In some places he is referred to as a "special agent," in some places as a "private agent," some authorities call him an "*ad hoc* agent," and some use the term "personal agent." It is highly likely that not all of the writers have the same kind of agents in mind, but one cannot always be sure from the context in which they are discussed, especially since their status under international law is defined approximately the same. Furthermore, some agents are given diplomatic rank and some are not. And to confuse the picture even more their status cannot be judged by their functions alone, for often there is little or no difference whether or not the agent has diplomatic rank.

Writer's Definition of the Term "Special Agent"

Special or *ad hoc* agents, it would seem, should be defined as those individuals assigned by a State to temporary missions, whose duties do not have the breadth of scope normally assumed to be a part of the regular diplomat's, and who may or may not have diplomatic rank.

In the introduction to Sändstrom's Report for the ILC, the author characterizes the work of the special agent as "performing temporarily an act which ordinarily is taken care of by the permanent mission." [1] The definition here is more sharply drawn than that which appears under article 1 of his draft, which merely defines the special mission as one sent by a State "for a special diplomatic assignment." [2] Probably the most crucial aspect of the definition is that he is sent by the State, i.e. by a duly authorized official of the sending Government. It is true that such a definition allows great leeway in determining his status, particularly with regard to the extent of the privileges and immunities to which he is entitled, for it lumps together agents with no diplomatic rank sent by a postmaster general, with those having the rank of Ambassador sent by a president or a prime minister. Nevertheless, in either case he is a representative of the State which sends him from the viewpoint of international law. The question of the difference in treatment which *should* be accorded two such different agents will be dealt with later.

[1] "Ad Hoc Diplomacy," *op. cit.*, A/CN.4/129, p. 4.
[2] *Ibid.*, p. 13.

Relationship of the Special Agent to the State

The relationship of such a special agent to his State will, to a large extent, be determined by the municipal law of the State. But this cannot be the end of the matter. In the United States, for example, it is clear that special executive agents are not officers in the constitutional sense. They are therefore considered under the United States Constitution as private agents. And yet this cannot be taken to mean that they are not public agents in international law. For they represent the President who "alone has the power to speak or listen as a representative of the nation." [1] In addition the mission of the Presidential agent is undertaken for the purpose of gathering information which the Executive needs to determine state policy. That is to say, there are not several organs or branches of our government which are authorized to communicate with other nations. Thus, the latter must depend for their official communications with the United States upon the President, or some agency which is authorized to speak for him. And when an agent is sent abroad by the President the agent acts as his representative in the Executive's official capacity.

It is not as if the agent were carrying out a mission in which the President as a private individual was interested, e.g., the purchase of real estate, vacation interests, publication of memoirs, etc. Under these circumstances it does not seem possible or proper to consider the agent as a private agent while abroad, a classification which would make his position tantamount to that of a visiting alien. In other words, although he is not an officer he ought to be considered as an agent of the State regardless of how he was appointed, if he is carrying out a mission for the President, pertaining to State affairs.

In attempting to assess the place of the special agent in international law the traditional methodology of that discipline has been followed, i.e., application by analogy and extension from court decisions, foreign office statements and the writings of scholars.

Position of the Courts

No court cases or arbitrative decisions have been uncovered in which a determination of the status of a special executive agent was required. But in any case in which the status of an envoy was in need of determination the courts almost always seemed to rely upon the foreign office for the decision. The question would generally be, has the individual been received as a person with representative character,

[1] *U.S.* v. *Curtis-Wright Export Corp.* 239 U.S. 304.

or is he a member of a diplomatic mission? Occasionally the question of his functions would be raised, but almost always this seemed to be secondary to the opinions of the Foreign Office.

Position of the Foreign Offices

So far as the foreign offices are concerned the conclusion is inescapable that the special agent does not *ipso facto* have the qualities of a diplomat. No state official with whom the writer has corresponded has ever considered him to have such, and all who have discussed this point have taken the position that diplomatic privileges and immunities are not his due according to international law. Nevertheless, most of the states have indicated that they do allow the privileges of a diplomat and are willing to grant a special degree of protection. Some have even indicated that although the agent is not strictly entitled to the privileges and immunities of a diplomat they will grant them, generally upon the basis of reciprocity. This is true, for example, of the governments of the Republic of China, of France, of Canada, and of the Soviet Union. Although the idea of reciprocity was usually mentioned and, in the case of Canada, the requirement of a diplomatic passport, the basis in each case seemed to be courtesy, i.e., the desire to maintain good relations, and function, i.e., the need to allow the agent whose mission was accepted to have the freedom of action necessary to fulfill his assignment.

Position of Scholars

Those scholars who have addressed themselves to the subject or who have corresponded with the writer are almost without exception of the opinion that special agents have no diplomatic status. Yet several have indicated that the functions they perform are similar to the diplomats' and that they should therefore be given the same privileges. It was even suggested by some, a view in which the German Foreign Office official privately concurred, that inasmuch as agreements are made to give other agents who have similar responsibilities diplomatic immunities, e.g., commissioners and delegates to international conferences, there is no reason why the special executive agent should not be entitled to the same. It is interesting to note that all who are of this opinion base their stand on courtesy and function, a stand which corresponds to that of many of the foreign office replies. Kauffmann perhaps sums up this view best when he argues that the non-diplomat must be allowed those immunities without which he could not carry out his obligations effectively and efficiently – immunities therefore based upon the concept *officium ne impediatur*.[1]

Many writers are not at all explicit with regard to their opinions beyond the belief that special agents are not entitled to diplomatic privileges and immunities. Some imply that they should receive special consideration, but what this is is not always defined. When it is defined, the opinions generally are that the agent should be given special protection in order to make possible the accomplishment of his mission.

The matter of responsibility for his acts is open to some question. Since he is engaged on a public mission most authorities argue that the state must be responsible. But the nature of the responsibility with some authorities would depend upon the status he is thought to hold. Others insist that whether he is considered as a major or minor agent, or authorized acts his state must accept responsibility.

Writer's Views of the Status of the Special Agent

From the practices and opinions discussed in this study it would seem necessary to define the special agent's position as follows: Just as with any mission, the sending state must seek the *agréation* before dispatching the agent. Once this is obtained he should then be given a letter of recommendation, in which the nature and purpose of his mission is defined, and a diplomatic passport. As soon as possible after arrival in the foreign state he should present his letter of introduction to the Chief of State or to whomever he is expected to work with in order to complete his assignment. While in the host country he ought to receive all privileges which would normally be shown to a diplomatic envoy, and those immunities which are necessary to enable him to fulfill his functions. These would include the freedom of the port, i.e. exemption from customs, etc., exemption from the usual taxes (income and property), civil and criminal immunity and inviolability of person, papers and residence. Inasmuch as such agents rarely travel with any staff or families there would normally not be any need to consider their status. But if staff or family should accompany such an agent, and their number should be kept to an absolute minimum, they ought to receive the same status with regard to these privileges and immunities.

At this point a word should be said regarding the question of status for agents with diplomatic rank as compared to those without. In this

[1] *Supra*, pp. 141–142.

report they have been treated as one regardless of the nature of their assignment and regardless of the organ of Government which has authorized their mission. It is possible that at some later date when studies of *ad hoc* agents have increased in quantity and quality beyond that of the present, sufficient documentation will exist regarding the use of the different categories of special agents, as well as sufficient argumentation regarding the appropriateness of a particular status so that fine distinctions can be made among them. This study being in the nature of a pioneering work, no such differences have been attempted. But this does not mean that an effort of this nature should not be undertaken. Perhaps one of the best examples of the need, one of the best proofs of the prevailing confusion on the subject can be found in the effort of the ILC to come up with a draft on this subject. Ever since 1957 the Commission and a Special Rapporteur to whom it assigned the task of drawing up a draft, the General Assembly and its Sixth Committee, and subsequently the member States who received a copy of the initial draft, have been considering the rules of "diplomatic intercourse and immunities" for regular agents and, since 1958, the international status of special agents. At the 1961 Vienna Conference on Diplomatic Relations the subject was again taken up and the question of the special agent turned over to a sub-committee of delegates from Ecuador, Iraq, Italy, Japan, Senegal, the Soviet Union, the United Kingdom, the United States and Yugoslovia. The Chairman was Niftali Ponce Miranda of Ecuador. After three meetings the sub-committee decided insufficient study had been devoted to the topic and recommended that the ILC continue along this line. Thus, aside from the Sändstrom draft there has not yet been any agreement reached, even tentatively, of the international law status of special agents. Although this may in part be attributable to the pressures of other demands, in part it also reflects the confusion and uncertainty which surrounds the legal position of these agents. This conclusion is fortified when one examines the records of the Yearbook of the ILC, 1960, volume 1. Both Mr. Sändstrom's drafts on regular and *ad hoc* diplomacy had been before the members of the ILC for some time, and in fact the comments found on pages 327 and 328 of volume 1 come at the fourth meeting devoted to *ad hoc* diplomacy. (These meetings were held in Geneva on June 17th, 21st, 22nd and 29th, 1960). It is quite apparent that even at that late date there was much doubt as to the categories of agents the members had been discussing, as to the relationship the agents had to their own States, and as to their appropriate standing in international law. A proposal to change the term "diplomatic mission" to "official mission" brought forth the protest that this might mean that even agents who were pursuing matters of a commercial or cultural nature might then get immunity. The Rapporteur indicated that the reason he chose to use the adjective "diplomatic" was to eliminate missions which conducted negotiations at a low level. Another member ventured the view that the heads of special missions were not diplomatic agents. (In light of this remark one is entitled to raise the question what purpose there was in considering the subject at all.) One member admitted that the situation was far from clear and wondered whether they ought to be considering all special missions or only those of "career diplomats." Still another argued that although a group of men were sent on a mission by their Government, thus constituting an "official mission," they still might not be entitled to diplomatic privileges and immunities. The reasoning here was not clear, but the implication was that either the nature of their function (investigating trade conditions), or their own private status before going on the mission (businessmen) or both, was enough to disqualify them. Two of the members in attempting to dispel some of the doubts of the others pointed out very sagaciously that in order to qualify for diplomatic prerogatives "a special mission had to represent the State," but then one of them indicated his own doubts by questioning whether all members of such a mission might be entitled to these prerogatives.[1]

The writer would like to state that these views and misconceptions were introduced here only as further evidence of the uncertainty that has existed in many circles on the subject of special missions, and this uncertainty is undoubtedly due to the complexity of the subject. If the term special agent or special mission had not been so ambiguous, i.e. had not been used to cover such a wide variety of missions, and if statesmen and scholars had not ignored the practice for so long thus allowing it "to grow like Topsy" the uncertainties might have been reduced or even removed long ago.

This writer suggests that it is not possible to determine whether a special agent is entitled to a diplomatic status on the basis of function. The reason is quite apparent. Too often the functions of a special mission are similar or even identical to those of regular diplomatic missions. Furthermore, this same situation prevails for missions in which the agents have received diplomatic rank and those in which

[1] Yearbook of the International Law Commission, vol. I, *op. cit.*, pp. 327–28.

they have not. The cardinal point then is whether or not they represent the State, and if they do they should be entitled to all of the above discussed diplomatic prerogatives. However, there can be no doubt that the confusion and uncertainty would be greatly diminished if the sending State would follow the practice of indicating its desire to have such agents accorded such prerogatives by the simple device of bestowing upon them a diplomatic classification and issuing them a diplomatic passport. Thus when the *agréation* is undertaken, to the extent that it exists for special missions, this matter would be clarified in the exchange between the sending and receiving States. There would appear to be few good reasons why such a practice cannot be followed.

One might be that present classifications for heads of missions might not be deemed to be appropriate. If this view should prove to be widely held, certainly some new classification (s) could be agreed upon. Secondly, it is admitted that for some States constitutional provisions may make it difficult to bestow a diplomatic rank when the speedy dispatch of the mission is necessary. This would provide a much more valid objection to the proposal than the first, and would require consideration by the Governments interested in codification.

As for responsibilities, the doctrine of imputability for State sponsored missions must be followed. Oppenheim's view of original and vicarious responsibility seems justified.

And with regard to freedom to travel in the receiving State, and to communicate with one's own Government, restrictions should be kept to a minimum. In fact, excluding the problem of the use of radio, which use will undoubtedly become more and commonplace in the coming years, there ought not be any restrictions except for travel in those zones labelled "security." In some respects this freedom is even more crucial for special missions than it is for regular missions, because of the limited time within which they must usually conclude their work.

In conclusion it may be said that because such agents have not become involved in a large number of difficulties and controversies is no reason to continue to overlook this subject. It may be that contentious cases may not arise for some time. Yet, inasmuch as the use of such agents is neither rare nor recent, but on the contrary represents a very common practice ranging into thousands of cases, it would seem wise that the foreign offices and scholars concern themselves with the practice, and attempt to determine its place in the codification of the international law of diplomatic immunities. It is gratifying to note that at last the International Law Commission has appreciated the seriousness of the need and it is to be hoped that it will bring forth a draft agreement which will be acceptable to the States. Then the *lacuna* which now exists will be filled, and if a serious difficulty should arise the world would not be confronted with the sad spectacle of international friction arising over a situation which existed because of a "gap" in international law. An agreement of this nature would indicate that a practice which has remained unregulated for many years has finally been defined. With so many states willing to grant these privileges and immunities informally, reason no longer exists to eschew codification.

APPENDICES

APPENDIX A

This is a representative list of special agents who have been sent on foreign missions by Presidents of the United States. It is intended to show only the duration of time during which the practice has been followed, the variation in status of the agents used, and the variety in the kinds of missions established.

Name	*Date*	*Diplomatic Rank or Title*	*Nature of Mission*
John Quincy Adams	March 14, 1798	Commissioner	To conclude treaty of amity and commerce with Sweden
General O. E. Babcock	1869	None	To make inquiries about the resources of San Domingo. Negotiated treaty for lease of bay and peninsula of Samana.
Bernard M. Baruch	March 17, 1945	None	To explore subject of Germany's post-war economic position with British government officials.
James F. Bayard	March 25, 1887	None	To negotiate extradition treaty with Russia.
James H. Blount	1893	Commisioner (with Paramount Authority to Regular Agent)	To investigate influences of American officials and armed forces on Hawaiian Revolution.
James Buchanan	March 26, 1832	Commissioner	To conclude treaty of commerce and navigation with Austria.
William I. Buchanan	1907	Minister Plenipotentiary	To second Hague Peace Conference as U.S. Representative.
Lewis Cass	March 21, 1857	Commissioner	To Denmark for commercial matters.
Henry Clay	November 22, 1825	Envoy-Extraordinary and Minister Plenipotentiary	To conclude treaty of peace, friendship, and navigation with Central American Republics.
Dr. Frank P. Corrigan	November 11, 1937	Envoy Extraordinary and Minister Plenipotentiary	To facilitate pacific solution of the controversy between Honduras and Nicaragua over definition of their common boundary.
Brig. Gen. Benj. O. Davis	July 2, 1947	Ambassador	To represent the President of the United States at Liberia's Centennial Celebration.

Name	*Date*	*Diplomatic Rank or Title*	*Nature of Mission*
Norman H. Davis	December 30, 1931	Ambassador	To Geneva Disarmament Conference.
—	March 17, 1933	Ambassador	To London International Monetary and Economic Conference.
—	May, 1934	Ambassador	To Geneva Disarmament Conference
Col. Wm. Donovan	1941	None	To London to discuss the military situation with Winston Churchill; to Dublin to persuade Prime Minister de Valera to grant air and naval bases to Britain; to Greece, Bulgaria, Yugoslavia and the Near East to assess the political situation in light of the expanding military conflict.
Louis G. Dreyfus, Jr.	June 4, 1944	Ambassador	To attend ceremonies for the establishment of the Republic of Iceland as representative of President Roosevelt.
W. E. B. DuBois	1924	Envoy Extraordinary and Minister Plenipotentiary	To attend inauguration of the President of Liberia as representative of President Coolidge.
Stephen Early	January 14, 1945	None	To survey arrangements for handling war news in Europe.
Milton Eisenhower	January 24, 1953	Special Ambassador	To Latin America on Goodwill Tour.
—	July 13, 1958	Special Ambassador	To Panama, El Salvador, Costa Rica, Guatemala, Honduras, and Nicaragua to study economic conditions.
Maj. Gen. Philip B. Fleming	July 9, 1945	None	To Norway, Netherlands, Denmark, Belgium, France, Italy and Sweden to study their plans to meet post-war economic problems.
Albert Gallatin	April 5, 1817	Envoy Extraordinary and Minister Plenipotentiary	To conclude a treaty of commerce with Netherlands.
Walter F. George	May 9, 1956	Ambassador	To represent President Eisenhower at NATO talks in Paris.

Name	*Date*	*Diplomatic Rank or Title*	*Nature of Mission*
James W. Gerard	December 3, 1936	Ambassador	To represent President Roosevelt at the coronation of King Edward VIII.
—	January 26, 1937	Ambassador	To represent President Roosevelt at the coronation of King George VI.
Henry F. Grady	October 21, 1945	Ambassador	To represent President Truman as a member of an international delegation to observe the Greek elections.
John Hays Hammond	1911	Unknown	To represent the President at the coronation of King George V of England.
W. Averell Harriman	March 8, 1941 April 12, 1941	None Minister	To expedite war materials to Britain under Lend-Lease program.
Conrad Hilton	April 19, 1956	None	To Monaco to represent the President at the Grimaldi (Prince Rainier)-Kelly wedding.
Herbert Hoover	January 23, 1947	None	To Britain, France, U.S. zone of Germany, Italy, and "Central Europe" to study food and collateral problems.
Harry L. Hopkins	January, 1941	None	To confer with Winston Churchill on war needs.
—	July, 1941	None	To confer with Winston Churchill on Lend-Lease supplies; to confer with Premier Stalin on war needs.
—	April, 1942	None	To confer with Winston Churchill on war needs and other problems.
—	July, 1942	None	Same as above.
—	January, 1945	None	Same as above.
—	May, 1945	None	To confer with Premier Stalin on Polish government and Soviet participation in U.N.
Joseph C. Hutchenson	December 11, 1945	Unknown	American chairman of the Anglo-American Commission of Inquiry on Palestine.
H. M. Jacoby	1930	Ambassador Extraordinary and Minister Plenipotentiary	To attend coronation of Haile Selassie I of Ethiopia.

Name	*Date*	*Diplomatic Rank or Title*	*Nature of Mission*
Joseph Kennedy	March 8, 1939	Ambassador to London	To attend coronation of Pope Pius XII
Fiorello H. LaGuardia	January 5, 1946	Ambassador	To represent President Truman at the inauguration of President Dutra of Brazil.
Edwin A. Locke, Jr.	May 13, 1945	Personal Representative to Foreign Governments	Unknown
J. R. Leit	July 5, 1835	Agent	To conclude treaty of commerce and navigation with Morocco.
A. Dudley Mann	March 28, 1946	Agent	To Germany } To establish treaties of commerce.
			To Hungary
	June 18, 1849	Agent	To Switzer-
	June 15, 1850	Agent	land
Rep. Mike Mansfield	November 27, 1944	None	To study political and economic conditions in China.
Gen. George C. Marshall	November 28, 1945 April 13, 1946	Ambassador	To study political conditions within China.
Maury Maverick and Patrick W. McDonough	December 28, 1945	None	To study small business operations and prepare plans for stimulating trade with the Philippines, China, Korea, Australia, and New Zealand.
Basil Miles	1917	Minister Plenipotentiary	To assist United States Ambassador in representing the interests of foreign governments in Petrograd.
James G. McDonald	June 23, 1948	Unknown	To Israel during period United States extended *de facto* recognition as head of United States mission.
James Monroe	October 14, 1804	Minister Extraordinary and Plenipotentiary	To conclude treaty with Spain relative to Louisiana boundaries and claims of citizens of both countries.
Leland Morris	June 19, 1946	Ambassador	To head American section of Allied mission to observe revision of Greek electoral lists.
Gouverneur Morris	October 13, 1789	Agent	To ascertain intentions of Britain re Treaty of 1783 and to make treaty of commerce.
Donald M. Nelson	September 30, 1944	Personal Representative to Foreign Governments	To China to study problems relative to the war.

Name	*Date*	*Diplomatic Rank or Title*	*Nature of Mission*
Vice-President Richard Nixon	November, 1953	None	Round-the-World Goodwill Tour.
	February 6, 1955	None	Central America Goodwill Tour.
Nathaniel Niles	May 3, 1838	Agent	To conclude treaty of commerce with Sardinia.
Edwin W. Pauley	April 30, 1945	Ambassador	To head American delegation of the Reparations Commission of the Allies, meeting in Moscow.
William Phillips	December 12, 1942	Ambassador	To head United States mission in New Delhi.
Joel R. Poinsett	March 14, 1825	Envoy Extraordinary and Minister Plenipotentiary	To conclude treaty of commerce and settle boundary issues with Mexico.
Horace Porter	1907	Ambassador	To second Hague Conference as representative of the U.S.
Byron Price	August 31, 1945	Unknown	To act as liaison between American occupation forces and the German people.
John Randolph of Roanoke	June 18, 1830	Commissioner	To conclude treaties relative to principles of maritime war, commerce and navigation.
Senator David Reed	January 10, 1930	None	To London Naval Conference as a Representative of the President.
Philip D. Reed	October 20, 1943	Minister	To act as chief of the mission for economic affairs in London.
Edmund Roberts	1832	Unknown	To act as "roving ambassador" in region of Indian Ocean to obtain commercial rights from local rulers.
Senator Joseph Robinson	January 10, 1930	None	To London Naval Conference as a Representative of the President.
Elihu Root	1917	Ambassador	To Russia to encourage enthusiasm for remaining with Allies in the War.
Uriah M. Rose	1907	Ambassador	To second Hague Conference as U.S. Representative.
Samuel I. Rosenman	January 23, 1945	Minister	To Britain and Europe to examine problems regarding the flow of United States supplies other than military.

Name	*Date*	*Diplomatic Rank or Title*	*Nature of Mission*
Brig. Gen. John H. Russell	February 11, 1922	High Commissioner with rank of Ambassador	To represent President Harding in Haiti.
Edmund Schulthess	July 3, 1938	Commissioner	On Commission of Inquiry provided for by the treaty of conciliation between the U.S. and Yugoslavia.
R. W. Shufeldt	November 15, 1881	Special Envoy	To establish treaty of friendship and commerce with Korea.
Col. Robert M. Springer	August 1, 1946	Commissioner	To the United Nations War Crimes Commission in London.
Maj. Gen. Joseph W. Stilwell	February 10, 1942	None	To work in close cooperation with Premier Chiang-Kai-Shek.
Claude Swanson	December 17, 1931	Unknown	To Geneva Arms Conference
Myron Taylor	June 14, 1938	Ambassador Extraordinary and Plenipotentiary	To serve on special intergovernmental committee to facilitate emigration of political refugees from Austria and Germany.
—	February 4, 1939	Ambassador	To the Vatican as representative of President Roosevelt.
—	May 4, 1946	Ambassador	To the Vatican as representative of President Truman.
Abel P. Upshur	October 24, 1843	Agent	To conclude an extradition treaty with France.
Daniel Webster	February 24, 1851	Agent	To establish claims convention with Portugal.
Sumner Welles	April 24, 1924	Unknown	To arrange peace conference between the representatives of the *de facto* government of Honduras and revolutionary faction.
—	February 10, 1940	Unknown	To Europe including Italy, Germany, France, and Great Britain, to get information regarding political conditions.
Henry Wheaton	June 18, 1827	Envoy Extraordinary and Minister Plenipotentiary	To conclude claims convention with Denmark.
Wendell Willkie	1941	Unknown	To Britain to present personal message to Prime Minister Churchill.
—	August 22, 1942	Unknown	To Soviet Union, Egypt, Saudi Arabia, Palestine, Syria, Turkey, Iraq, Iran

Name	*Date*	*Diplomatic Rank or Title*	*Nature of Mission*
			"to tell the truth about America's war effort ... and to raise with the neutrals the question of the future which they faced when the war was over," and additional special tasks.
Henry Wise	May 25, 1844	Agent	To conclude a treaty of commerce and navigation with Brazil.

APPENDIX B

The following is a partial list of organizations, national and international, which the United States has created or joined since World War II, with the provisions for appointing the American members. It will be noted that no consistent policy of appointments exists, but it would seem that one criterion for judging the significance of the organization in the eyes of Congress is whether or not Congress has insisted on approving the appointments.

Organization	*Provisions for Appointment*	*Statutes, if any*
Economic Cooperation Administration	Administrator, Deputy Administrator, Public Advisory Board (12), U.S. Representative in Europe – appointed by the President with Senate approval.	62 Stat. 137–141 Public Law 472, April 2, 1948
Mutual Defense Assistance Act of 1949	"Four Persons to carry out the provisions of the Act," appointed by the President with Senate approval.	63 Stat. 719, Public Law 329, October 6, 1949
Mutual Security Act of 1951	Director, Deputy Director, Special Representative and Deputy Special Representative in Europe – appointed in Executive office of the President by the President with Senate approval.	65 Stat. 377 Public Law 165, October 10, 1951
South Pacific Commission	Commissioner and alternate appointed by President. No confirmation needed.	62 Stat. 16 Public Law 403, January 28, 1948
United Nations Security Council	One delegate and deputy appointed by President with Senate approval	59 Stat. 619 Public Law 264 December 20, 1945
United Nations General Assembly	Five delegates and alternates appointed by the President with Senate approval.	59 Stat. 619, Public Law 264, December 20, 1945
United Nations Economic and Social Council	The delegate is appointed by the President and confirmed by the Senate if not a member of Congress or an officer who has already been given Senate approval.	59 Stat. 620, Public Law 264, December 20, 1945
United Nations Trusteeship Council	The delegate is appointed by the President and confirmed by the Senate if not a member of Congress or an officer who has already been given Senate approval.	59 Stat. 620, Public Law 264, December 20, 1945
United Nations Economic, Scientific and Cultural Organization	Five delegates and five alternates appointed by the President with Senate approval.	60 Stat. 712, Public Law 565, July 3, 1946

Organization	*Provisions for Appointment*	*Statutes, if any*
United Nations International Monetary Fund and International Bank for Reconstruction and Rehabilitation	Governor of the Bank and Alternate (also serves as Governor of the Fund), Executive Director of the Bank and alternate, Executive Director of the Fund and alternate appointed by the President with Senate approval.	39 Stat. 512, Public Law 171, July 31, 1945
United Nations International Refugee Organization	One delegate and not more than two alternates to a specific session appointed by the President. No confirmation needed.	61 Stat. 215, Public Law 146, July 1, 1947
United Nations World Health Organization	Three delegates and alternates appointed by the President. No confirmation needed unless the representative is appointed to the Executive Board.	62 Stat. 441, Public Law 643, June 14, 1948
United Nations International Civil Aviation Organization	One delegate customarily appointed by President after being agreed to by the Air Co-ordinating Committee. No confirmation needed.	None*
United Nations Universal Postal Union	Delegates designated by the Postmaster General and the principal delegates approved by the President for each Congress of the organization.	48 Stat. 943, Public Law 315, June 12, 1934
United Nations International Tele-communications Union	Delegates for each session of the Plenipotentiary Conferences customarily appointed by the President. No confirmation needed.	None*
United Nations World Meteorological Organization	Permanent delegate is proposed by the Secretary of Commerce and appointed by the Secretary of State	None*
United Nations Food and Agricultural Organization	Delegate to the Council is a ranking officer of the Department of Agriculture proposed by the Secretary of Agriculture and appointed by the Secretary of State.	None*
United Nations International Labor Organization	Delegates to General Conference meetings, and the delegate to the Governing Body customarily appointed by the President.	None*
United Nations International Atomic Energy Agency	Permanent delegate appointed by the President with Senate approval.	71 Stat. 453, Public Law 85, August 28, 1957

* Correspondence, United States Department of State, Office of International Conferences, October 7, 1958.

APPENDIX C

VIENNA CONVENTION ON DIPLOMATIC RELATIONS*

The States Parties to the present Convention,

Recalling that peoples of all nations from ancient times have recognized the status of diplomatic agents,

Having in mind the purposes and principles of the Charter of the United Nations concerning the sovereign equality of States, the maintenance of international peace and security, and the promotion of friendly relations among nations,

Believing that an international convention on diplomatic intercourse, privileges and immunities would contribute to the development of friendly relations among nations, irrespective of their differing constitutional and social systems,

Realizing that the purpose of such privileges and immunities is not to benefit individuals but to ensure the efficient performance of the functions of diplomatic missions as representing States,

Affirming that the rules of customary international law should continue to govern questions not expressly regulated by the provisions of the present Convention,

Have agreed as follows:

Article 1

For the purpose of the present Convention, the following expressions shall have the meanings hereunder assigned to them:

(*a*) the "head of the mission" is the person charged by the sending State with the duty of acting in that capacity;

(*b*) the "members of the mission" are the head of the mission and the members of the staff of the mission;

(*c*) the "members of the staff of the mission" are the members of the diplomatic staff, of the administrative and technical staff and of the service staff of the mission;

(*d*) the "members of the diplomatic staff" are the members of the staff of the mission having diplomatic rank;

(*e*) a "diplomatic agent" is the head of the mission or a member of the diplomatic staff of the mission;

(*f*) the "members of the administrative and technical staff" are the members of the staff of the mission employed in the administrative and technical service of the mission;

(*g*) the "members of the service staff" are the members of the staff of the mission in the domestic service of the mission;

(*h*) a "private servant" is a person who is in the domestic service of a member of the mission and who is not an employee of the sending State;

* A/CONF. 20/13/16 April 1961

(*i*) the "premises of the mission" are the buildings or parts of buildings and the land ancillary thereto, irrespective of ownership, used for the purposes of the mission including the residence of the head of the mission.

Article 2

The establishment of diplomatic relations between States, and of permanent diplomatic missions, takes place by mutual consent.

Article 3

1. The functions of a diplomatic mission consist *inter alia* in:
(*a*) representing the sending State in the receiving State;
(*b*) protecting in the receiving State the interests of the sending State and of its nationals, within the limits permitted by international law;
(*c*) negotiating with the Government of the receiving State;
(*d*) ascertaining by all lawful means conditions and developments in the receiving State, and reporting thereon to the Government of the sending State;
(*e*) promoting friendly relations between the sending State and the receiving State, and developing their economic, cultural and scientific relations.

2. Nothing in the present Convention shall be construed as preventing the performance of consular functions by a diplomatic mission.

Article 4

1. The sending State must make certain that the *agrément* of the receiving State has been given for the person it proposes to accredit as head of the mission to that State.

2. The receiving State is not obliged to give reasons to the sending State for a refusal of *agrément*.

Article 5

1. The sending State may, after it has given due notification to the receiving States concerned, accredit a head of mission or assign any member of the diplomatic staff, as the case may be, to more than one State, unless there is express objection by any of the receiving States.

2. If the sending State accredits a head of mission to one or more other States it may establish a diplomatic mission headed by a *chargé d'affaires ad interim* in each State where the head of mission has not his permanent seat.

3. A head of mission or any member of the diplomatic staff of the mission may act as representative of the sending State to any international organization.

Article 6

Two or more States may accredit the same person as head of mission to another State, unless objection is offered by the receiving State.

Article 7

Subject to the provisions of Articles 5, 8, 9 and 11, the sending State may freely appoint the members of the staff of the mission. In the case of military, naval or air attachés, the receiving State may require their names to be submitted beforehand, for its approval.

Article 8

1. Members of the diplomatic staff of the mission should in principle be of the nationality of the sending State.

2. Members of the diplomatic staff of the mission may not be appointed from among persons having the nationality of the receiving State, except with the consent of that State which may be withdrawn at any time.

3. The receiving State may reserve the same right with regard to nationals of a third State who are not also nationals of the sending State.

Article 9

1. The receiving State may at any time and without having to explain its decision, notify the sending State that the head of the mission or any member of the diplomatic staff of the mission is *persona non garta* or that any other member of the staff of the mission is not acceptable. In any such case, the sending State shall, as appropriate, either recall the person concerned or terminate his functions with the mission. A person may be declared *non grata* or not acceptable before arriving in the territory of the receiving State.

2. If the sending State refuses or fails within a reasonable period to carry out its obligations under paragraph 1 of this Article, the receiving State may refuse to recognize the person concerned as a member of the mission.

Article 10

1. The Ministry for Foreign Affairs of the receiving State, or such other ministry as may be agreed, shall be notified of:

(*a*) the appointment of members of the mission, their arrival and their final departure or the termination of their functions with the mission;

(*b*) the arrival and final departure of a person belonging to the family of a member of the mission and, where appropriate, the fact that a person becomes or ceases to be a member of the family of a member of the mission;

(*c*) the arrival and final departure of private servants in the employ of persons referred to in sub-paragraph (*a*) of this paragraph and, where appropriate, the fact that they are leaving the employ of such persons;

(*d*) the engagement and discharge of persons resident in the receiving State as members of the mission or private servants entitled to privileges and immunities.

2. Where possible, prior notification of arrival and final departure shall also be given.

Article 11

1. In the absence of specific agreement as to the size of the mission, the receiving State may require that the size of a mission be kept within limits considered by it to be reasonable and normal, having regard to circumstances and conditions in the receiving State and to the needs of the particular mission.

2. The receiving State may equally, within similar bounds and on a non-discriminatory basis, refuse to accept officials of a particular category.

Article 12

The sending State may not, without the prior express consent of the receiving State, establish offices forming part of the mission in localities other than those in which the mission itself is established.

Article 13

1. The head of the mission is considered as having taken up his functions in the receiving State either when he has presented his credentials or when he has notified his arrival and a true copy of his credentials has been presented to the Ministry for Foreign Affairs of the receiving State, or such other ministry as may be agreed, in accordance with the practice prevailing in the receiving State which shall be applied in a uniform manner.

2. The order of presentation of credentials or of a true copy thereof will be determined by the date and time of the arrival of the head of the mission.

Article 14

1. Heads of mission are divided into three classes, namely:

(*a*) that of ambassadors or nuncios accredited to Heads of State, and other heads of mission of equivalent rank;

(*b*) that of envoys, ministers and internuncios accredited to Heads of State;

(*c*) that of *chargé d'affaires* accredited to Ministers for Foreign Affairs.

2. Except as concerns precedence and etiquette, there shall be no differentiation between heads of mission by reason of their class.

Article 15

The class to which the heads of their missions are to be assigned shall be agreed between States.

Article 16

1. Heads of mission shall take precedence in their respective classes in the order of the date and time of taking up their functions in accordance with Article 13.

2. Alterations in the credentials of a head of mission not involving any change of class shall not affect his precedence.

3. This article is without prejudice to any practice accepted by the receiving State regarding the precedence of the representative of the Holy See.

Article 17

The precedence of the members of the diplomatic staff of the mission shall be notified by the head of the mission to the Ministry for Foreign Affairs or such other ministry as may be agreed.

Article 18

The procedure to be observed in each State for the reception of heads of mission shall be uniform in respect of each class.

Article 19

1. If the post of head of the mission is vacant, or if the head of the mission is unable to perform his functions, a *chargé d'affaires ad interim* shall act provisionally as head of the mission. The name of the *chargé d'affaires ad interim* shall be notified, either by the head of the mission or, in case he is unable to do so, by the Ministry for Foreign Affairs of the sending State to the Ministry for Foreign Affairs of the receiving State or such other ministry as may be agreed.

2. In cases where no member of the diplomatic staff of the mission is present in the receiving State, a member of the administrative and technical staff may, with the consent of the receiving State, be designated by the sending State to be in charge of the current administrative affairs of the mission.

Article 20

The mission and its head shall have the right to use the flag and emblem of the sending State on the premises of the mission, including the residence of the head of the mission, and on his means of transport.

Article 21

1. The receiving State shall either facilitate the acquisition on its territory, in accordance with its laws, by the sending State of premises necessary for its mission or assist the latter in obtaining accommodation in some other way.
2. It shall also, where necessary, assist missions in obtaining suitable accommodation for their members.

Article 22

1. The premises of the mission shall be inviolable. The agents of the receiving State may not enter them, except with the consent of the head of the mission.
2. The receiving State is under a special duty to take all appropriate steps to protect the premises of the mission against any intrusion or damage and to prevent any disturbance of the peace of the mission or impairment of its dignity.
3. The premises of the mission, their furnishings and other property thereon and the means of transport of the mission shall be immune from search, requisition, attachment or execution.

Article 23

1. The sending State and the head of the mission shall be exempt from all national, regional or municipal dues and taxes in respect of the premises of the mission, whether owned or leased, other than such as represent payment for specific services rendered.
2. The exemption from taxation referred to in this Article shall not apply to such dues and taxes payable under the law of the receiving State by persons contracting with the sending State or the head of the mission.

Article 24

The archives and documents of the mission shall be inviolable at any time and wherever their may be.

Article 25

The receiving State shall accord full facilities for the performance of the functions of the mission.

Article 26

Subject to its laws and regulations concerning zones entry into which is prohibited or regulated for reasons of national security, the receiving State shall ensure to all members of the mission freedom of movement and travel in its territory.

Article 27

1. The receiving State shall permit and protect free communication on the part of the mission for all official purposes. In communicating with the Government and the other missions and consulates of the sending State, wherever situated, the mission may employ all appropriate means, including diplomatic couriers and messages in code or cipher. However, the mission may install and use a wireless transmitter only with the consent of the receiving State.

2. The official correspondence of the mission shall be inviolable. Official correspondence means all correspondence relating to the mission and its functions.

3. The diplomatic bag shall not be opened or detained.

4. The packages constituting the diplomatic bag must bear visible external marks of their character and may contain only diplomatic documents or articles intended for official use.

5. The diplomatic courier, who shall be provided with an official document indicating his status and the number of packages constituting the diplomatic bag, shall be protected by the receiving State in the performance of his functions. He shall enjoy personal inviolability and shall not be liable to any form of arrest or detention.

6. The sending State or the mission may designate diplomatic couriers *ad hoc*. In such cases the provisions of paragraph 5 of this Article shall also apply, except that the immunities therein mentioned shall cease to apply when such a courier has delivered to the consignee the diplomatic bag in his charge.

7. A diplomatic bag may be entrusted to the captain of a commercial aircraft scheduled to land at an authorized port of entry. He shall be provided with an official document indicating the number of packages constituting the bag but he shall not be considered to be a diplomatic courier. The mission may send one of its members to take possession of the diplomatic bag directly and freely from the captain of the aircraft.

Article 28

The fees and charges levied by the mission in the course of its official duties shall be exempt from all dues and taxes.

Article 29

The person of a diplomatic agent shall be inviolable. He shall not be liable to any form of arrest or detention. The receiving State shall treat him with due respect and shall take all appropriate steps to prevent any attack on his person, freedom or dignity.

Article 30

1. The private residence of a diplomatic agent shall enjoy the same inviolability and protection as the premises of the mission.

2. His papers, correspondence and, except as provided in paragraph 3 of Article 31, his property, shall likewise enjoy inviolability.

Article 31

1. A diplomatic agent shall enjoy immunity from the criminal jurisdiction of the receiving State. He shall also enjoy immunity from its civil and administrative jurisdiction, except in the case of:

(*a*) a real action relating to private immovable property situated in the territory of the receiving State, unless he holds it on behalf of the sending State for the purposes of the mission;
(*b*) an action relating to succession in which the diplomatic agent is involved as executor, administrator, heir or legatee as a private person and not on behalf of the sending State;
(*c*) an action relating to any professional or commercial activity exercised by the diplomatic agent in the receiving State outside his official functions.

2. A diplomatic agent is not obliged to give evidence as a witness.

3. No measures of execution may be taken in respect of a diplomatic agent except in the cases coming under sub-paragraphs (*a*), (*b*) and (*c*) of paragraph 1 of this Article, and provided that the measures concerned can be taken without infringing the inviolability of his person or of his residence.

4. The immunity of a diplomatic agent from the jurisdiction of the receiving State does not exempt him from the jurisdiction of the sending State.

Article 32

1. The immunity from jurisdiction of diplomatic agents and of persons enjoying immunity under Article 37 may be waived by the sending State.

2. Waiver must always be express.

3. The initiation of proceedings by a diplomatic agent or by a person enjoying immunity from jurisdiction under Article 37 shall preclude him from invoking immunity from jurisdiction in respect of any counter-claim directly connected with the principal claim.

4. Waiver of immunity from jurisdiction in respect of civil or administrative proceedings shall not be held to imply waiver of immunity in respect of the execution of the judgment, for which a separate waiver shall be necessary.

Article 33

1. Subject to the provisions of paragraph 3 of this Article, a diplomatic agent shall with respect to services rendered for the sending State be exempt from social security provisions which may be in force in the receiving State.

2. The exemption provided for in paragraph 1 of this Article shall also apply to private servants who are in the sole employ of a diplomatic agent, on condition:

(*a*) that they are not nationals of or permanently resident in the receiving State; and
(*b*) that they are covered by the social security provisions which may be in force in the sending State or a third State.

3. A diplomatic agent who employs persons to whom the exemption provided for in paragraph 2 of this Article does not apply shall observe the obligations which the social security provisions of the receiving State impose upon employers.

4. The exemption provided for in paragraphs 1 and 2 of this Article shall not preclude voluntary participation in the social security system of the receiving State provided that such participation is permitted by that State.

5. The provisions of this Article shall not affect bilateral or multilateral agreements concerning social security concluded previously and shall not prevent the conclusion of such agreements in the future.

Article 34

A diplomatic agent shall be exempt from all dues and taxes, personal or real, national, regional or municipal, except:

(*a*) indirect taxes of a kind which are normally incorporated in the price of goods or services;
(*b*) dues and taxes on private immovable property situated in the territory of the receiving State, unless he holds it on behalf of the sending State for the purposes of the mission;
(*c*) estate, succession or inheritance duties levied by the receiving State, subject to the provisions of paragraph 4 of Article 39;
(*d*) dues and taxes on private income having its source in the receiving State and capital taxes on investments made in commercial undertakings in the receiving State;
(*e*) charges levied for specific services rendered;
(*f*) registration, court or record fees, mortgage dues and stamp duty, with respect to immovable property, subject to the provisions of Article 23.

Article 35

The receiving State shall exempt diplomatic agents from all personal services, from all public service of any kind whatsoever, and from military obligations such as those connected with requisitioning, military contributions and billeting.

Article 36

1. The receiving State shall, in accordance with such laws and regulations as it may adopt, permit entry of and grant exemption from all customs duties, taxes, and related charges other than charges for storage, cartage and similar services, on:
(*a*) articles for the official use of the mission;
(*b*) articles for the personal use of a diplomatic agent or members of his family forming part of his household, including articles intended for his establishment.

2. The personal baggage of a diplomatic agent shall be exempt from inspection unless there are serious grounds for presuming that it contains articles not covered by the exemptions mentioned in paragraph 1 of this Article, or articles the import or export of which is prohibited by the law or controlled by the quarantine regulations of the receiving State. Such inspection shall be conducted only in the presence of the diplomatic agent or of his authorized representative.

Article 37

1. The members of the family of a diplomatic agent forming part of his household shall, if they are not nationals of the receiving State, enjoy the privileges and immunities specified in Articles 29 to 36.

2. Members of the administrative and technical staff of the mission, together with members of their families forming part of their respective households, shall, if they are not nationals of or permanently resident in the receiving State, enjoy the privileges and immunities specified in Articles 29 to 35, except that the immunity from civil and administrative jurisdiction of the receiving State specified in paragraph 1 of Article 31 shall not extend to acts performed outside the course of their duties. They shall also enjoy the privileges specified in Article 36, paragraph 1, in respect of articles imported at the time of first installation.

3. Members of the service staff of the mission who are not nationals of or permanently resident in the receiving State shall enjoy immunity in respect of

acts performed in the course of their duties, exemption from dues and taxes on the emoluments they receive by reason of their employment and the exemption contained in Article 33.

4. Private servants of members of the mission shall, if they are not nationals of or permanently resident in the receiving State, be exempt from dues and taxes on the emoluments they receive by reason of their employment. In other respects, they may enjoy privileges and immunities only to the extent admitted by the receiving State. However, the receiving State must exercise its jurisdiction over those persons in such a manner as not to interfere unduly with the performance of the functions of the mission.

Article 38

1. Except insofar as additional privileges and immunities may be granted by the receiving State, a diplomatic agent who is a national of or permanently resident in that State shall enjoy only immunity from jurisdiction, and inviolability, in respect of official acts performed in the exercise of his functions.

2. Other members of the staff of the mission and private servants who are nationals of or permanently resident in the receiving State shall enjoy privileges and immunities only to the extent admitted by the receiving State. However, the receiving State must exercise its jurisdiction over those persons in such a manner as not to interfere unduly with the performance of the functions of the mission.

Article 39

1. Every person entitled to privileges and immunities shall enjoy them from the moment he enters the territory of the receiving State on proceeding to take up his post or, if already in its territory, from the moment when his appointment is notified to the Ministry for Foreign Affairs or such other ministry as may be agreed.

2. When the functions of a person enjoying privileges and immunities have come to an end, such privileges and immunities shall normally cease at the moment when he leaves the country, or on expiry of a reasonable period in which to do so, but shall subsist until that time, even in case of armed conflict. However, with respect to acts performed by such a person in the exercise of his functions as a member of the mission, immunity shall continue to subsist.

3. In case of the death of a member of the mission, the members of his family shall continue to enjoy the privileges and immunities to which they are entitled until the expiry of a reasonable period in which to leave the country.

4. In the event of the death of a member of the mission not a national of or permanently resident in the receiving State or a member of his family forming part of his household, the receiving State shall permit the withdrawal of the movable property of the deceased, with the exception of any property acquired in the country the export of which was prohibited at the time of his death. Estate, succession and inheritance duties shall not be levied on movable property the presence of which in the receiving State was due solely to the presence there of the deceased as a member of the mission or as a member of the family of a member of the mission.

Article 40

1. If a diplomatic agent passes through or is in the territory of a third State, which has granted him a passport visa if such visa was necessary, while pro-

ceeding to take up or to return to his post, or when returning to his own country, the third State shall accord him inviolability and such other immunities as may be required to ensure his transit or return. The same shall apply in the case of any members of his family enjoying privileges or immunities who are accompanying the diplomatic agent, or travelling separately to join him or to return to their country.

2. In circumstances similar to those specified in paragraph 1 of this Article, third States shall not hinder the passage of members of the administrative and technical or service staff of a mission, and of members of their families, through their territories.

3. Third States shall accord to official correspondence and other official communications in transit, including messages in code or cipher, the same freedom and protection as is accorded by the receiving State. They shall accord to diplomatic couriers, who have been granted a passport visa if such visa was necessary, and diplomatic bags in transit the same inviolability and protection as the receiving State is bound to accord.

4. The obligations of third States under paragraphs 1, 2 and 3 of this Article shall also apply to the persons mentioned respectively in those paragraphs, and to official communications and diplomatic bags, whose presence in the territory of the third State is due to *force majeure*.

Article 41

1. Without prejudice to their privileges and immunities, it is the duty of all persons enjoying such privileges and immunities to respect the laws and regulations of the receiving State. They also have a duty not to interfere in the internal affairs of that State.

2. All official business with the receiving State entrusted to the mission by the sending State shall be conducted with or through the Ministry for Foreign Affairs of the receiving State or such other ministry as may be agreed.

3. The premises of the mission must not be used in any manner incompatible with the functions of the mission as laid down in the present Convention or by other rules of general international law or by any special agreements in force between the sending and the receiving State.

Article 42

A diplomatic agent shall not in the receiving State practise for personal profit any professional or commercial activity.

Article 43

The function of a diplomatic agent comes to an end, *inter alia:*

(*a*) on notification by the sending State to the receiving State that the function of the diplomatic agent has come to an end;

(*b*) on notification by the receiving State to the sending State that, in accordance with paragraph 2 of Article 9, it refuses to recognize the diplomatic agent as a member of the mission.

Article 44

The receiving State must, even in case of armed conflict, grant facilities in order to enable persons enjoying privileges and immunities, other than nationals of the receiving State, and members of the families of such persons irrespective of their nationality, to leave at the earliest possible moment. It must, in particular, in case of need, place at their disposal the necessary means of transport for themselves and their property.

Article 45

If diplomatic relations are broken off between two States, or if a mission is permanently or temporarily recalled:

(*a*) the receiving State must, even in case of armed conflict, respect and protect the premises of the mission, together with its property and archives;

(*b*) the sending State may entrust the custody of the premises of the mission, together with its property and archives, to a third State acceptable to the receiving State;

(*c*) the sending State may entrust the protection of its interests and those of its nationals to a third State acceptable to the receiving State.

Article 46

A sending State may with the prior consent of a receiving State, and at the request of a third State not represented in the receiving State, undertake the temporary protection of the interests of the third State and of its nationals.

Article 47

1. In the application of the provisions of the present Convention, the receiving State shall not discriminate as between States.

2. However, discrimination shall not be regarded as taking place:

(*a*) where the receiving State applies any of the provisions of the present Convention restrictively because of a restrictive application of that provision to its mission in the sending State;

(*b*) where by custom or agreement States extend to each other more favourable treatment than is required by the provisions of the present Convention.

Article 48

The present Convention shall be open for signature by all States Members of the United Nations or of any of the specialized agencies or Parties to the Statute of the International Court of Justice, and by any other State invited by the General Assembly of the United Nations to become a Party to the Convention, as follows: until 31 October 1961 at the Federal Ministry for Foreign Affairs of Austria and subsequently, until 31 March 1962, at the United Nations Headquarters in New York.

Article 49

The present Convention is subject to ratification. The instruments of ratification shall be deposited with the Secretary-General of the United Nations.

Article 50

The present Convention shall remain open for accession by any State belonging to any of the four categories mentioned in Article 48. The instruments of accession shall be deposited with the Secretary-General of the United Nations.

Article 51

1. The present Convention shall enter into force on the thirtieth day following the date of deposit of the twenty-second instrument of ratification or accession with the Secretary-General of the United Nations.

2. For each State ratifying or acceding to the Convention after the deposit of the twenty-second instrument of ratification or accession, the Convention shall enter into force on the thirtieth day after deposit by such State of its instrument of ratification or accession.

Article 52

The Secretary-General of the United Nations shall inform all States belonging to any of the four categories mentioned in Article 48:

a) of signature to the present Convention and of the deposit of instruments of ratification or accession, in accordance with Articles 48, 49 and 50;

(*b*) of the date on which the present Convention will enter into force, in accordance with Article 51.

Article 53

The original of the present Convention, of which the Chinese, English, French, Russian and Spanish texts are equally authentic, shall be deposited with the Secretary-General of the United Nations, who shall send certified copies thereof to all States belonging to any of the four categories mentioned in Article 48.

IN WITNESS WHEREOF the undersigned Plenipotentiaries, being duly authorized thereto by their respective Governments, have signed the present Convention.

DONE AT VIENNA, this eighteenth day of April one thousand nine hundred and sixty-one.

APPENDIX D

THE AGENCIES OF COLONEL HOUSE AND HARRY HOPKINS

It has seemed desirable in a work of this kind to include two brief case studies of special agents. This appendix presents a discussion of their specific status as the writer interprets it under the municipal law of the United States and under international law. But it goes beyond the merely legal discussion and attempts what may be called a socio-political analysis of the way these agents operated, the reasons for their use and the resultant effect.

Although it is true that the two men who will be discussed, Edward M. House and Harry L. Hopkins, are not typical of executive agents, they have been chosen in part because of the greater wealth of material on them than on others, and also because in their activities one sees the farthest extension of the practice. In other words in such a study, the full panoply of advantages and disadvantages, dangers and values becomes revealed. The writer tried to approach the study of both agents in the same way but was not completely successful in this because of the impossibility of obtaining access to many of the papers concerning Hopkins, a problem referred to in the preface, and one which did not exist regarding House.

EDWARD M. HOUSE

House's Background

House was born in 1858 in Houston, Texas, into an environment where a lack of social consciousness was a prevailing characteristic. As a child he was never a very good student, but possibly took up an interest in politics as a result of an accident which kept him from living the robust life he had begun to lead. Through a friendship with the son of Senator Morton of Indiana his interest in politics flowered, especially because he was permitted to overhear the discussions of prominent Republicans, some of which took place in the White House during Grant's administration.

From 1880 to 1910 his time was taken up mainly with managing his fairly large Texas estates and with Texas politics. He was apparently very successful in directing the campaigns of numerous Texas Governors and in acting as their unofficial advisor after election. In fact his skill in political organization and his adroitness in dealing with men became known even beyond Texas. Thus, his mode of behavior, the refusal to accept office, his ability to compromise the differences between those who held conflicting views, and his activities in a broad variety of affairs as an agent for several governors were a forerunner of his future work as an executive agent.

In Washington he impressed Wilson with his willingness to serve selflessly, in no sense profiting financially from his association with the President. He also held a political philosophy which was much more compatible to that of Wilson than any other man in the Department of State or in the diplomatic service.[1]

The Nature of the House-Wilson Relationship

The nature of the House-Wilson relationship will undoubtedly remain a fascinating one for students of politics for years to come. Writers such as Baker, Link and the Georges either do not weigh his importance to Wilson heavily or belittle the value of his contribution. Others such as Millis depict him as a naive advisor who did not understand the intrigue of English diplomacy. Still other scholars, such as Seymour and Buehrig give him credit for much of the success Wilson achieved in foreign affairs, crediting him with the ability to season Wilson's idealism with realism.

That House and Wilson had a relationship that can be described as unique in the truest sense of the term cannot be denied. Although the President had other foreign affairs agents and advisors there is no doubt that no other person compared to House in the way he combined these roles.

The colonel had waited a long time for the "right" moment to arrive and it finally did in 1912. An affection between him and the President flowered rapidly and was so deep as to choke off friendships with almost all others. The two would visit each other frequently, House going to Washington or the President to New York or Massachusetts. When they weren't visiting they were exchanging views by mail or by a private telephone line between the two residences. To keep their exchange of views secret they used a "cypher" which "the President suggested." [2]

The genuine affection which existed is profusely illustrated by the many terms of endearment that stud the correspondence between them. Possibly one of the best examples of this is the notation in House's Diary just prior to and subsequent to his second mission to Europe, February to June, 1915. House wrote,

> He asked me to tell Sir Edward Grey his entire mind, so he would know what his intentions were about everything ... He said, "Let him know that while you are abroad I expect to act directly through you and to eliminate all intermediaries." He approved all I had in mind to say to Sir Edward and to the Germans. He said there is not much for us to talk over, for the reason we are both of the same mind and it is not necessary to go into details with you.[3]

When House returned he received a letter requesting him to visit Wilson because, "you are the only person in the world with whom I can discuss everything. There are some I can discuss one thing and others, another, but you are the only one to whom I can make an entire clearance of mind." [4] When House replied he could not come to Washington because of the heat the President traveled to Long Island to visit him.[5]

[1] Although there is a paucity of material dealing with House's early life, the writer has been able to develop the above description by relying upon the following sources: Charles Seymour, *The Intimate Papers of Colonel House* (New York: Houghton Mifflin Co., 1926) (hereafter cited as *House Papers*); Arthur Smith, *The Real Colonel House* (New York: George R. Doran Co., 1918); Josephus Daniels, *The Wilson Era, Years of War and After, 1917–1923* (Chapel Hill: University of North Carolina Press, 1946); Charles Seymour, *Woodrow Wilson and the World War: A Chronicle of Our Times* (New Haven: Yale University Press, 1921); Arthur S. Link, "Wilson the Diplomatist" in Earl Latham, ed., *The Philosophy and Policies of Woodrow Wilson* (Chicago: University of Chicago Press, 1958).

[2] "House Diary," *op. cit.*, March 28, 1913, I, 128.

[3] Seymour, *House Papers*, *op. cit.*, I, 356.

[4] *Ibid.*, I, 116.

[5] Correspondence, House to Wilson, June 20, 1915, Wilson MSS, Library of Congress.

It was not difficult for others to perceive that House held a special and rare position and it is understandable that hundreds of persons should have used him as the avenue to the President. But this was not limited to Americans. Foreign diplomats and men of unofficial but important connections would approach House with suggestions which they wanted Wilson to receive. This even included England's Foreign Minister Sir Edward Grey whose use of House was bound still further to enhance the latter's status. For example, after House and Grey had worked out their famous *Memorandum*, House asked Grey to make Lord Reading available any time he (House) cabled for him so that he could carry back a message from the President regarding application of the Agreement.[1] Grey, incidentally, states in his own memoirs that he arranged his day while House was in England so that he could drop by in the evening "whenever he wanted to have a talk." [2]

It is appropriate to ask how it is that House was not only able to establish but also to maintain such a friendship. In the first place it is fairly clear that Wilson had a kind of personality that required from others a deep affection and unswerving loyalty. Furthermore, he had a great reluctance to meet large numbers of people and to work out plans in detail. In both cases House served very satisfactorily. For example, he not only took charge of many of the patronage problems, but also spoke frequently with cabinet members and explained the President's ideas to them. In addition he was not only able to dwell upon the details of programs but could organize the talents of others to do this. Hence the President put him in charge of the Inquiry, the committee to prepare the data necessary to establish the peace treaty.

In order to fill this role he had to be "a keen student of Wilson's character. It was his own estimate that he learned to know his subject well enough to be able to influence him, but 'I could never really understand him.'" [3] It is the George's opinion that in large measure House's success could be attributed to a keen insight into Wilson's personality and an awareness of his "extraordinary need for, and responsiveness to praise, approval and personal devotion." [4]

It is quite probable that at times House became very frustrated in his role. He had a practical aspect about him which Wilson never seemed to have but which nevertheless the President seemed, for the most part, to appreciate in his friend. The President disliked to compromise and conciliate, but it was a practiced art with the Colonel. In many ways, therefore, House complemented Wilson or filled the gaps in his character so necessary to the successful filling of his office. It should not be assumed that House dominated the President or always was able to convince him of the correctness of his views. When Wilson made up his mind, when he became adamant, House was limited to the concessions he could wring from others. He knew that by disagreeing too much with the President he would only jeopardize his own position. The thing that House had to remember above all else was that the basis for his power lay in his being acceptable to the President. Thus he was tethered, and the degrees of freedom with which he operated were strictly related to the extent to which he could convince the President to accept his ideas. Such a restriction must, at

[1] House Diary, February 22, 1916, as cited in Edward H. Buehrig, *Woodrow Wilson and the Balance of Power* (Bloomington: Indiana University Press, 1955), pp. 313–314.

[2] Viscount Grey of Fallodon, *Twenty-Five Years: 1892–1916* (New York: Frederick A. Stokes Co., 1925), II, 124.

[3] Alexander L. George and Juliette L. George, *Woodrow Wilson and Colonel House, A Personality Study* (New York: The John Day Co., 1956), p. 124.

[4] *Ibid.*

times, have been quite painful to House. And the pain must have grown as, in House's eyes, the stakes grew larger and the President more inflexible.

The Paris Peace Conference represented just such a culminating point. Although one finds frequent criticism of Wilson before that time in the House Diary, particularly with regard to Wilson's reluctance to arm the nation during peace time, it does not really take on a tone of bitterness until 1919. This is not the place to present a detailed discussion of what happened between the two, but a few facts may be noted. In the first place House was now not only an adviser but also an official peace commissioner. And since he had also headed the Inquiry he was probably more familiar with the intricacies of the many problems that were raised than Wilson. Furthermore, it is a certainty that he made himself more available to the other delegates and their advisors and was therefore more familiar with their viewpoints. On the other hand Wilson was being criticized and condemned for his stands both in Paris and in Washington. Furthermore he failed to cultivate the Press, an error to which House did not fall prey. Thus House was more familiar with the reasons for the viewpoints of the other nations and United States Senators and probably made a stronger effort than usual to have Wilson change his mind. To what extent he followed the same procedure which he later told Seymour he frequently used with the President, namely winning him over by suggesting that a certain stand would earn him a place in history, is not certain.[1] But it seems clear that from Wilson's viewpoint, at the time he felt the strongest need for someone to stand by him, his "dearest friend" seemed to have deserted him.

In other words House's failure at Paris in his relationship with Wilson may have been due to altering his usual approach of trying to get others to accommodate their views to Wilson's. Instead he seems to have supported the others against Wilson. If this is so it destroys one of Edith Bolling Wilson's charges that House was nothing but a "yes-yes" man, but substantiates another, that he deserted his chief. On the other hand one would have to acknowledge that any agent would be more likely to be successful when (1) he is operating without his chief's presence hovering over him, and (2) when he is dealing in generalities rather than in the hard facts that detailed decisions force to light. Once Wilson discerned this shift in House's role he excluded House as he did the other commissioners from any important part in the decision making.[2]

There is no doubt that their relationship had become less sanguine even before the conference, and the George's go to great lengths to try to document this.[3] But it is also quite possible that the earlier critical comments in House's Diary could have been written from the dual need to "let-off steam" and the desire to preserve his good name for posterity. At any rate, until the Conference, parallel with the critical comments were the continued evidences of mutual affection and confidence.

His Influence and Methods of Operation

There were many ways for House to be influential with Wilson. Around the White House there are always many "shifting jealousies and ambitions," and as Blum points out, because Wilson was intent on ignoring the rivalries it became quite possible for House to utilize his talents effectively.[4] Although Blum does not deal with this aspect in detail it is clear that the problems that become

[1] *Ibid.*, p. 125.

[2] *Ibid.*, p. 249.

[3] *Ibid.*, see especially pp. 182–190.

[4] John Morton Blum, *Woodrow Wilson and the Politics of Morality* (Boston: Little Brown and Co., 1956), p. 112.

a part of the struggle for patronage were numerous in large measure because of the political "famine" that had existed since the Civil War with regard to appointments for "deserving" Democrats. By helping to take the "load" off of Wilson in such matters House was able to put himself in a position in which many would owe him a debt. He thus performed a service for Wilson and at the same time obtained a corps of "informers" who kept him abreast of the events which it was necessary for him to know about in order to play his role properly.

In addition to private letters from American diplomats abroad House also received letters and personal visits from officials of other countries. As a result he was not only in a position of getting information and insight into matters which the Department of State did not have, but also of apprising the President of the results, a performance which the Department often could not match.

Even critics of the Colonel acknowledge that "at the zenith of his career [he] exercised tremendous influence upon the course of diplomatic negotiations." [1] Probably an outstanding example of this was the situation in the early winter of 1915. Wilson was greatly distressed by the British attitude regarding the blockade and the problem of allowing British armed merchantmen to use American ports. This was one of those periods when his annoyance with the British seemed even greater than with the Germans. House, who was in England at the time, cautioned very strongly against the President's pushing the British too far for fear that this might force Grey out of the Foreign Office. He further warned against a break in the relations with Germany.[2]

> The colonel's views prevailed. He had the satisfaction of being informed by the President that "We are trying to be guided by what you think and shall await your full report upon your return home before taking any steps that might alter our opportunity, providing the sea operations of the Central Powers make it possible for us to maintain the status quo." House on February 14 ventured a direct cable to Lansing concerning the armed merchantmen: "There are so many other issues involved in the controversy concerning armed merchantmen that I sincerely hope you will be able to hold it in abeyance until I return. I cannot emphasize too strongly the importance of this." Accordingly, Lansing at a press conference on the sixteenth did an about-face, reverting to the orthodox position on arming merchantmen. In consequence Wilson proceeded to ride out the storm in Congress on an issue which could not have been more unpropitious – the right of Americans to travel on armed belligerent merchantmen.[3]

Shortly after House returned from abroad another opportunity presented itself for him to use his influence in an important matter. In the midst of the Sussex crisis Wilson had received and declined an invitation to speak before the League to Enforce Peace. Then he changed his mind and House obtained a second invitation for him. The speech was to "identify the policy of the United States with the league idea and announce the President's purpose of calling a peace conference. To assure favorable reception of the speech by the Allies, Wilson desired his proposal for a league to conform with what had passed between House and Grey. He requested House "to formulate what you would say, in my place, if you were seeking to make the proposal as nearly what you deem Grey and his colleagues have agreed upon in principle." [4]

[1] George and George, *op. cit.*, p. 192.

[2] House to Wilson, January 13, 1916, as cited in Buehrig, *Woodrow Wilson and the Balance of Power*, pp. 216–217.

[3] Wilson to House, February 13, 1915, *ibid.*, p. 217; House to Lansing, February 14, 1916, *ibid.*

[4] Wilson to House, May 18, 1916, as cited in Buehrig, *Woodrow Wilson and the Balance of Power*, *op. cit.*, p. 238.

One of Wilson's greatest weaknesses at least until 1916, was his lack of interest in and knowledge of foreign policy issues. House was continually trying to awaken this interest and continually urging a preparedness program on the President.

While abroad House's ability to draw people out, his tendency to act as a magnet in attracting all who wanted to impart or gather information and his generally good judgment in assessing the value of the information helped provide Wilson with insight into events. In filling this role he undoubtedly conciliated opposing viewpoints and helped explain the behavior of the United States to the statesmen of other countries. In fact he frequently did the same thing with the other powers making some effort to clarify what he thought the position of Britain, Germany and France was to one another.

Grey wrote that his "relations with House were quite informal." [1] This opportunity to be informal enhanced his value to Wilson because apparently both Grey and House operated much better in this fashion. The opportunity to avoid official dispatches and official explanations was greatly appreciated by both.

> Whatever I said to House, or he to me, was private and informal, to be repeated direct to President Wilson as House might think fit, sure not to be misunderstood, and not to be in any way binding except when it was written down and agreed between us, as a definite expression of view.[2]

His activities even reached the point where he would explain to members of a government what their superiors' plans and policies were much as an American Assistant Secretary of State might explain to an American Ambassador the intentions of the Secretary of State or of the President.[3] Thus he had the opportunity to disclose, explain, camouflage, etc., the activities of leading Western statesmen and because of his skill in doing this was on intimate terms with most of them. House thereby was able to circumvent not only the Department of State channels but at times that of the British Foreign Office as well. In addition to the ambassadors, American and foreign, writing and seeking him out, House was also able to keep informed through the numerous extremely important conferences he would hold with Sir William Tyrrell, Grey's Secretary, and Sir William Wiseman, Britain's Chief of Intelligence in the United States. At times these men revealed such important plans and problems of their Government that House wrote to Wilson during his second mission that the information he had just received was too important to send even by code.[4]

One of the reasons why he was in such a strategic position was that Wilson had so little confidence in the ability of this country's diplomats, a dissatisfaction that was almost as strongly felt by House and Lansing, the Secretary of State. This disapproval was likewise felt toward some of the foreign diplomats in Washington and there is some reason to believe that the British may have had a similar feeling toward their Ambassador Spring-Rice.[5] It should also be noted

[1] Grey, *op. cit.*, p. 123.

[2] *Ibid.*

[3] See for example the revealing discussion recounted in House's Diary in which House explained Grey's views on the Panama tolls and Mexican controversies to Spring-Rice of the British Embassy, or House's statement to Sir Horace Plunkett that he could not reveal to Sir Horace the British government's plans regarding Ireland. "House Diary," *op. cit.*, December 29, 1913, III, 407.

[4] Correspondence, House to Wilson, February 12, 1915, Wilson MSS, Library of Congress.

[5] Correspondence, House to Wilson, August 25, 1914 and March 27, 1915, Wilson MSS, Library of Congress; "House Diary," December 15, 1915, VII, 324–326; Correspondence, Wilson to C. W. Eliot, September 17, 1913, Wilson MSS, Library of Congress; "House Diary," December 29, 1913, III, 406.

that the President also had very little confidence in his first Secretary of State, Bryan, and not much more in his second, Lansing, feelings in which House concurred. Perhaps the best proof of this is that the President and House corresponded in code quite frequently and in fact House had the same kind of arrangement with Grey, at the latter's request.[1]

If one were to seek two terms which defined House's activities one would probably call him a pacificator and an instigator. Many hours were spent in smoothing out difficulties and feelings (Secretary of the Navy Daniels called him Mr. Smooth-It-Away) and many more in suggesting plans of action along many fronts, requesting the President or others to put them in motion.

Five Missions Abroad

To aid Wilson along these lines House undertook five missions abroad, May to July, 1914, February to June, 1915, January to February, 1916, November to December, 1917, and October, 1918 to October, 1919.

During his first trip abroad he went without any credentials, as a private citizen who was a personal friend of the President. His purpose apparently was to strengthen the ties of friendship between Britain, Germany, France, and the United States, to reduce the friction that was developing especially between the British, French and Germans, and to divert some of the large expenditures for armaments to economic exploitation of undeveloped parts of the world, e.g., South America. This was House's "Great Adventure." [2] His conferences with German officialdom, including the Kaiser, and British leaders were arranged by the American Ambassadors Gerard and Page who were highly successful in getting invitations for House. (In fact, he had insisted he would only go to Berlin upon invitation).[3] His intention was to speak in his own name, leaving the leaders to draw their own inferences as to whether he was also speaking for the President.[4] But he really left little to doubt, telling the Kaiser, for example, that the President was concerned about the distrust that existed in European capitals and believed that an American would have a better chance "to compose the difficulties." [5] He proposed to keep each Chief of State informed regarding the plans of the others, a proposal which they readily accepted. From the beginning, therefore, he not only undertook the most difficult and delicate assignments, but proceeded to act as an agent of other Executives in addition to Wilson.

By 1915 the shipping problem had already become serious even for the neutrals. Germany had declared a submarine blockade of Britain in February and the British had replied with Orders in Council, which practically wiped out the distinction between contraband and non-contraband. Merchant ships were being stopped and taken to Port by the British or sunk by the Germans. Hence House went to Europe again in February, interestingly, on the Lusitania, which was sunk three months later while he was still abroad. During this trip his objective was to get the three western states to agree to a convention which would consider defining the concept "freedom of the seas" in such a way as to reduce greatly the contraband list to just the actual implements of war. Merchant vessels, neutral or belligerent, would proceed freely providing they did not carry

[1] *Ibid.*, June 4, 1915, VI, 156.

[2] Seymour, *House Papers*, *op. cit.*, I, 242, 247.

[3] "House Diary," *op. cit.*, May 28. 1914, IV, 34.

[4] Correspondence, House to Wilson, May 29, 1914, as cited in Seymour, *House Papers*, *op. cit.*, I, 249.

[5] "House Diary," *op. cit.*, June 1, 1914, IV, 40.

contraband. They would be permitted to enter any port unless it were effectively blockaded.[1] He believed that all states would benefit from such an agreement but especially Great Britain. Much to House's disappointment the German government seemed much more willing to take it up than the British, who were quite reluctant to come to a definite agreement. To get British support House coupled this plan with the idea of arms limitations, a proposition which, if acceptable, would reduce the power of the German land forces as much as the other would reduce the need for British naval forces.

We find House in the spring of 1915 not only entreating important leaders such as Sir Edward Grey, Lord Kitchner and Lloyd George to show due consideration for his proposals but also appealing to the press, especially in Britain. By cultivating publishers and editors he thought he could build up support among the populace at large. He hoped they would then act as a pressure point on the government.[2]

This time House's expenses were paid but he still carried no official papers nor even instructions from the President, having received a letter telling him they were unnecessary for "we are both of the same mind." [3]

The problems confronting the United States as a result of the belligerents' actions on the high seas became more and more severe. The Gulfflight, Lusitania, Arabic and Ancona had been sunk with the loss of a number of American lives. But the very idea of sinking passenger ships without warning or safeguard for civilian ives greatly disturbed House and Wilson, and the possibility of entering the war seemed very real. The convention idea had not been acceptable and Grey, for one, was beginning to regret it. He wrote several letters to House expressing the belief that some kind of a League of Nations seemed the only way to curb aggressive international behavior.[4] House seized upon this idea and coupled to it the possibility that the United States might join with others to mediate the present dispute. If Germany refused to consider any terms which entailed the idea of collective security and the diminution of militarism, the United States might throw in its weight on the side of the Allies and thus bring about the end of the war. Hence the development of the idea of intervention to which Wilson gave his approval. It was to be left to the British, however, in conjunction with her allies, to determine when the moment was ripe to propose this daring step. At the "right" moment, House told Grey, he would go to Germany to get them to agree to end the war. If they refused the United States would (Wilson added "probably") join the Allies.[5] But the British again dragged their feet, and House, and especially Wilson, became alarmed. Hence the President proposed that House make a third trip on the alleged grounds of informing the United States' ambassadors of the most recent thoughts of the President. While abroad he could push their ideas.[6]

The third journey took House to most of the Western capitals. Although he was not successful in getting the belligerents to agree on peace terms, he managed to see many influential members in and out of government in each country and possibly accomplished some real measure of good in moderating the antagonism that had developed in each country toward the United States. He was especially popular with the press in each country, many of the papers, in-

[1] Seymour, *House Papers*, *op. cit.*, I, 406–410.

[2] House to Wilson, March 5, 1915, Wilson MSS, Library of Congress.

[3] "House Diary," *op. cit.*, January 24, 1915, VII, 28.

[4] Grey to House, August 10, 1915, August 26, 1915, September 22, 1915, as cited in Seymour, *House Papers*, *op. cit.*, II, 87–89.

[5] *Ibid.*, II, 90–91.

[6] *Ibid.*, pp. 101–102.

cluding even some in the United States which had been opposing the Administration, had laudatory things to say regarding both his efforts and manner of conducting himself.[1] From several sources came suggestions that other state leaders would do well to emulate Wilson in the matter of using special agents.[2] This was a period of great popularity for House. His friendship with Wilson was never closer, his acceptance in the capitals of the West never greater and his popularity at home and abroad never higher. This despite the fact that so little was known of what he was really doing!

When House undertook his third mission to Europe he held a status different from any he had held heretofore. The British ambassador, Spring-Rice, in one of his frequent excitable moments, had apparently listened to the views of some enemies of the Administration who argued that House's activities were illegal in that he was meeting leaders of foreign governments and possibly making agreements with them, in the capacity of a private citizen and not as a government official. It was alleged that this was a violation of the Logan Act. Spring-Rice, in accepting this view, warned other Britons not to treat House diplomatically. The latter informed Wilson of this matter, whereupon he became extremely angry. Although he declared "there was nothing in it" he decided to accept Lansing's and House's suggestion that House "be appointed a special agent of the State Department." Attorney-General Gregory approved of this.[3]

Apparently none of them was aware of the true nature of House's status, nor of the fact that hundreds of others had preceded him in the category of special executive agent, nor for that matter that Wilson had himself used others in that same capacity, e.g., Hale and Lind. House wrote in his Diary

> It was further agreed that no one abroad should know that I was a special agent, for we both thought it would minimize my influence. We are using it simply for a protection in the event of trouble with the Senate. There is some evidence that the opposition in the Senate wish to make an issue of me if it can be done, and if they attempt it, it will be along the lines of my acting for the Government without having any legal authority to do so.[4]

This is an extremely revealing statement for not only does it indicate that his true status was not appreciated, but it also reveals that they too believed he might be acting illegally, or at least extralegally. Nevertheless, because of the size of the stakes involved, it was considered to be worth going ahead. Any deficiencies in his status would be overcome by assigning him a position of agent of the Department of State. However, this was to be kept secret, thus allowing others to think he might be acting without proper authority!

When House went abroad on his next two missions, November, 1917, to try to bring co-ordination to the Allied military efforts, and in October, 1918, as a member of the United States Supreme War Council, he carried credentials from the President. On the fourth mission he carried two letters. One was to the Prime Ministers of Britain, France and Italy but simply headed "Gentlemen" and without a date. (Seymour gives it the date of October 24 in the *House Papers*.) In this the President merely stated that House had been authorized to represent him at the Conference, "and in any other conferences he may be invited and think it best to take part in ..." [5] There is still another letter in the House collection which was apparently for the American ambassadors to the

[1] *Ibid.*, chapters vi and vii, *passim.*

[2] *Ibid.*

[3] "House Diary," December 15, 1915, VII, 326.

[4] *Ibid.*, p. 328.

[5] "House Diary," *op. cit.*, October 24, 1917, cited in Seymour, *House Papers, op. cit.*, III, 206. House never showed these credentials.

major allied states. It is very much along the same lines as the one to the Prime Ministers except that it also contained a request that House be given all the cooperation possible.[1]

On the fifth and last mission he carried official credentials as a United States member of the Supreme War Council, and he remained abroad as a member of the Peace Commission. Wilson was informed of German peace overtures but was rightly afraid that the German High Command wanted terms that would allow Germany to remain too strong. He decided to send House to France in order to assure control of the situation. House was commissioned a "Special Representative of the United States of America" and received a letter denoting him as the "personal representative" of the President.[2] For the first time he was given the honorary rank of Special Ambassador.[3]

This suffices to indicate the nature of House's activities, the relationship he had with leaders of several governments, and the status he held as a special agent on his various missions.

Advantages and Disadvantages in Using House

What of the dangers and benefits which were incurred from using House? Numerous examples of both exist. House thoroughly immersed himself in his work and there is probably much truth in his belief that his numerous sources of information gave him a very full picture of each situation. But he eventually became imbued with the idea that his knowledge and understanding of international events exceeded that of all others. In a moment of candor he wrote, "I believe I am the only one who gets a view of the entire [international] picture. Some get one corner and some another, but I seem to have it all." [4]

As a result he was bound to feel rather critical from time to time of what others were doing. For example, when Wilson and Lansing proposed that merchant men should be disarmed on the assumption that if they were submarines would probably not strike them, they precipitated a "controversy with Congress" and with Germany which House felt "largely interfered with my efforts abroad." He was very upset that "they ... [have not] held the situation quiescent as I [have] urged them to ... I am deeply disappointed ..." [5] This feeling of concern that others were not doing their job well, or that they did not understand what it was they should be doing is frequently revealed in House's diary. We do not get the feeling that House is only an agent of the President, but rather a tutor. He was also highly critical at times of the chiefs of other states. House once told Balfour that Prime Minister Asquith "did not hold the reins of government enough" and he "confessed to a feeling of disappointment" in him.[6]

There is no reason to doubt that House's special relations with so many people of importance was by and large highly beneficial to the nation. Yet for this very reason he was not able to operate with that degree of detachment so necessary for those in advisory positions. For example, it was clear for some time that the British Ambassador, Spring-Rice, was not capable, for emotional and physical reasons, of fulfilling his assignment. As a result, House was expected to suggest to the British government the desirability of recalling him. However,

[1] House MSS, October 23, 1917, Yale University Library.

[2] Seymour, *House Papers*, *op. cit.*, IV, 87.

[3] *Papers Relating to the Foreign Relations of the United States*, 1917, Sup. 2, I, 334, file No. 763. 72/13326 a.

[4] "House Diary," March 10, 1916, VIII, 105.

[5] *Ibid.*, p. 98.

[6] *Ibid.*, p. 78.

one day before House departed for England the Ambassador visited him and was

> never ... more entertaining, affectionate and reasonable ... He complimented me so extravagantly that I almost lost countenance ... The whole conversation was along lines of friendly and personal affection for me. How can I go to London and demand his head? I am trying to think of some way to save him and it will probably result in some modification of the President's, Lansing's and my wishes to have him recalled.[1]

Doubtless his behavior in many situations helped create some of the antagonism in the Department of State. One finds much evidence of a feeling that House was in control of foreign relations to the extent of running the Department. He and Lansing differed radically in their ideas of what was practical regarding Germany's U-boat campaign.[2] Both Bryan and Lansing knew they were made Secretary because House supported them. And both knew that many of the members of the United States foreign missions corresponded directly with him. In addition when he was abroad he would stop in to see them and would sometimes arrange for several of them to meet with him at conferences. Once he went so far as to arrange with the Ambassador to Austria (Penfield) to have himself kept informed "even to the extent of sending a special messenger to London if its importance justifies it." [3] "We will soon have [he wrote to Wilson] a fairly reliable bureau of information in each belligerent capital and there will not be as much guesswork as in the past." [4] And about the same time he wrote to Wilson that he planned to organize the United States officials abroad into a team to push *his* ideas.[5] There is no indication that he was specifically instructed to make such arrangements. The same applies to the suggestions he made to Billy Phillips, the First Assistant Secretary of State that, "Clifford Carver's salary be raised to $2000 ... and [that] Lanier Wilson ['s name be placed] on the State Department payroll ..." [6]

The net effect of these and other situations was a feeling of Bryan's that he did not hold the President's confidence, which in fact was true. But the point is he had never held it from the beginning, and the actions of House were not of such a nature as to induce him to stay with his job. Bryan had a rather poignant final meeting with the President in which, Wilson reported to House, he remarked "with a quiver in his voice and on his lips 'Colonel House has been Secretary of State, not I, and I have never had your full confidence.'" The diary continues, "The President tried to minimize what I had done, but this was not very successful for acts were against him, *although Mr. Bryan knew but a small part of my work.*" [7]

The same kinds of problems arose with Lansing. Wilson, realizing that this might happen, suggested that House have a talk with the New Secretary right at the start, but when House asked whether he should reveal "the whole story regarding my European work," the President replied "'no, not fully, but enough to get him to work in harmony with us.'" [8] Nevertheless, slips were bound to occur and oversights to take place. Once when House and Wilson worked out

[1] "House Diary," December 17, 1915, VII, 330.

[2] Buehrig, *Woodrow Wilson and the Balance of Power, op. cit.*, p. 215.

[3] Correspondence, House to Wilson, March 27, 1915, Wilson MSS, Library of Congress.

[4] *Ibid.*

[5] Correspondence, House to Wilson, March 26, 1915, Wilson MSS, Library of Congress. The writer's emphasis.

[6] "House Diary," July 4, 1915, VII, 182.

[7] *Ibid.*, p. 174.

[8] *Ibid.*, p. 177.

plans the President notified the Chairman of the Foreign Relations Committee but forgot to tell the Secretary. The latter found out only when he read of them in the paper. Frank Polk, who was Counselor for the Department, knew of Lansing's hurt feelings and told House that Lansing felt that House was attending to matters entirely within his province.[1] Certainly the Inquiry which operated under House's direction replaced the State Department in Paris.

The House-Wilson relations and the nature of House's activities and interests were bound to have repercussions beyond the Department of State. There seems little reason to doubt that foreign governments preferred to deal with House than with an Embassy official or the Secretary himself. But this was, at times, the result of House's actions. For example, shortly after meeting the Foreign Secretary Grey, House told him that Wilson and Bryan were not completely *en rapport.*[2] Slightly more than a year later House wrote to Wilson not to allow Bryan to make any overtures regarding the European situation because the belligerents had very little confidence in and regard for Bryan.[3] This kind of behavior naturally brought dissatisfaction with the President's use of House. Secretary of the Navy Daniels revealed in his memoirs that he did not believe the President was wise in using a private citizen for such assignments. His opinion was based on the same unhappy feeling we noted before in this study, viz., that an agent should not carry out such assignments without a formal commission.[4]

And as might also be expected House was subject to criticism by members of Congress who were at times very distrustful of his activities. When it was learned that he would be the chief American delegate at the Allied War Council meeting in Paris, Senator Penrose gave a long speech in Congress attacking him and President Wilson for using him. His chief complaints were that he was not a government official whereas the chiefs of other delegations would be high ranking officers. Furthermore, Penrose thought the whole idea of using personal representatives was obnoxious for a democracy and he likened it to the behavior of autocrats. He called House a "mysterious traveller," a "Texas lobbyist," and was provoked because he was being paid out of the contingent fund.[5]

Senator Sherman sometime later also lashed out at House by ridiculing his book, *Philip Dru,* which House had published anonymously, because it smacked of statism and showed great contempt for tradition.[6]

One might also question the wisdom of Wilson relying so heavily upon one man for so many important decisions. In the first place Grey reveals that House, almost from the start, was pro-Ally. Although one may agree with House's analysis of the true nature of the struggle, it is hard to agree with his taking a position contrary to the President's stand of neutrality, if in fact Grey is right.

Secondly, one may question House's wisdom in pushing his agreement with Grey, which was never lived up to by the latter. Perhaps, one might argue, that if several advisors had been working on the problem there would have been less likelihood of their not realizing the true nature of the Allied situation. Ending the war in 1916 was highly remote, as desirable as it may have seemed later on to Grey.[7] Here is where one agent operating alone was at a disadvantage and where such an agency as a National Security Council or at least the appropriate

[1] *Ibid.*, March 28, 1916, VIII, 145.

[2] *Ibid.*, July 3, 1913, II, 247.

[3] Correspondence, House to Wilson, September 1, 1914, Wilson MSS, Library of Congress.

[4] Josephus Daniels, *The Wilson Era – Years of Peace: 1910–1917* (Chapel Hill: University of North Carolina Press, 1944), p. 568.

[5] *Congressional Record,* 65th Cong., 2nd Sess., LVI, 1089–1098.

[6] *Ibid.*, pp. 9873–9879.

[7] Grey, *op. cit.*, p. 136.

officials of the Department of State might have brought a more seasoned judgment to bear.

Of course there were many ways in which House performed yeoman's service for Wilson. In addition to taking care of many political appointments, House also gathered information from a variety of sources and made this available to Wilson. As Buehrig points out, this activity was extremely beneficial because a man like Ambassador Page, for example, distrusted many people. Thus Wilson was kept informed not only of the official position in various countries but also of that of critics of the government, e.g., Norman Angell, Ramsay Mac Donald, etc.[1]

Another value that resulted from the use of House stemmed particularly from his unofficial position. It enabled him to operate with greater freedom than would have been likely had he held high governmental position. For example, Sir William Wiseman, head of the British Intelligence Service, resided in the same apartment building as House and they saw each other frequently. Wiseman, on the other hand, was in immediate contact with Eric Drummond, the secretary to Balfour who headed the Foreign Office after the Asquith government fell. Wiseman also reported directly to Lloyd George.[2]

House also was in frequent communication with numerous foreign ambassadors and with publishers from this country and abroad. This enabled him not only to pick up information but also to place stories or stop them without their carrying an official source. And he was generally able to do this with tact and finesse. Grey found that "his suggestions were fertile, and ... were conveyed with a sympathy that made it pleasant to listen to ..." [3]

But perhaps his greatest contribution as a special agent and advisor was what the Georges described as his ability to provide a "synthesis of both realist and idealist views of world politics." [4] This quality showed up in his efforts to get a rearmament program started so that Wilson could play his part in ending the war more effectively than he did before 1918. After the British blockade and use of armed merchantmen aroused the President's ire, it was primarily House who tried to keep him from taking a position which would force Britain's hand.

In Paris House showed a greater understanding of the need to have a "good press" than Wilson did. And his ability to conciliate opposing forces not only at the Conference but also in the Senate was valuable until he lost importance in Wilson's eyes. Once this decline in status occurred he could no longer act as a catalytic agent, which meant that he was not in a position of lining up the forces which the President so badly needed on his side.

Summary

From the foregoing it will be seen that the variety of House's activities had almost no limit and that he built up so many important confidences that he understandably felt better informed on world affairs than any other person in this country and western Europe. In carrying out his missions and in building up his network of intelligence he undoubtedly created antagonism within the cabinet, and especially Department of State, within Congress, and among some of the members of the press. That this would happen was probably inevitable, partly because of the natural jealousies and partly because of the pervasiveness of his activities and the secretive way in which he performed them.

[1] Buehrig, *Wilson's Foreign Policy in Perspective*, *op. cit.*, p. 21.

[2] *Ibid.*, p. 24.

[3] Grey, *op. cit.*, p. 124.

[4] George and George, *op. cit.*, pp. 163–64.

But the President's natural lack of confidence in the traditional channels of information, and the requirements of a political patronage system which aggravated this by imposing upon him men who were not always of a caliber adequate to the task, made him turn to a "second personality," an "independent self." [1] Without such a person, under the circumstances in which the President had to operate, the situation might have been even much more trying for him than it was. House was probably of material assistance, and the results of his efforts probably weighed more heavily on the beneficial than on the harmful side of the ledger.

> Like all great public men, Wilson needed a friend to whom he could unburden his secret thoughts and turn for advice and spiritual support. A man of intellect and moral strength, House was perfectly equipped to meet Wilson's peculiar needs. Wilson demanded the total loyalty of his friend, and House knew when to speak or be silent, when to agree or to demur. Yet in thus subordinating his will to Wilson's, House did not compromise his own integrity, judgment, or critical capacities ... [His] influence by and large was salutary, for in times of crisis House proved a wise counselor and a stabilizing force.[2]

Out of his five trips abroad House carried official papers from the President twice, and had diplomatic rank only once. In 1917 he was the American representative on the Allied War Council with credentials (which he never showed) but with no rank,[3] and in 1918 he was given the title "Special Representative of the United States of America" and "Personal Representative of the President" with the honorary rank of ambassador.[4] In addition, because he was expected to be a member of the American peace mission he was also given the *pleins pouvoirs*.[5]

On his first trip he carried a letter from the President wishing him good luck (House showed this to the Kaiser after their conversation was finished),[6] and on his second trip he apparently carried no letters, the President telling him he (House) knew his mind well enough not to need any.[7] With regard to his third trip his status is not clear. Presumably he carried papers indicating he either held a position with the Department of State or was its agent. His papers are not clear on this point and the official papers of the Department reveal nothing, possibly because he was to remain as a personal presidential agent unless a furor arose regarding his status, at which time he would make known his other status. At no time did he receive any salary, but from his second trip on his expenses were paid out of the contingent fund.

There would seem to be no doubt that because of the nature of his work and the relationship to the President he must be considered a special executive agent while he was abroad, one for whom the state would have to assume responsibility for all authorized acts. It is true that because he so rarely received instructions the President's word as to what was or was not authorized would have to be accepted, but generally speaking this would usually be the case anyway.

[1] Seymour, *House Papers*, *op. cit.*, I, 114.

[2] Arthur S. Link, *Woodrow Wilson and the Progressive Era, 1910–1917* (New York: Harper and Bros., 1954), p. 26.

[3] *Supra*, p. 204.

[4] *Supra*, p. 205.

[5] *Supra*, p. 205.

[6] "House Diary," June 24, 1914, IV, 110.

[7] *Ibid.*, January 24, 1915, VII, 10.

HARRY L. HOPKINS

Hopkins' Background

Harry L. Hopkins was born in 1890 in Sioux City, Iowa, and lived in the Midwest until he finished college. As a student he made fair grades and was keenly interested in politics. He espoused political reform during his college days, an interest which he maintained through much of his life.

His first job was as a social worker in New York, and although he continued in social work most of his activities were as an administrator in private and public affairs. He served under Franklin Roosevelt in New York State as chairman of the Temporary Emergency Relief Administration, and in 1933 followed his chief to Washington where he directed several relief agencies and the Department of Commerce. By 1940 he was known as Roosevelt's closest *confidante* and lived for several years in the White House. In 1941 with fascism on the verge of what appeared to be a conquest of all of Europe, Roosevelt sent him abroad on the first of several missions as a special executive agent.

Whereas Colonel House had great ability in conciliating the differences of men with whom Wilson had to deal, Hopkins' most significant contribution seemed to be in his ability to "get to the heart of a matter," to strip away the tissues surrounding a problem and, like a surgeon to lay bare the vital spot. Then he would act as a catalyst, urging and even goading others to take the action he believed necessary. His was a "sharp" mind, but with a practical rather than a theoretical bent. It was not the kind of a mind which could create a League of Nations, but was eminently successful in understanding the basic wartime problems other nations had, and the ways in which the United States would help resolve them, and then in finding the means of providing that help.[1]

The Nature of the Hopkins-Roosevelt Relationship

Like House, Hopkins seemed to epitomize a selfless attitude and conscientious solicitude for his chief. And, as with House, he seemed to define his tasks in the very broadest terms. As he set about resolving problems new problems would arise which would result in new avenues of approach. Therefore he frequently went well beyond the original scope of his task. He seemed unable to abide by limitations and restrictions.

This tendency to expand authority and ask others to carry out assignments which would not normally be within his province, was not peculiar to Hopkins. Dean Acheson recalled that it was a common practice for those who were on the White House staff to begin a request with "the White House wants," whether or not "it" really did.[2] Many of those who knew him believe that Hopkins was cautious about going this far, but others disagree.

At the same time it should be pointed out that Hopkins often made no effort to publicize his work and in fact would go out of his way, if it seemed desirable to do so, to remain anonymous. For example when Sir Gerald Campbell of the British Embassy requested a copy of Hopkins' speech on British production which he gave before the War Munitions Board, Hopkins refused, stating,

[1] The material for this background description comes from Geoffrey T. Hillman, "Profiles" *The New Yorker*, August, 1943; Robert E. Sherwood, *Roosevelt and Hopkins, An Intimate History* (New York: Harper and Bros., 1950), chapters i–viii, *passim*, and interviews with Eleanor Roosevelt, July 27, 1955 and Isador Lubin, April 5, 1956.

[2] Interview, April 2, 1956.

"... on the whole I would rather not have any publicity about anything that concerns me ..." [1] This desire to shun publicity, which was not so typical of Hopkins pre-1940 as it was after that date, reminds one very much of Colonel House. But his methods of operating probably were very valuable during the war when all problems were so greatly intertwined. In effect the nature of his work seemed to require taking a broad rather than narrow view of his assignments.

Being limited in the financial remuneration he could receive from his kind of work, it is quite possible that some of Hopkins' reward came in the form of a desire for authority and widespread influence. And certainly in the role he filled these objectives were well within reach. At the same time, his devotion to Roosevelt was a factor that seemed to keep self-aggrandizement in check.

Hopkins' affection for Roosevelt was undoubtedly reciprocated. Although there is not the voluminous correspondence between them that existed between House and Wilson, mainly because much of the time Hopkins lived in the White House, there are letters among their papers which Roosevelt signed "Affectionately." [2] And the statements of the President to Wendell Willkie and Mrs. Roosevelt in 1941 give further testimony to this fact. When Willkie asked Roosevelt why he kept Hopkins on, the President replied,

> "... someday you may well be sitting here where I am now as President of the United States. And when you are, you'll be looking at that door over there and knowing that practically everybody who walks through it wants something out of you. You'll learn what a lonely job this is, and you'll discover the need for somebody like Harry Hopkins who asks for nothing except to serve you." [3]

To Mrs. Roosevelt who raised the same kind of question and referred to the gossip of Hopkins living on government expense at the White House, the President replied, "There is a tremendous job to be done. I need what Harry has to give and I need him here in this house." [4] Hopkins' informality, his ability to cut through red tape, and his "unprotocol mannerisms" endeared him to the President who was never fond of career diplomats anyway.

Probably one of the best examples of the faith the President had in him is the fact that he was chosen to go to Britain and Soviet Russia when both were sustaining severe punishment from the Nazi power and when dire predictions were coming forth of the impossibility of either nation surviving for long. The President needed a man who could make shrewd calculated guesses of the resiliency and determination of the leadership and people of these states. Hopkins' training in the social welfare programs of the early '30s gave him many opportunities to form judgments of a person's mettle in the face of adversity.

When Hull resigned his position, probably with some of the same feelings that Bryan had regarding the extent to which the President relied upon a special agent and advisor rather than upon the duly appointed officer of the Department, it was probably this same agent who had a major voice in suggesting his successor. Stettinius was "generally said to have been a Hopkins' choice." [5] Although it seems highly unlikely that Stettinius would ever have

[1] Hopkins MSS, April 25, 1942, April 29, 1942, Franklin D. Roosevelt Library.

[2] Hopkins MSS, May 18, 1944, Franklin D. Roosevelt Library.

[3] Sherwood, *op. cit.*, p. 3.

[4] Eleanor Roosevelt, *This I Remember* (New York: Harper and Bros., 1948), p. 238.

[5] Rexford G. Tugwell, *The Democratic Roosevelt, A Biography of Franklin D. Roosevelt* (New York: Doubleday and Co., Inc., 1957), p. 668.

been a "strong" Secretary of State, there was too little time left serving Roosevelt to determine to what extent Hopkins would have been able to dominate the Department as House had earlier. That Stettinius would have been willing to follow suggestions from Hopkins seems probable, but that Roosevelt would have permitted this is not at all certain. At any rate, it will be clear from facts produced later, that Roosevelt and Hopkins had a very deep friendship, but the tutor-pupil relationship that at times seemed to have existed between House and Wilson was, if anything, just the opposite with the President and Hopkins, the latter generally being much more willing to be led.

Five Missions Abroad

Hopkins' work in the foreign field, which he began in 1941, by far eclipsed the prestige and power he had enjoyed until then. In a column for the *New York Times* Arthur Krock wrote, "His power as the Presidential liaison with all the allied governments, his influence as chairman of the group that allocates and re-allocates the flow of lend-lease munitions, and his unparalleled intimacy with the President makes his lightest word an event of moment." [1]

Hopkins moved into this situation despite his lack of training in transportation, production, raw materials, purchase and allocation, and diplomacy. It is interesting to note that he did not even comprehend the seriousness of the event when the war started. He wrote to his brother in 1939, "I believe we can really keep out of it." [2] But he learned fast with Roosevelt as his guide. And he apparently was very capable in dealing with people and in analyzing facts.[3] It has been suggested to this writer that the kind of talent and experience the President needed was precisely that in which Hopkins excelled. And much of this came from his early social work experience.[4] This is quite different from the House-Wilson relationship in which House often seemed to sense the kind of role the United States would have to play before the President did.

In January, 1941, Great Britain and the Commonwealth stood alone against the Rome-Berlin Axis. Roosevelt wanted to find out what the picture in Britain was like and he wanted to do this through a representative who would have easy access to top British officials, someone upon whose judgment he could rely. (One close observer suggests that he began to use a special agent partly because the regular diplomat must move so slowly).[5] Hence he announced that Hopkins would go to London as his personal representative for a couple of weeks. The Press was further informed that he would have no powers and that his expenses would be paid. This was the first of five missions he was sent on by Presidents Roosevelt and Truman.[6]

The following letter of authorization and instruction was given to Hopkins by the President.

January 4, 1941

My dear Mr. Hopkins:

Reposing special faith and confidence in you, I am asking you to proceed at your early convenience to Great Britain, there to act as my personal representative. I am also asking you to convey a communication in this sense to His Majesty King George VI.

You will of course communicate to this Government any matters which may come to your

[1] *New York Times*, May 27, 1943.
[2] Sherwood, *op. cit.*, p. 124.
[3] Interview, Oscar Cox, April 2, 1956.
[4] Interview, Phillip Young, April 4, 1956.
[5] *Ibid.*
[6] He also went to all of the wartime conferences except the second Quebec Conference.

attention in the performance of your mission which you may feel will serve the best interests of the United States. With all best wishes for the success of your mission, I am,

Very sincerely yours,
Franklin D. Roosevelt[1]

The letter to the King read:

January 4, 1941

Your Majesty:

I have designated the honorable Harry L. Hopkins as my personal representative on a special mission to Great Britain. Mr. Hopkins is a very good friend of mine in whom I repose the utmost confidence. I am asking him to convey to you and to Her Majesty the Queen my cordial greetings and my sincere hope that his mission may advance the common ideals of our two nations.

Cordially your friend,
Franklin D. Roosevelt[2]

With as casual and uninstructive letters as these, Hopkins undertook his first mission of the war. From the comments of Herschel Johnson, American *chargé d'affaires* in Britain, he was neither given nor had any clear-cut plan as to how to proceed. But the objective apparently was to try to determine how the British were standing up against the Axis onslaught and what they might need in the way of assistance.

Apparently he worked very hard to familiarize himself with the situation in Britain. In reporting to Roosevelt he painted a picture that was not bleak but disturbing, seasoned, however, with the conviction that the people would fight. But Hopkins was still unschooled enough to believe that "if we act boldly and promptly on a few major fronts we can get enough material to Britain within the next few weeks to give her the additional strength she needs to turn back Hitler.[3]

Mainly because he was so close to the President, Hopkins was quickly taken to the bosom of British officialdom. He was permitted to see reports on the military situation which were of the utmost secrecy. And he was also informed of important government plans and expectations. For example, he informed Roosevelt of a highly secret report he had been shown which consisted of the reports and replies between the Minister of Defense (Churchill) and the Middle East Commander (Wavell). Hopkins was not only impressed by the fact that he saw this highly secret information but also because it reflected a spirit of dogged determination to push an offensive even in the face of adversity.[4] As a result of these feelings which took hold of him shortly after he arrived, he began to write with a favorable view toward helping the British. In May he wrote, "... this island needs our help now Mr. President with everything we can give them ..." [5]

Churchill frequently took advantage of his presence and introduced him to the public wherever they went. Naturally this built up the impression of a closer relationship between Britain and the United States than Roosevelt was

[1] Hopkins MSS, Franklin D. Roosevelt Library.

[2] *Ibid.*

[3] Sherwood, *op. cit.*, p. 258. This same optimism was reflected in later reports from the Soviet Union.

[4] *Ibid.*, p. 256.

[5] *Ibid.*, p. 243.

yet willing to imply, an impression that Churchill wanted to create to improve morale.[1]

There soon developed a personal relationship between Hopkins and Churchill. The latter began to use Hopkins' services just as Roosevelt did. Frequently when the Prime Minister was uncertain about a diplomatic move regarding the United States he would seek and receive Hopkins' advice. Hopkins urged, for example, that during Congressional debate on the Lend-Lease Bill that the British government do nothing which might accentuate any differences with the United States.[2] And a short time later when Churchill decided to make a world address but with special consideration for the United States, "he consulted Hopkins on many of its points. There was by now an intimacy between the two men which developed to such a degree that it is no exaggeration to say that Churchill reposed the same confidence in Hopkins that Roosevelt did." [3] This great feeling of confidence remained a characteristic of the relationship between the two throughout the war. It was very natural, therefore, for the Prime Minister to use Hopkins as a channel to the President. This feeling for Hopkins is revealed in Churchill's own writings. He refers to Hopkins as "that extraordinary man who played, ... a sometimes decisive part in the whole movement of the war. ... He was the most faithful and perfect channel of communication between the President and me." [4] Hopkins performed such a service even when he was in Washington. Thus, Churchill cabled Hopkins on October 27, 1943 that Lord — was in the United States, and since he was such a good friend of the Prime Minister and staunch supporter of the government, it would be of great value if he would be permitted to visit the President.[5] Thus the agent became, in effect, an aide and advisor to the leaders of both of the English speaking democracies. In this way his position of importance *vis à vis* officialdom of both of these countries was greatly enhanced.

One of the most important parts of Hopkins' functions while abroad was to ascertain the specific military needs of the government. This information he was able to provide because of the complete confidence the officials felt in him. It is little short of remarkable to see how quickly he was accepted and how thoroughly familiar he became with the situation despite the fact that there was no military alliance, nor, in fact, was the United States even a belligerent yet.

While in Britain he went on tours with Churchill and spoke to groups wherever the Prime Minister encouraged him to do so. He expressed the sympathy Americans felt toward the English people and in other ways attempted to create a feeling of solidarity. In fact during his second visit in July, 1941, he even delivered a radio address over the BBC in which this sympathy was plainly revealed.[6]

With each public appearance or address it is quite likely that he led some of his audience to infer that American aid was coming in great quantities, and it is even possible that they concluded that the United States would soon be marching with Britain. To some extent this may have been unavoidable, but it is quite probable that it did not greatly concern Hopkins.

While in England Hopkins spent several weekends at Churchill's home and had long talks with him. He inspected units of the British fleet, addressed a

[1] *Ibid.*, p. 247.
[2] *Ibid.*, p. 242.
[3] *Ibid.*, p. 261.
[4] Winston S. Churchill, *The Second World War: The Grand Alliance* (Boston: Houghton Mifflin Co., 1951), III, 23.
[5] Hopkins MSS, September 27, 1942, Franklin D. Roosevelt Library.
[6] Sherwood, *op. cit.*, p. 319.

meeting of newspaper editors, and of course had conferences with the King and Queen.

In July of the same year he again went to Britain. The mission was primarily concerned with allocating naval patrol assignments in the Atlantic, questions of British strategy in the Middle East, and the resolution of difficulties that had started to arise because Ambassador Winant and the Department of State were being by-passed in favor of Lend-Lease Expeditor Harriman and Hopkins. Plans for the Argentia (Atlantic) Conference were also discussed.[1] One important result of the meeting was the realization on the part of Hopkins that differences in military thinking between the Americans and British could best be overcome, or at least moderated, by having Roosevelt bring Generals Marshall and Arnold with him to the forthcoming Argentia conference.

Although it has not been verified it appears that Hopkins got the idea during this second mission that a trip to the Soviet Union would be highly desirable. The situation inside Russia was very uncertain. The four-week period that many had given the Russian army before it collapsed was already past, and although the reports were still gloomy it was clear that a re-calculation was required of Soviet strength and determination. These factors were precisely the ones Hopkins was expected to analyze when Roosevelt first sent him to England. And, inasmuch as the British Cabinet had already decided to aid Russia the question of allocating Lend-Lease supplies was pressing. Hopkins and Winant drafted the following cable to Roosevelt on July 25:

> ... I am wondering whether you would think it important and useful for me to go to Moscow. Air transportation good and can reach there in 24 hours. I have a feeling that everything possible should be done to make certain the Russians maintain a permanent front even though they be defeated in this immediate battle. If Stalin could in any way be influenced at a critical time I think it would be worth doing by a direct communication from you through a personal envoy. I think the stakes are so great that it should be done. Stalin would then know in an unmistakable way that we mean business on a long-term supply job. I of course have made no moves in regard to this and will await your advice. If you think Moscow trip inadvisable I will leave here not later than Wednesday.[2]

Roosevelt cabled his approval and Hopkins left on the 27th. Although Hopkins carried no credentials with him to Britain this time he was given two important documents of identification for the Moscow trip, a diplomatic visa from Ambassador Maisky in London (which no one even asked to see) and a letter from Roosevelt to Stalin. In the latter Roosevelt asked that, "... you ... treat Mr. Hopkins with the identical confidence you would feel if you were talking directly to me. He will communicate directly to me the views that you express to him and will tell me what you consider are the most pressing individual problems on which we could be of aid." [3]

When he met Stalin he told him his mission wasn't a diplomatic one because he didn't come to propose "any formal understanding of any kind" but wanted primarily to learn what were Russia's immediate and long term needs.[4] Because of his special position he was able to get vital information that had not been made available to either the American or British officials who were stationed there. This information considerably aided America and Britain in getting a clearer picture of Russia's needs and determination to fight. His interpretation of the situation was at variance with that of many other officials in Moscow, but

[1] *Ibid.*, pp. 311–313, 318.

[2] *Ibid.*, p. 318.

[3] *Ibid.*, p. 322. Roosevelt also agreed that he take General Lee to show United States intentions were serious. Hopkins MSS, July 27, 1941, Franklin D. Roosevelt Library.

[4] Sherwood, *op. cit.*, pp. 327, 328.

his proved to be the correct one. Furthermore, this third mission helped pave the way for a closer relationship between the two Western powers and the Soviet Union which was so essential to winning the war.

In 1945 while on his way to Yalta Hopkins carried out his fourth overseas assignment, which was really two assignments in one. However, the purpose of the two was the same. Just prior to the Yalta Conference a strain had developed between the United States and Britain, and relations were not too good either, nor had they ever been, between Roosevelt and De Gaulle. The disagreements with the British resulted from differences in point of view between the two governments over the composition of the newly created Italian government,and also over the crisis in the eastern Mediterranean. Admiral King had denied the use of American LST's in the Greek campaign and Churchill became infuriated because of the political overtones of King's action. Although Hopkins got Admiral Leahy to ask King to withdraw the order, which was done, Churchill's feelings were still ruffled. Hopkins spent two or three days with Churchill and radioed Roosevelt that his efforts had been very satisfactory.[1]

His mission to France was not so successful. Hoping to penetrate De Gaulle's austerity he acknowledged that the United States might have made some errors of judgment, and even urged De Gaulle to consider coming to Yalta toward the end of the conference when European political matters were discussed. Apparently De Gaulle did not thaw. Bidault, who was also there, reported however that Hopkins left a favorable impression.[2] This was a mission quite limited in its objective, but also probably the least successful of all. So far as is known he carried no special credentials with him.

The fifth, and last, special mission abroad was undertaken for a new President. Roosevelt had died and President Truman was confronted with a serious deterioration in Russo-American relations. The San Francisco Conference seemed to be foundering and Molotov, the chief of the Russian delegation was on his way back to the Soviet Union. Charles Bohlen, a liaison officer in the White House with the Department of State, and Averell Harriman, the Ambassador to Russia, thought that it would be beneficial if President Truman sent Hopkins to Moscow to try to come to an understanding. The important questions which needed airing and resolving dealt with the following: the sudden curtailment of Lend-Lease supplies which the Soviet government felt was a move designed to intimidate it with regard to the differences that existed between it and the United States, the question of the disposition of the German navy and merchant fleet, which Stalin said was not being shared as per agreement, and, most important of all, the question of the composition of the newly established Polish government, which Russia believed had to be friendly to it but doubted that this view was held in the United States or in Britain.[3] These are the questions which were discussed when President Truman gave his assent to a very sick but eager Hopkins to fly to Moscow. Not all of these issues were resolved happily. Unfortunately, the most crucial, the Polish, was one of those that was not. Two positive results that were accomplished were the appointment of Marshal Zukov to the Control Council of Berlin, and the acceptance on the part of Stalin of the United States position regarding voting in the Security Council of the United Nations.

These agreements in themselves proved very helpful in clearing the air and may be considered a fitting capstone to Hopkins' work as a special agent. On this trip as on most of the others he carried no special credentials.

[1] *Ibid.*, pp. 838–47.
[2] *Ibid.*, pp. 847–48.
[3] *Ibid.*, pp. 888–895.

His Influence and Methods of Operation

As was true with Colonel House, Hopkins was an agent who was very much involved in domestic as well as international affairs. To analyze his performance in detail is not the function of this study, but a brief picture of how he operated would be of value.

From what has been said already it is clear that Hopkins did not conceive of his role as one that was played within a narrowly-restricted area. From his earlier career as an executive with the Association for Improving the Conditions of the Poor (A.I.C.P.) it is patently clear that he tended to see a problem in its broadest perspectives. In wartime this type of mind could prove very beneficial. It revealed administrative talent in the broadest sense and it is perhaps this ability that led Roosevelt to choose him for his missions and to operate as an administrative assistant who would not be restricted to a specific agency. That this was clearly his intention is illustrated by the letter he sent to Hopkins March 27, 1941. It said, "I hereby designate you to advise and assist me in carrying out the responsibility placed upon me by the Act of March 11, 1941," the Lend-Lease Act.[1]

In addition to the "generalissimo" type of post he was also given specific assignments, e.g., Roosevelt telegraphed Churchill that Hopkins and others would be put on three boards that he was proposing be created which included a "Combined Shipping Adjustment Board," a "Munitions Assignment Board," and a "Combined Raw Materials Board." [2] In addition to this he was chairman of the President's Soviet Protocol Committee and a member of the War Production Board. This broad set of duties provided great latitude within which to operate. Hence we find in the Hopkins papers numerous indications, some in the form of memos and letters, of his tendency to "put his nose into" many different kinds of things, a form of behavior which was quite readily tolerated by the President.

For example, we find a memo to Grace Tully, the President's Secretary. "I understand the army is going to send the President a recommendation to take over the Persian Railroad. I wonder if I might see that memo before the President approves it. H.L.H." [3] And, after a supposed deterioration in the relationship between the two, a matter of some dispute between those who knew the two men well, Hopkins felt free to order stopped the dispatch of a cable by Roosevelt to Churchill which Hopkins felt was dangerous. The cable implied that Churchill and Stalin could have a joint meeting regarding developments in the Balkans and come to decisions without Roosevelt's participation. Hopkins thought this was unwise and after stopping the cable he went to Roosevelt and told him so. Roosevelt agreed and instead informed Stalin that he was very much interested in this area.[4] The incident referred to above in which Hopkins managed to get Admiral King to rescind an order barring use of American naval units to the British in the Greek campaign is not only an example of the way in which he conceived of his job but also one in which he solved a major problem without the President's even knowing of it.[5]

None of these annoying characteristics appears in Cordell Hull's *Memoirs* where one might expect to find them. His only negative comment refers to the problems and "havoc" personal missions sometimes caused, particularly for

[1] Hopkins MSS, Franklin D. Roosevelt Library.

[2] Roosevelt MSS, January 26, 1942, Franklin D. Roosevelt Library.

[3] Hopkins MSS, September 2, 1942, Franklin D. Roosevelt Library.

[4] Sherwood, *op. cit.*, pp. 833–834.

[5] *Ibid.*, pp. 840–841.

ambassadors,[1] and the difficulties which arise for Cabinet oficers when unofficial advisers are allowed to intervene.[2] But whenever Hull writes these things he seems to exclude Hopkins from his criticism, and in fact praises his overall effort quite highly. Yet Acheson definitely believes there was friction.[3] Hull omits any examples of friction, even those cited in Sherwood.[4]

At the Arcadia Conference he was again in a position to perform a valuable service because of the nature of his role. Roosevelt and Marshall wanted unity of command in the Pacific but Churchill was opposed. When Beaverbrook informed Hopkins that the Prime Minister had not yet completely made up his mind, Hopkins arranged for a private meeting between Churchill and Marshall in which the former agreed to revise his position in favor of the American one. Sherwood refers to this as a demonstration of the role played by Hopkins at all the major conferences of the next three years. Sherwood writes that,

> Because of the utter informality of his position as well as of his character he could act in an extra official capacity and thus bring about ready settlement of disputes which might have been greatly prolonged or completely stalled if left to the traditional, antiquated machinery of international negotiation. There were many more notes passed to Hopkins under conference tables and many more examples of his effective, off-the-record action. He was rarely confined by the "customary channels." [5]

He was so successful in this kind of situation that at Teheran, which was probably the high point of his career in terms of prestige and influence, he acted on a par with Eden and Molotov, performing functions much like a Secretary of State who, in addition, enjoyed excellent relations with his chief. Churchill has summed up very neatly the influence that Hopkins attained. He writes, "... Together these two men [Roosevelt and Hopkins] ... were capable of taking decisions of the highest consequence over the whole area of the English-speaking world." [6]

Advantages and Disadvantages in Using Hopkins

Let us now examine some of the effects which stemmed from Hopkins' missions and from the way he operated. In both Moscow and London Hopkins' special relation to the President gave him an opportunity to gather much information that was needed regarding morale, war production and governmental views. It is quite likely that the information Hopkins sent to Roosevelt would not have been available to anyone other than a presidential agent. Both foreign governments during war time were naturally most reluctant to reveal their true predicaments unless they felt assured of two things: (1) a receptive and understanding audience, (2) a transmission of their information to the President without leaks. Both of these *desiderata* would be satisfied in Hopkins. One or the other could not be found in the existing official representatives. Ambassadors Kennedy and Standley did not have the confidence of the governments of Britain and Russia. And the succeeding ambassadors, Winant and Steinhardt, who were more sympathetic, both suffered from the disadvantage that they had to report through State Department channels which were not completely sympathetic. Furthermore information which was transmitted through the regular channels had to pass through several hands and the risk of leaks increased pro-

[1] Cordell Hull, *The Memoirs of Cordell Hull* (New York: Macmillan Co., 1948), p. 200.
[2] *Ibid.*, p. 205.
[3] Interview, April 2, 1956.
[4] Sherwood, *op. cit.*, p. 679.
[5] *Ibid.*, p. 457.
[6] Churchill, *op. cit.*, p. 23.

portionately. Hopkins' reports often went directly to the President, and from the point of speed alone this was an advantage.

Hopkins also made a number of public statements while in Britain which would surely have brought rebukes from Secretary of State Hull had Hopkins been an ambassador. In his speech over the BBC he said that Britain was fighting the war for the democracies, and that the Atlantic should be thought of as joining not separating the two English-speaking countries. He further added, "Like most Americans,I feel that your fight is a fight for freedom in the world and that it must not and will not fail." [1] At a private dinner attended by prominent Britons he quoted the Book of Ruth, "whither thou goest I will go ... even to the end." [2] Not being a public official his degree of freedom was much greater. Yet, being so close to the President allowed for interferences which might have been desired. Davis and Lindley point out that his special status "attracted confidences which would escape an ambassador. And, coming directly from the White House he could speak with unrivaled authority." [3] On one occasion a British official told Sherwood, "'We came to think of Hopkins as Roosevelt's own, personal Foreign Office.'" [4]

To Roosevelt the advantages were also obvious. He could communicate through an agent in whom he had the utmost confidence, and one whose views were quite similar to his own. Furthermore there were many ways in which the very informality of his status could prove invaluable. Acheson recalls that at the small private conferences which Churchill and Roosevelt frequently held, Churchill would often have a plan written out which he would pull from his pocket at an opportune moment and ask Roosevelt to sign. Before the President could act, however, Hopkins would reach over, pick up the paper and say, "We'll take care of this in the morning." [5] And the fact that the President was using one agent instead of several ambassadors made it possible for the agent to develop, and consequently for the President to receive, an integrated view of the situation that several men working on separate phases could not have had. Furthermore, the fact that the agent's files and information would be less likely to come under the scrutiny of Congressional investigation could be considered as providing a desirable advantage.

There were, of course, numerous disadvantages that arose from the use of Hopkins as a special agent. State Department leaders were often ill informed or completely ignorant of Hopkins' accomplishments. He sometimes wrote to the President on his own stationery and either sent the reports by special messengers or delivered them himself. Frequently he would use the cables but not the State Department's because of a strong feeling on the part of many, including Roosevelt, that they could not be trusted.[6] Even when, as was true during the first Russian mission, some of his discussions concerned political matters the Department was not fully informed.

There was undoubtedly a strong undercurrent of disagreement that existed between Hull and Hopkins although it never amounted to the kind of situation in which Wilson's Secretaries found themselves. Hull found Hopkins "too free

[1] *New York Times*, July 27, 1941.

[2] Sherwood, *op. cit.*, p. 247.

[3] Forrest Davis and Ernest K. Lindley, *How War Came, An American White Paper: From the Fall of France to Pearl Harbor* (New York: Simon and Shuster, 1942), p. 180.

[4] Sherwood, *op. cit.*, p. 202.

[5] Dean Acheson interview, April 2, 1956.

[6] Sherwood, *op. cit.*, pp. 134–136, 227, 269.

and easy-going," and they clashed strongly on their evaluations of De Gaulle, Hull feeling a personal distaste for the General.[1]

But the tensions in the Department were very natural since it frequently felt it was not informed of all the matters it should have been, and therefore was not always capable of providing a policy which could satisfactorily meet the vicissitudes of foreign relations. Former Secretary Acheson points out that not only was the Department ill-informed but so were the ambassadors on the spot. The latter difficulty was well highlighted by some of the unpleasantness that developed for Winant, with Harriman in the same capital as Lend-Lease Expeditor.[2] Hence, Acheson points out, the morale of the staff and foreign service suffered adversely. In addition, he believes, the situation was not improved by the President's manner, which usually was one of deprecating the significance of the mission.[3] This is illustrated by Roosevelt's announcement of the first Hopkins' mission. At the press conference of January 3, 1941, he denied that Hopkins had any special mission, said that he would only get his expenses paid, that he had no powers, and that he was "just going over to say, 'How do you do to a lot of my friends.'"[4]

There was almost an outright clash between Hull and Hopkins over French civilian control in Algeria. At Casablanca Hopkins suggested that Jean Monnet be given the job. Roosevelt asked Hull for his opinion and he opposed Monnet because of his close linkage with the Free French. Peyrouton, probably an unwise choice, was the man finally selected. But Hopkins, not willing to accept defeat in this matter, suggested the following month to Roosevelt that he authorize Monnet to serve as Lend-Lease expeditor in North Africa, which the President did. This was a deliberate circumvention of the State Department.[5] One of course could conclude that some of the difficulties might not have arisen if the President had made sure that the appropriate officials in various departments of the government had been kept informed. But in this matter he was somewhat like Wilson and had a suspicious attitude regarding career diplomats and State Department personnel. Also, like Wilson, he had a Secretary of State who was popular with Congress and the public, and it was therefore necessary to continue with his services for the sake of party harmony.

There were other disadvantages too. Criticism of the President would frequently be levied in Congress and in the press because of the use of Hopkins. In large measure this antagonism was already there before Hopkins' foreign affairs work began due to his association with the radical wing of the New Deal. Clare Booth Luce was pleased that James Byrnes was placed in charge of the Office of War Mobilization because at last someone would be able to check on Hopkins and it would now be possible for Congress to investigate his activities.[6] When it was announced that Hopkins had landed in Moscow for his first Russian mission, Representative Clare Hoffman of Michigan said, "this makes the [Communist] circle complete."[7] And Representative Plumely, by inserting a

[1] Dean Acheson interview, April 2, 1956. Although there is some reason to accept Acheson's statement, it should be remembered that Hull is laudatory of Hopkins in his *Memoirs*; see p. 923.

[2] Sherwood, *op. cit.*, p. 269.

[3] Acheson interview, April 2, 1956.

[4] Sherwood, *op. cit.*, p. 231.

[5] Sherwood, *op. cit.*, p. 679. Hull does not even mention this in his *Memoirs*, and in correspondence with Hopkins he passes over it diplomatically. Hopkins MSS, April 8, 1943, Franklin D. Roosevelt Library.

[6] *New York Times*, May 30, 1943.

[7] *Congressional Record*, 77th Cong., 1st Sess., LXXXVII, 6457.

Boston Post editorial into the *Congressional Record*, gave implicit approval to the belief that there was something sinister in the use of Hopkins for so many different kinds of chores.[1]

Summary

Like Colonel House, Hopkins had a highly varied career. Unlike House, however, much of the time that Hopkins carried out his special missions he had an administrative position in the White House. This position was deliberately kept vague, and this vagueness enhanced the natural proclivities of Hopkins to administer programs with a liberal interpretation of his duties and powers.

Because Hopkins was in government there was no problem of how to provide money for his expenses, except during his first mission. At that time he was paid out of the contingent fund as an emissary of the President. Thereafter, the expenses necessary for travel were available to him as they would be for any government employee of the White House.

It was apparently the practice of the President to provide official credentials of an introductory nature only for the first mission that Hopkins made to a country. Thus, he had a letter of introduction on his first trip to England in January, 1941, and on his first trip to Russia in July, 1941. It is interesting to note that for his first international conference abroad, Casablanca, he also carried identification. It was a letter which read: "To Whom It May Concern: This is to certify that the bearer, Mr. Harry L. Hopkins, whose description appears below, is a member of the party of the President of the United States." [2] Perhaps it was the location of the conference which seemed to require this. But these are the only occasions known to this writer when he carried such papers.

So far as any privileges or immunities extended to either House or Hopkins are concerned, it has not been possible to obtain any specific statements from the three governments involved. However, as has been indicated above, the governments, through official spokesmen, did acknowledge after much correspondence, that such agents would normally be considered as meriting the kind of treatment which is shown to a regular diplomat, based, however, upon courtesy and not established law. Generally speaking, they carried no diplomatic rank and apparently no special considerations were ever requested for them. Yet there can be little doubt from the replies to the questions raised by the writer, and the evidence that has come to light in each case, that each of these agents was given the utmost consideration and was in a position tantamount to that of regular diplomats under international law.

That the state was responsible for their authorized actions even though they were not regularly accredited agents, there can be no doubt. They were on missions that eventually affected or helped create State policy. They, through the inherent powers of the President of the United States in foreign affairs, were *bona fide* agents who, by representing the President, were entitled to receive special protection and special consideration.

[1] *Ibid.*, p. A 1794.

[2] Sherwood, *op. cit.*, p. 668.

BIBLIOGRAPHY

BOOKS

Adams, Charles F. (ed.) *Memoirs of John Quincy Adams, Comprising Portions of His Diary from 1795 to 1848*. Vol. IX. Philadelphia: J. B. Lippincott and Co., 1876.

Baker, Ray Stannard. *Woodrow Wilson Life and Letters*. Vols. IV–VIII. New York: Doubleday, Page and Co., 1929–1939.

Benton, Thomas H. *Abridgment of Debates of Congress, 1789–1856*. Vol. IX. New York: D. Appleton and Co., 1857–1861.

Bishop, William W. Jr. *International Law, Cases and Materials*. New York: Prentice Hall, Inc., 1953.

Blum, John Morton. *Woodrow Wilson and the Politics of Morality*. Boston: Little, Brown and Co., 1956.

Bluntschli, J. L. *Das Moderne Völkerrecht der Civilisierten Staaten*. Nordlingen: H. Beck, 1878.

Briggs, Herbert W. *The Law of Nations: Cases, Documents, and Notes*. 2nd ed. New York: Appleton-Century-Crofts, Inc., 1952.

Buehrig, Edward H. (ed.) *Wilson's Foreign Policy in Perspective*. Bloomington: Indiana University Press, 1957.

—. *Woodrow Wilson and the Balance of Power*. Bloomington: Indiana University Press, 1955.

Calvo, M. Charles. *Le Droit International Théorique et Pratique*. Paris: Librairie Nouvelle de Droit et de Jurisprudence, 1896.

Cheever, Daniel S., and Haviland, H. Field Jr. *American Foreign Policy and the Separation of Powers*. Cambridge: Harvard University Press, 1952.

Childs, J. Rives. *American Foreign Service*. New York: Henry Holt and Co., 1948.

Churchill, Winston. *The Second World War*. Vols. III–VI. Boston: Houghton Mifflin Co., 1950–1953.

Corwin, E. S., and Koenig, Louis. *The Presidency Today*. New York: New York University Press, 1956.

Corwin, E. S. *The President's Control of Foreign Relations*. Princeton: Princeton University Press, 1917.

—. *The Constitution and What It Means Today*. 11th ed. Princeton: Princeton University Press, 1954.

—. *The President Office and Powers, 1787–1957: History and Analysis of Practice and Opinion*. 1st ed.; 4th ed. revised. New York: New York University Press, 1957.

Dangerfield, Royden J. *In Defense of the Senate: A Study in Treaty Making*. Norman: University of Oklahoma Press, 1933.

Daniels, Josephus. *The Wilson Era: Years of Peace, 1910–1917*. Chapel Hill: The University of North Carolina Press, 1944.

—. *The Wilson Era: Years of War and After, 1917–1923.* Chapel Hill: The University of North Carolina Press, 1946.

Davis, Forrest, and Lindley, Ernest K. *How War Came, An American Wihte Paper: From the Fall of France to Pearl Harbor.* New York: Simon and Shuster, 1942.

Dennison, Eleanor E. *The Senate Foreign Relations Committee.* California: Stanford University Press, 1942.

Eagleton, Clyde. *International Government.* 3rd ed. New York: The Ronald Press Co., 1957.

Farrand, Max. *The Framing of the Constitution of the United States.* New Haven: Yale University Press, 1913.

— (ed.). *The Records of the Federal Convention.* 3 vols. New Haven: Yale University Press, 1911.

Feis, Herbert. *Churchill, Roosevelt, Stalin. The War They Waged and The Peace They Sought.* Princeton: Princeton University Press, 1957.

Fenwick, Charles G. *International Law.* 3rd ed. New York: Appleton Century-Crofts, Inc., 1948.

Fiore, Pasquale. *International Law Codified and Its Legal Sanction.* Translated by E. M. Borchard. New York: Baker, Voorhis and Co., 1918.

Foster, John W. *A Century of American Diplomacy: Being A Brief Review of the Foreign Relations of the United States, 1776–1876.* Boston and New York: Houghton Mifflin Co., 1900.

—. *The Practice of Diplomacy as Illustrated in the Foreign Relations of the United States.* Boston and New York: Houghton Mifflin Co., 1906.

Genet, Raoul. *Traité de Diplomatie et de Droit Diplomatique.* Vol. I. Paris: Revue Générale de Droit International Public, 1931.

George, Alexander L., and George, Juliette L. *Woodrow Wilson and Colonel House: A Personality Study.* New York: John Day Co., 1956.

Gould, Wesley L. *An Introduction to International Law.* New York: Harper and Bros., 1957.

Grey, Viscount of Falloden. *Twenty-Five Years: 1892–1916.* 2 vols. New York: Frederick A. Stokes Co., 1925.

Grotius, Hugo. *The Rights of War and Peace Including the Law of Nature and of Nations.* Translated by A. C. Campbell. London: M. Walter Dunne, 1901.

Hackworth, Green H. *Digest of International Law.* 8 vols. Washington: Government Printing Office, 1940.

Hall, William E. *A Treatise on International Law.* 8th ed. A. Pearce Higgins, ed. Oxford: The Clarendon Press, 1924.

Hamilton, Alexander, Jay, John, and Madison, James. *The Federalist.* New York: Modern Library, 1941.

Harris, Joseph P. *The Advice and Consent of the Senate, A Study of the Confirmation of Appointments by the United States Senate.* Berkeley and Los Angeles: University of California Press, 1953.

Harvard Law School. *Research in International Law.* Cambridge: Harvard Law School, 1932.

Haynes, George H. *The Senate of the United States, Its History and Practice.* 2 vols. Boston: Houghton Mifflin Co., 1938.

Heatley, D. P. *Diplomacy and the Study of International Relations.* London: Clarendon Press, 1919.

Heffter, August W. *Das europäische Völkerrecht der Gegenwart auf den Bisherigen Grundlagen.* Berlin: H. W. Müller, 1888.

Hershey, Amos S. *Essentials of International Public Law and Organization.* Revised Edition. New York: Macmillan Co., 1927.

—. *Diplomatic Agents and Immunities.* Washington: Department of State, 1919.

Hill, Norman. *International Organization.* New York: Harper and Bros., 1952.

Horwill, Herbert W. *The Usages of the American Constitution.* London: Oxford University Press, 1925.

Hull, Cordell. *The Memoirs of Cordell Hull.* 2 vols. New York: Macmillan Co., 1948.

Hunt, Gaillard (ed.). *Writings of James Madison.* Vol. IX. New York: G. P. Putnam's Sons, 1910.

Hyde, Charles C. *International Law Chiefly as Interpreted and Applied by the United States.* Vol. I. 2nd ed. rev. Boston: Little, Brown and Co., 1945.

Kauffmann, Siegmund. *Die Immunität der Nicht-Diplomaten, ein Beitrag zur Kodifikation des Völkerrechts.* "Frankfurter Abhandlungen Zum Modernen Völkerrecht," Hft. 33. Leipzig: Robert Noske, 1932.

Kelsen, Hans. *Principles of International Law.* New York: Rinehart and Co., Inc., 1952.

Koenig, Louis W. *The Presidency and the Crisis, Powers of the Office from the Invasion of Poland to Pearl Harbor.* New York: Morningside Heights: King's Crown Press, 1944.

Latané, John H., and Wainhouse, David W. *A History of American Foreign Policy, 1776–1940.* New York: Doubleday Doran and Co., 1941.

Latham, Earl (ed.). *The Philosophy and Policies of Woodrow Wilson.* Translated by Jacques Dumas and A. De Lapradelle. 5th ed. London: Oxford University Press, 1920.

Lay, Tracy H. *The Foreign Service of the United States.* New York: Prentice Hall, 1925.

Link, Arthur S. *Woodrow Wilson and the Progressive Era, 1910–1917.* New York: Harper Bros., 1954.

—. *Wilson, the Diplomatist: A Look at His Major Foreign Policies.* Baltimore: Johns Hopkins University Press, 1957.

Mathews, John M. *American Foreign Relations, Conduct and Policies.* New York: D. Appleton-Century Co., 1938.

—. *The Conduct of American Foreign Relations.* New York: The Century Co., 1922.

Lord McNair, William Lennox. *International Law and Opinions.* 3 vols. Cambridge: Cambridge University Press, 1956.

Mechem, F. R. *Treatise on the Law of Public Offices and Officers.* Chicago: Callaghan and Co., 1890.

Moore, John Bassett. *A Digest of International Law.* Vol. IV. Washington: Government Printing Office, 1906.

Ogdon, Montell. *Juridical Bases of Diplomatic Immunity.* Washington: John Byrne and Co., 1936.

Oppenheim, L. *International Law: A Treatise.* Vol. I, *Peace.* London: Longmans, Green and Co., 1905 (1st ed.), 1948–52, (7th ed.), 1955 (8th ed.).

Paullin, C. O. *Diplomatic Negotiations of American Naval Officers, 1778–1883.* Baltimore: Johns Hopkins Press, 1912.

Pepper, George W. *Family Quarrels, President, Senate and House.* New York: Baker, Voorhis and Co., 1931.

Poole, De Witt C. *The Conduct of Foreign Relations Under Modern Democratic Conditions.* New Haven: Yale University Press, 1924.

Richardson, James D. *A Compilation of the Messages and Papers of the Presidents.* Vol. IV. New York: Bureau of National Literature, 1908.

Rivier, Alphonse. *Principes Du Droit Des Gens.* Paris: Librairie Nouvelle de Droit et de Jurisprudence, 1896.

Roosevelt, Eleanor. *This I Remember*. New York: Harper, 1949.

Salmon, Lucy. *The History of the Appointing Power of the President*. New York: G. P. Putnam's Sons, 1886.

Satow, Sir Ernest. *A Guide to Diplomatic Practice*. London: Longmans Green and Co., 1932 (3rd ed.), 1957 (4th ed.).

Seymour, Charles. *The Intimate Papers of Colonel House*. 4 vols. New York: Houghton Mifflin Co., 1926 (2 vols.), 1928 (2 vols.).

—. *Woodrow Wilson and the World War: A Chronicle of Our Own Times:* New Haven: Yale University Press, 1921.

Sherwood, Robert E. *Roosevelt and Hopkins, An Intimate History*. New York: Harper and Bros., 1950.

Skilling, H. Gordon. *Canadian Representatives Abroad from Agency to Embassy*. Boston: Bruce Humphries, Inc., 1945.

Smith, Arthur D. H. *Mr. House of Texas*. New York and London: Funk and Wagnalls Co., 1940.

—. *The Real Colonel House*. New York: George H. Doran Co., 1918.

Stuart, Graham H. *American Diplomatic and Consular Practice*. New York: D. Appleton-Century Co., Inc. 1936. Also 2nd ed., 1952.

Tugwell, Rexford G. *The Democratic Roosevelt: A Biography of Franklin D. Roosevelt*. New York: Doubleday and Co., Inc., 1957.

Twiss, Sir Travers. *The Law of Nations Considered as Independent Political Communities*. 2nd ed. Oxford: Clarendon Press, 1884.

Van Essen, J. L. F., and Landheer, B. *Selected Bibliography of the Library of the Peace Palace*. 3 vols. Leyden: A. W. Sijthoff, 1953.

Von Martens, G. F. *The Law of Nations: Being the Science of Natural Law, Covenants, Power, Etc.* London: William Cobbett, 1829.

Wharton, Francis (ed.). *A Digest of the International Law of the United States*. Vol. I. Washington: Government Publications Office, 1886.

Williams, Benjamin H. *American Diplomacy, Policies and Practice*. New York and London: McGraw-Hill Book Co., Inc., 1936.

Willoughby, Westel W. *The Constitutional Law of the United States*. New York: Baker Vorhis and Co., 1910 (1st ed.), 1929 (2nd ed.).

Wilmerding, Lucius Jr. *The Spending Power: A History of the Efforts of Congress to Control Expenditures*. New Haven: Yale University Press, 1943.

Wilson, Edith B. *My Memoir*. New York: Bobbs Merrill Co., 1939.

Wilson, Woodrow. *Constitutional Government in the United States*. New York: Columbia University Press, 1908.

Wright, Quincy. *The Control of American Foreign Relations*. New York: Macmillan Co., 1922.

Wriston, Henry M. *Executive Agents in American Foreign Relations*. Baltimore: Johns Hopkins Press, 1929.

ARTICLES

Becker, Joseph D. "The State Department White List and Diplomatic Immunity," *American Journal of International Law*, Vol. XLVII (October, 1953).

Deak, Francis. "Classification, Immunities and Privileges of Diplomatic Agents" *Southern California Law Review*, Vol. I, No. 3 (March, 1928), and No. 4 (May, 1928).

Deener, David R. "Some Problems of the Law of Diplomatic Immunity," *American Journal of International Law*, Vol. L (January, 1956).

Eagleton, Clyde. "The Responsibility of the State for the Protection of Foreign Officials," *American Journal of International Law*, Vol. XIX (April, 1925).

Flanders, Henry. "Power of the President To Appoint Special Diplomatic Agents without the Advice and Consent of the Senate," *The American Law Register and Review*, First Series, Vol. XXXIII (New Series, Vol. I), p. 1894.

Gutteridge, Joyce A. C. "Immunities of the Subordinate Diplomatic Staff," *British Yearbook of International Law*, Vol. XXIV (1947).

Hill, David Jayne. "The Classification of Diplomatic Agents," *American Journal of International Law*, Vol. XXI (1927).

Hurst, Sir Cecil J. B. "Diplomatic Immunities – Modern Developments," *British Yearbook of International Law*, Vol. X (1929).

—. "Les Immunités Diplomatiques," *Recueil Des Cours*, Vol. XII (1926).

Jenks, Wilfred C. "Some Constitutional Problems of International Organizations," *British Yearbook of International Law*, Vol. XXII (1945).

Jones, Harry W. "The President, Congress and Foreign Relations," *California Law Review*, Vol. XXIX (July, 1941).

Kunz, Josef. "Privileges and Immunities of International Organizations," *American Journal of International Law*, Vol. XLI (October, 1947).

Lyons, A. B. "The Conclusiveness of the Foreign Office Certificate," *British Yearbook of International Law*, Vol. XXIII (1946).

—. "Conclusiveness of the Statements of the Executive – Continental and Latin American Practice," *British Yearbook of International Law*, Vol. XXV (1948).

Macmahon, Arthur W. "Senatorial Confirmation," *Public Administration Review*, Vol. III, No. 4 (Autumn, 1943).

Meron, Theodore. "International Responsibility of States for Unauthorized Acts of Their Officials," *British Yearbook of International Law*, Vol. XXXIII (1957)

Parry, Clive. "Constitutions of International Organizations," *British Yearbook of International Law*, Vol. XXIII (1946).

Preuss, Lawrence. "Diplomatic Privileges and Immunities of Agents Invested with Functions of an International Interest," *American Journal of International Law*, Vol. XXV (1931).

Schwebel, S. M. "The International Character of the Secretariat of the United Nations," *British Yearbook of International Law*, Vol. XXX (1953).

Thorpe, Francis N. "Is the President of the United States Vested with Authority Under the Constitution To Appoint a Special Diplomatic Agent with Paramount Power without the Advice and Consent of the Senate," *The American Law Register and Review*, First Series, Vol. XXXIII (New Series, Vol. I) (1894).

Van Vollenhoven, Clyde. "Diplomatic Prerogatives of Non-Diplomats," *American Journal of International Law*, Vol. XIX (1925).

Woolsey, Lester. "The Personal Diplomacy of Colonel House," *American Journal of International Law*, Vol. XXI (1927).

LEGAL REFERENCES

Canada. *Privileges and Immunities (United Nations) Act, 1947. Revised Statutes of Canada.* Vol. IV, 1952.

Great Britain. *International Organization (Immunities and Privileges) Act.* 14 Geo. VI, 1950.

Great Britain. *Privileges and Immunities of International Organization.* 7 Geo. VI, 1944.

United States Code. Title 18, Sec. 112; Title 22,, Secs. 252, 253, 254, 287.

U.S. *Federal Register.* Vol. X.

U.S. *Official Opinions of the Attorneys-General.* Vols. IV, VII, XX, XXII, XXIII XXVII, LII.
U.S. *Revised Statutes.* 1st ed.
U.S. *Statutes at Large.* Vols. I, V, XI, XXVII, XXXIV, XXXV, LII.

Cases: Foreign

Belgium. *Taco Mesdag* c. *Marie Heyermans.* Cour de Cassation, Pas. Belg .98 I 202 (1898).
France. *L'Affaire Gravenhoff.* Trib. Civ. Seine (1918).
France. *Drtilik* v. *Barbier. Ann. Dig.*, 1925–26, Case 242.
Great Britain. *Barbuitt's Case.* Cases T. Talbott, 281 (1737).
Great Britain. *Engelke* v. *Mussmann.* A C. 1928 433.
Great Britain. *Fenton Textile Association* v. *Karassin and Others.* 38 *T.L.R.* 259 (1921).
Great Britain. *In Re Cloete.* 65 L.T.R. (1891)
Great Britain. *In Re Serventi. Ann. Dig.*, 1919–1922, Case No. 211.
Great Britain. *Margaret Roper Case. Ann. Dig.*, 1927–1928, Case No. 150.
Great Britain. *Mattueoff Case.* 10 Mod. 4 (1710).
Great Britain. *F. Quintanilla Case. Ann. Dig.*, 1925–1926, Case No. 163.
Great Britain. *Re The Turkish Inspector of Students. Ann. Dig.*, 1946, Case No. 80.
Great Britain. *Triquet* v. *Bath.* 3 Burr. 1478.

Cases: United States

Durand v. *Hollins.* 4 Blatch. 451 (1860).
In Re Baiz. 135 U.S. 403 (1890).
In Re Neagle. 135 U.S. L (1890).
Little v. *Barrieme.* 2 Cranch 170 (1804).
Marbury v. *Madison.* 1 Cranch 137 (1803).
Respublica v. *De Longchamps.* 1 Dallas 111 (1784).
Tsiang v. *Tsiang.* 86 NYS 2nd 556 (1949).
U.S. v. *Coplon and Gubitchev.* 88 F. Supp. 915 (1950).
U.S. v. *Curtis Wright Export Corp.* 299 U.S. 304 (1936).
U.S. v. *Germaine.* 99 U.S. 508 (1878).
U.S. v. *Hartwell.* 6 Wall. 385 (1867).
U.S. (*Massey Claim*) v. *Mexico.* Opinions of the Commissioners. 228 (1927).
U.S. v. *Maurice.* 24 Fed. Case 36 (1823).
U.S. v. *Smith.* 124 U.S. 525 (1888).

PUBLIC DOCUMENTS

American State Papers. Documents Legislative and Executive of the Congress of the United States. Vol. I.
Journal of the Executive Proceedings of the Sendte of the United States of America. Vol. XXIII.
U.S. Annals of Congress. Vol. XXVI.
U.S. *Register of Debates in Congress.* Vol. VII.
U.S. *Congressional Globe.* Vols. XI, XXIV, XXV, XLIII.
U.S. *Congressional Record,* Vols. XIX, XXVI, XXXVI, XXXVIII, XL, XLIX, LVI, LXI, LXXXVII, LXXXIX, XCI, XCII, XCIII, XCIX.
U.S. Department of State. *Instructions to Diplomatic Officers of the United States.* 1897.

U.S. Senate. *Appointing and Removal Power*. Senate Document No. 172, 70th Cong., 2nd Sess., 1929.

U.S. House of Representatives. *Appointment of Members of Congress to Military, and Other Offices*. House Report 2205, 55th Cong., 3rd Sess., February 21 1899.

U.S. Senate. *Hawaiian Islands*. Senate Report 227, 53rd Cong., 2nd Sess., February 26, 1894.

U.S. House of Representatives. *Minority Report: Conference on International Communication To Accompany H.R. 9822 To Authorize the President of the United States To Participate in International Conferences, and Other Matters*. House Report 387, 66th Cong., 1st Sess., October 21, 1919.

U.S. Senate. *Report on the Treaty between the United States and Great Britain Concerning the Interpretation of the Convention of October 20, 1818*. Senate Miscellaneous Document 109, 50th Cong., 1st Sess., May 10, 1888.

League of Nations. *Report of the Committee of Experts for the Progressive Codification of International Law*. C. 196. M. 70. 1927. V.

United Nations. *Privileges and Immunities of the United Nations*. General Assembly, 1st Sess., Document a/43, Annex 22, 1946.

United Nations. *Report of the International Law Commission*. General Assembly, 13th Sess., Sup. No. 9 (A/3859), 1958.

United Nations, General Assembly, United Nations Conference on Diplomatic Intercourse and Immunities, Committee of the Whole, Provisional Summary, Records, Series A/CONF. 20/CI/SR.

—, United Nations Conference on Diplomatic Intercourse and Immunities, Provisional Summary, Records of the Plenary Meetings, series A/CONF. 20/SR.

—, United Nations Conference on Diplomatic Intercourse and Immunities, Vienna Convention on Diplomatic Relations, A/CONF. 20/13.

—, United Nations Conference on Diplomatic Intercourse and Immunities, Final Act of the United Nations Conference on Diplomatic Intercourse and Immunities, A/CONF. 20/10.

—, United Nations Conference on Diplomatic Intercourse and Immunities, Guide to the Draft Articles on Diplomatic Intercourse and Immunities Adopted by the International Law Commission, A/CONF. 20/8.

—, International Law Commission, 12th session, "Ad Hoc Diplomacy", A/CN 4/129.

—, General Assembly Official Records, 13th sess., Supplement No. 9 (A/3859), Report of the International Law Commission, 10 th session, 1958.

—, 15th session, Supplement No. 9 (A/4425) Report of the International Law Commission, 12th session.

—, Yearbook of the International Law Commission, 1960, vol. 1, Summary Records of the 12th session, A/CN 4/SER. A/1960.

OTHER SOURCES

Correspondence – Scholars

Bishop, William W. Jr., May 19, 1958.

Bland, Sir Nevile, August 5, 1958.

Briggs, Herbert W., May 20, 1958.

Corwin, Edward S., September 27, 1958, October 23, 1958.

Deener, David R., June 3, 1958.

Kelsen, Hans, May 15, 1958.
Kunz, Joseph L., April 14, 1958, May 16, 1958.
Lord McNair, July 31, 1958.
Plischke, Elmer, May 20, 1958.
Schwarzenberger, G., August 8, 1958.

Correspondence – Governments

Canada. Department of External Affairs. Under-secretary of State for External Affairs, March 10, 1958.
Canada. Canadian Consulate – Detroit, Vice-Consul of Canada, April 11, 1958.
Canada. Department of External Affairs. Under-secretary of State for External Affairs, September 25, 1958.
China. Chinese Embassy – Washington. Counselor, September 4, 1958.
France. French Embassy – Washington. Minister Plenipotentiary, October 13, 1958.
Great Britain. Foreign Office, March 21, 1958.
Great Britain. Foreign Office, September 4, 1958.
Germany. Ministry of Justice. April 21, 1958, August 28, 1958.
Germany. Foreign Office, Chief of Protocol, September 16, 1958.
Italy. Ministry of Justice. Chief Legislative Officer, April 1, 1958.
United States. Department of State, Assistant Legal Adviser, April 10, 1958, August 9, 1958.
United States. Department of State, Office of International Conferences, October 7, 1958.
United States. Department of State, Historical Division, November 17, 1958.
Union of Soviet Socialist Republics. Embassy – Washington. Attaché, November 3, 1958.

Correspondence: United Nations

United Nations. Deputy Under-Secretary for Economic and Social Affairs September 12, 1958.

Personal Interviews

Acheson, Dean, April 2, 1956.
Baruch, Bernard, April 5, 1956.
Cohen, Benjamin V., April 3, 1956.
Cox, Oscar, April 2, 1956.
Hyman, Sidney, April 4, 1956.
Lubin, Isador, April 5, 1956.
Roosevelt, Eleanor, July 27, 1955.
Rosenman, Judge Samuel I., August 23, 1955.
Seymour, Charles, August 20, 1956.
Tully, Grace, April 4, 1956.
Wriston, Henry M., April 5, 1956.
Young, Phillip, April 4, 1956.

Unpublished Materials

Canada. Department of External Affairs. "Privileges Granted in Canada to Representatives of Other Governments," August 15, 1955. (Mimeographed.)

Nigro, Felix A. "Senate Confirmation." Unpublished Ph. D. dissertation, Department of Political Science, University of Wisconsin, 1948.

United States. Department of State. "Rights and Privileges Accorded Representatives of Foreign Governments in the United States," July 25, 1955. (Mimeographed.)

United States. Department of State. "Information Taken from Card Files in the Department of State That Are Based on Those Appointment Papers Which Required the Imprint of the Seal of the United States," undated. (Typewritten.)

INDEX

MAURICE WATERS

THE AD HOC DIPLOMAT

A Study in Municipal and International Law

WITH A FOREWORD BY

HANS MORGENTHAU

MARTINUS NIJHOFF / THE HAGUE

Ever since the existence of organized societies diplomatic agents have been used as a channel of communication. For a long period of time these agents had *ad hoc* assignments, but in the 14th and 15th centuries their missions took on a more formal character. This practice commenced among the States of the Italian peninsula, particularly on the part of the Holy See. By the 15th century resident embassies began to be used and slowly an elaborate diplomatic code of behavior, or rights, privileges, and immunities developed. From that time on, although *ad hoc* missions did not disappear, they were diminished in importance by the use of permanent missions and the lack of attention paid to them. Nevertheless, such agents continue to be used, and in this century alone probably number in the hundreds.

This study is an attempt to focus on the *ad hoc* diplomat in terms of his municipal and international law status. The United States, which employs such agents more than any other state was chosen as the example upon which to focus. The authority of the President to use such agencies, the status they hold in its constitutional system, and the nature of the assignments they have been given is the subject of the first part of the book.

The second part examines the status of the special agent from the point of view of international law. It opens with a presentation of the views of major scholars on the subject of the law of diplomats. From these and from other sources those characteristics which were deemed useful as a framework of analysis were singled out for consideration. Against this backdrop, the discussion of the status of the special agent is presented.

Because so little published material was available as a means of comprehending the practice, the writer had to turn to other sources. Hence the appropriate legal officers of the governments of many states to which these agents are known to have been sent were questioned as to the status and treatment accorded these agents when they appeared in their countries. In addition those scholars whose published studies of recent years indicated a relevant interest were questioned for their views. These were given and are revealed in the body of this work. Finally, through attendence as an observer at the United Nations International Law Conference in Vienna, 1961, the author was able to speak with statesmen and scholars who participated, thereby rounding out his knowledge. Where appropriate, pertinent law cases have been introduced in both parts.

Recognizing the importance of case studies as a means of illuminating the principles and problems of the subject, two have been included. The men selected are undoubtedly the two most celebrated special agents in United States history, Colonel House, the agent of Woodrow Wilson, and Harry Hopkins, who carried out foreign assignments for Franklin

Roosevelt. In order to add to an understanding of the problems which arise in using special agents, interviews were conducted with individuals familiar with the work of these men and the reasons they were chosen. The net result of this research is the first comprehensive examination of the legal status of the *ad hoc* agent, and a political analysis of why he is used and how.

About the author: Undergraduate study, Le Havre (France) and Shrivenham (England); A.B. Antioch College (1951); Ph. D., International relations, University of Chicago (1959); Instructor, Political Science, University of Wisconsin (1954-1956); Instructor, Assistant Professor, Political Science, Wayne State University (1956); Visiting Assistant Professor, Antioch College (1961-1963).

1963. XII and 233 pages. roy. 8vo. Cloth Guilders 20.—

Elbert M. Byrd Jr. - Treaties and executive agreements in the United States. Their separate roles and limitations. With a foreword by Elmer Plischke. 1960. 286 pages Guilders 21.—

S. I. P. van Campen - The quest for security. Some aspects of Netherlands foreign policy 1945-1950. 1958. XVI and 308 pages. Guilders 19.—

= Publications under the direction of the Netherlands Institute of International Affairs, no. 2.

Yves Collart - Le désarmement. Etude et bibliographie sur les efforts des Nations Unies. / Disarmament. A study guide and bibliography on the efforts of the United Nations. 1958. XII and 110 pages. Guilders 3.—

David R. Deener, The United States attorneys general and international law. 1957. XVI et 416 pages. Cloth Guilders 26.50

H. Drion - Limitation of liabilities in international air law. 1954. XIII and 389 pages. Cloth Guilders 24.50

P. A. M. van der Esch - Prelude to war. The international repercussions of the Spanish civil war (1936-1939). 1951. XI and 190 pages. Cloth Guilders 15.—

Werner Feld - Reunification and West German-Soviet relations. The role of the reunification issue in the foreign policy of the Federal Republic of Germany, 1949-1957 with special attention to policy toward the Soviet Union. 1963. X and 204 pages. Cloth Guilders 18.—

Manuel R. Garcia Mora - International responsibility for hostile acts of private persons against foreign states. 1962. XVII and 207 pages. Guilders 20.—

Leon Gordenker - The United Nations and the peaceful unification of Korea. The politics of field operations 1947-1950. 1959. XIII and 306 pages. Guilders 18.75

Edwin C. Hoyt - The unanimity rule in the revision of treaties. A re-examination. With a foreword by Philip C. Jessup. 1959. XII and 264 pages. Guilders 21.85

W. M. Laird Kleine-Ahlbrandt - The policy of simmering. A study of British policy during the Spanish civil war, 1936-1939. With a foreword by Sir Harold Mitchell. 1962. XII and 161 pages. Guilders 16.75

E. J. Baron Lewe van Aduard - Japan from surrender to peace. With a foreword by John Foster Dulles. 1953. XVI and 351 pages. With 7 plates. Cloth Guilders 19.—

Stuart Hull McIntyre - Legal effect of World War II on treaties of the United States. 1958. IX and 392 pages. Cloth Guilders 28.50

Joseph A. Obieta, S. J. - The international status of the Suez canal. With a foreword by Richard R. Baxter. 1960. XI and 137 pages. Guilders 13.85

Ernst Presseisen - Germany and Japan. A study in totalitarian diplomacy 1933-1941. 1958. XII and 360 pages. Cloth Guilders 28.50
=International Scholars Forum. A series of books by American scholars. Vol. XII.

Marc Raeff - Michael Speransky. Statesman of Imperial Russia 1772-1839. 1957. XII and 387 pages. Cloth Guilders 27.50

Herbert H. Rowen, The ambassador prepares for war. The Dutch embassy of Arnauld de Pomponne 1669-1671. 1957. X and 210 pages. Cloth Guilders 19.—
=International Scholars Forum. A series of books by American scholars. Vol. VII.

Amry Vandenbosch - Dutch foreign policy since 1815. A study in small power politics. 1959. XII and 318 pages. Cloth Guilders 25.50

Walpole - An honest diplomat at the Hague. The private letters of Horatio Walpole, 1715-1716. Edited with an introduction by John J. Murray. 1955. 394 pages. Guilders 24.75
=Indiana University Publications, Social Sciences Series, no. 13

H. A. Wassenbergh - Post-war international civil aviation policy and law of the air. Second revised edition. 1962. XII and 197 pages. Guilders 15.—

One Guilder = ab. $ 0.278 = ab. 2 sh = env Fr. 1.36 = ca. DMW 1.10

Obtainable through any bookseller or direct from the publisher

MAURICE WATERS

THE AD HOC DIPLOMAT

A Study in Municipal and International Law

WITH A FOREWORD BY

HANS MORGENTHAU

MARTINUS NIJHOFF / THE HAGUE

Ever since the existence of organized societies diplomatic agents have been used as a channel of communication. For a long period of time these agents had *ad hoc* assignments, but in the 14th and 15th centuries their missions took on a more formal character. This practice commenced among the States of the Italian peninsula, particularly on the part of the Holy See. By the 15th century resident embassies began to be used and slowly an elaborate diplomatic code of behavior, or rights, privileges, and immunities developed. From that time on, although *ad hoc* missions did not disappear, they were diminished in importance by the use of permanent missions and the lack of attention paid to them. Nevertheless, such agents continue to be used, and in this century alone probably number in the hundreds.

This study is an attempt to focus on the *ad hoc* diplomat in terms of his municipal and international law status. The United States, which employs such agents more than any other state was chosen as the example upon which to focus. The authority of the President to use such agencies, the status they hold in its constitutional system, and the nature of the assignments they have been given is the subject of the first part of the book.

The second part examines the status of the special agent from the point of view of international law. It opens with a presentation of the views of major scholars on the subject of the law of diplomats. From these and from other sources those characteristics which were deemed useful as a framework of analysis were singled out for consideration. Against this backdrop, the discussion of the status of the special agent is presented.

Because so little published material was available as a means of comprehending the practice, the writer had to turn to other sources. Hence the appropriate legal officers of the governments of many states to which these agents are known to have been sent were questioned as to the status and treatment accorded these agents when they appeared in their countries. In addition those scholars whose published studies of recent years indicated a relevant interest were questioned for their views. These were given and are revealed in the body of this work. Finally, through attendence as an observer at the United Nations International Law Conference in Vienna, 1961, the author was able to speak with statesmen and scholars who participated, thereby rounding out his knowledge. Where appropriate, pertinent law cases have been introduced in both parts.

Recognizing the importance of case studies as a means of illuminating the principles and problems of the subject, two have been included. The men selected are undoubtedly the two most celebrated special agents in United States history, Colonel House, the agent of Woodrow Wilson, and Harry Hopkins, who carried out foreign assignments for Franklin

Roosevelt. In order to add to an understanding of the problems which arise in using special agents, interviews were conducted with individuals familiar with the work of these men and the reasons they were chosen. The net result of this research is the first comprehensive examination of the legal status of the *ad hoc* agent, and a political analysis of why he is used and how.

About the author: Undergraduate study, Le Havre (France) and Shrivenham (England); A.B. Antioch College (1951); Ph. D., International relations, University of Chicago (1959); Instructor, Political Science, University of Wisconsin (1954-1956); Instructor, Assistant Professor, Political Science, Wayne State University (1956); Visiting Assistant Professor, Antioch College (1961-1963).

1963. XII and 233 pages. roy. 8vo. Cloth Guilders 20.—

Elbert M. Byrd Jr. - Treaties and executive agreements in the United States. Their separate roles and limitations. With a foreword by Elmer Plischke. 1960. 286 pages Guilders 21.—

S. I. P. van Campen - The quest for security. Some aspects of Netherlands foreign policy 1945-1950. 1958. XVI and 308 pages. Guilders 19.—

= Publications under the direction of the Netherlands Institute of International Affairs, no. 2.

Yves Collart - Le désarmement. Etude et bibliographie sur les efforts des Nations Unies. / Disarmament. A study guide and bibliography on the efforts of the United Nations. 1958. XII and 110 pages. Guilders 3.—

David R. Deener, The United States attorneys general and international law. 1957. XVI et 416 pages. Cloth Guilders 26.50

H. Drion - Limitation of liabilities in international air law. 1954. XIII and 389 pages. Cloth Guilders 24.50

P. A. M. van der Esch - Prelude to war. The international repercussions of the Spanish civil war (1936-1939). 1951. XI and 190 pages. Cloth Guilders 15.—

Werner Feld - Reunification and West German-Soviet relations. The role of the reunification issue in the foreign policy of the Federal Republic of Germany, 1949-1957 with special attention to policy toward the Soviet Union. 1963. X and 204 pages. Cloth Guilders 18.—

Manuel R. Garcia Mora - International responsibility for hostile acts of private persons against foreign states. 1962. XVII and 207 pages. Guilders 20.—

Leon Gordenker - The United Nations and the peaceful unification of Korea. The politics of field operations 1947-1950. 1959. XIII and 306 pages. Guilders 18.75

Edwin C. Hoyt - The unanimity rule in the revision of treaties. A re-examination. With a foreword by Philip C. Jessup. 1959. XII and 264 pages. Guilders 21.85

W. M. Laird Kleine-Ahlbrandt - The policy of simmering. A study of British policy during the Spanish civil war, 1936-1939. With a foreword by Sir Harold Mitchell. 1962. XII and 161 pages. Guilders 16.75

E. J. Baron Lewe van Aduard - Japan from surrender to peace. With a foreword by John Foster Dulles. 1953. XVI and 351 pages. With 7 plates. Cloth Guilders 19.—

Stuart Hull McIntyre - Legal effect of World War II on treaties of the United States. 1958. IX and 392 pages. Cloth Guilders 28.50

Joseph A. Obieta, S. J. - The international status of the Suez canal. With a foreword by Richard R. Baxter. 1960. XI and 137 pages. Guilders 13.85

Ernst Presseisen - Germany and Japan. A study in totalitarian diplomacy 1933-1941. 1958. XII and 360 pages. Cloth Guilders 28.50
= International Scholars Forum. A series of books by American scholars. Vol. XII.

Marc Raeff - Michael Speransky. Statesman of Imperial Russia 1772-1839. 1957. XII and 387 pages. Cloth Guilders 27.50

Herbert H. Rowen, The ambassador prepares for war. The Dutch embassy of Arnauld de Pomponne 1669-1671. 1957. X and 210 pages. Cloth Guilders 19.—
= International Scholars Forum. A series of books by American scholars. Vol. VII.

Amry Vandenbosch - Dutch foreign policy since 1815. A study in small power politics. 1959. XII and 318 pages. Cloth Guilders 25.50

Walpole - An honest diplomat at the Hague. The private letters of Horatio Walpole, 1715-1716. Edited with an introduction by John J. Murray. 1955. 394 pages. Guilders 24.75
= Indiana University Publications, Social Sciences Series, no. 13

H. A. Wassenbergh - Post-war international civil aviation policy and law of the air. Second revised edition. 1962. XII and 197 pages. Guilders 15.—

One Guilder = ab. $ 0.278 = ab. 2 sh = env Fr. 1.36 = ca. DMW 1.10

Obtainable through any bookseller or direct from the publisher

GPSR Compliance

The European Union's (EU) General Product Safety Regulation (GPSR) is a set of rules that requires consumer products to be safe and our obligations to ensure this.

If you have any concerns about our products, you can contact us on ProductSafety@springernature.com

In case Publisher is established outside the EU, the EU authorized representative is:

Springer Nature Customer Service Center GmbH
Europaplatz 3
69115 Heidelberg, Germany

Batch number: 10830943

Printed by Printforce, the Netherlands